Eyewitness to Evil

By

G. Scott McGregor

To David -
Best wishes to you - you're a
brave guy.
GS McG

Avid Readers Publishing Group

Lakewood, California

Eyewitness to Evil

Avid Readers Publishing Group

http://www.avidreaderspg.com

ISBN-13: 978-1-935105-36-7

Printed in the United States

Dedication

This book is dedicated to the men and women of the Armed Forces of The United States. We remain free because of you. Of that, there can be no doubt.

Acknowledgements

I would like to thank my colleague and friend, Brigitte, for her inspiration and encouragement; also my friend, Winston, who listened and challenged me on a daily basis, and my close friend, Cesar, who knew just what to say at the right time to keep me going. There is a special thanks that must go to all the members of my small fellowship group. Each one helped me in a special way that played a part in completing the project. I especially want to thank my friend, Howard, who recognized the PTSD that surfaced as I wrote this book. And a final thank you to Avid Readers Publishing Group who were such a pleasure to work with.

Eyewitness to Evil

Table of Contents by Chapters

Preface

I've divided this book into four sections to present the events and facts in an organized manner. Since 1000 years is as one day in the Middle East, events that take place today have their reference points in past centuries.

The first section introduces the reader to specific events in America, Israel and Lebanon that show why we have fallen in love with socialism and are on the verge of choosing tyranny. That very tyranny raised its ugly head on the other side of the world in the conflict between Israel and Lebanon and set its goal to bring down America.

The second section looks back at specific historical events that make today's jihad against Western Civilization. The astounding and humiliating defeat of the united Arab armies by the Israeli Defense Forces in the Six Day War of 1967 led to the Khartoum Conference of Arab states. Their resolutions resorted to Islamic tradition, no peace, no treaties, and only endless war. They blamed America for Israel's success, and Arab propaganda infected the Western media disguising their jihad with images of freedom fighters and Arab unity. We bought it.

Section three explains why America misunderstood the events surrounding twenty years of Middle East conflict that was heading towards Western Civilization. From technical limitations, to an elite media's worldview to a third religion destined to conquer the world… the West was in darkness about the resumption of jihad that stopped at the gates of Vienna, Austria September 11, 1683.

Section four shows how the Christian Church built Western Civilization through science, scholarship, economic development and law leading to the rights of man and the founding of an independent United States. It also warns that tyrannical organizations within our shores call for the overthrow of America with Islamic law by both legislation and violence. We are within two or three election cycles of losing our liberties through economic desperation and energy dependence. It's exactly what our enemies want us to do. What will we decide?

Introduction

I want every American to know and consider that we are caught in a war for the survival of our democracy…and you can help us win. Our enemy has a full-blown strategy including infiltration, media manipulation, terrorism, and legal changes. Their goal is simple, destroy America or change it to an Islamic state. Think that sounds fantastic? Then why did one of the most recognized Islamic rights groups advocate replacing The United States Constitution with the Koran?[1] Read on.

I'll present my case by using more than 400 references. I've consulted Islamic, Jewish, Christian and secular sources to glean the points of conflict and leave you, the reader, with the distillation. Here you'll read what teachers and news commentators don't tell you because it isn't politically correct.

You'll read how Islam does not separate religion and government.[2] Then, you'll read about the development of the rights of man and the separation of religion and state on which America was founded. And I'll demonstrate how those rights began with Judaism and were refined by Christian scholarship through the ages. You'll read about the emergence of Islam, their conquest of the Christian Middle East and The Crusades that relieved 400 years of Islamic oppression. You'll read about six days that changed the world and how Islamic fascism fooled Americans with phrases and images.

But most of all, this book will bring you up to date on our current situation. Then, it will empower you to recognize the cunning of fascism and enable you to strike it down by your knowledge and love of our great republic. After all, freedom is created within our hearts and there it must be defended by alert minds filled with the light of truth. This generation of Americans will decide if America stays free or wanders into a trap of tyranny. The struggle will take years but the victory is ours to win.

For me the story began on a beautiful cloudless morning in 1985 when two teenage boys approached me on the streets of Bent Jbeil, South Lebanon. One of them asked to talk with me but refused to be put on camera. This was normal since Lebanon was filled with violent factions and people feared their neighbors. However, what followed took me by surprise as one of the teens broke into clear English explaining that they were both chosen as holy warriors to go to the United States and kill Americans. Bragging that we could do nothing to stop them, this boy ranted that they would punish America for all the evils committed against Islam and further promised that Islam would triumph over America because Allah willed it.

Added to other stories I'd reported, this teen's diatribe seemed the tip of an iceberg, but I couldn't verify their claims. Bent Jbeil is closely connected to Iranian influence through the Shiite Crescent that stretches from Lebanon through Iraq and into Iran.[3] I suspected these teens represented part of an unconventional overall war strategy against America. Their own words and actions demonstrated that the strategy included media manipulation, immigration, and terrorism. But I couldn't verify it at the time. I even contacted the CIA by telephone and requested to talk to somebody who studied Lebanon. The man I spoke to never identified himself and after listening to a brief explanation of how I came upon the story, he told me never to call back.

But it couldn't be denied that bad things were happening to Americans in Lebanon. April 18, 1983 a suicide car bomber blew himself up destroying the U.S. Embassy in Beirut and killing 18 Americans.[4] Six months later on October 23rd, 241 United States Marines were killed in Beirut by an Iranian car bomber. Hezbollah leader Imad Fayez Mugniyah planned both the Beirut events and was on the FBI's Most Wanted List until his death in 2008.[5] Sadly, both these tragic events in Beirut may have been avoided if prior warnings were heeded and policies changed.

Five months before the attack on the embassy as 1982 ended, the top counter terrorist unit, SEAL Team Six, secretly infiltrated Beirut to check out the security of American installations. Their twenty-four hour a day surveillance of the U.S. Embassy and its surroundings revealed troubling facts. The SEALs discovered identical cars with identical bearded figures observing the embassy at irregular hours.[6]

Judging from their intelligence gathered over three weeks the team concluded the embassy would likely be car bombed. In a meeting with a senior diplomat of the embassy these facts were presented by the SEAL team's commander along with a "black box" device that would detonate a car bomber's trigger mechanisms within a 1000-foot perimeter away from the building.[7]

According to the commander's own account, the senior diplomat me by surprise as one of the teens broke into clear English explaining that they were both chosen as holy warriors to go to the United States and kill Americans. Bragging that we could do nothing to stop them, this boy ranted that they would punish America for all the evils committed against Islam and further promised that Islam would triumph over America because Allah willed it.

Added to other stories I'd reported, this teen's diatribe seemed the tip of an iceberg, but I couldn't verify their claims. Bent Jbeil is closely connected to Iranian influence through the Shiite Crescent that stretches from Lebanon through Iraq and into Iran.[3] I suspected these teens represented part of an unconventional overall war strategy against America. Their own words and actions demonstrated that the strategy included media manipulation, immigration, and terrorism. But I couldn't verify it at the time. I even contacted the CIA by telephone and requested to talk to somebody who studied Lebanon. The man I spoke to never identified himself and after listening to a brief explanation of how I came upon the story, he told me never to call back.

But it couldn't be denied that bad things were happening to Americans in Lebanon. April 18, 1983 a suicide car bomber blew himself up destroying the U.S. Embassy in Beirut and killing 18 Americans.[4] Six months later on October 23rd, 241 United States Marines were killed in Beirut by an Iranian car bomber. Hezbollah leader Imad Fayez Mugniyah planned both the Beirut events and was on the FBI's Most Wanted List until his death in 2008.[5] Sadly, both these tragic events in Beirut may have been avoided if prior warnings were heeded and policies changed.

Five months before the attack on the embassy as1982 ended, the top counter terrorist unit, SEAL Team Six, secretly infiltrated Beirut to check out the security of American installations. Their twenty-four hour a day surveillance of the U.S. Embassy and its surroundings revealed troubling facts. The SEALs discovered identical cars with identical bearded figures observing the embassy at irregular hours.[6]

Judging from their intelligence gathered over three weeks the team concluded the embassy would likely be car bombed. In a meeting with a senior diplomat of the embassy these facts were presented by the SEAL team's commander along with a "black box" device that would detonate a car bomber's trigger mechanisms within a 1000-foot perimeter away from the building.[7]

According to the commander's own account, the senior diplomat belittled the SEAL team's vulnerability assessment of the embassy. He also refused the "black box" device because it would explode the car bomb *before* it reached the embassy. According to the diplomat, "If the explosion caused Lebanese casualties it might damage America's diplomatic image." [8]

Less than three months later a suicide bomber drove his truck trough the flimsy wire gates up to the front entrance of the embassy and blew himself up. Sixty-three people were killed when the seven-story building was reduced to ruble. It was the first offensive attack on the U.S. by Hezbollah and it was a complete success.

A member of the same SEAL team evaluated the rules of engagement given to the 1st Battalion 8th Marines stationed at Beirut International Airport and termed them *lunacy*. Marines were not allowed to have a round in the chamber of their rifles and could not load and fire without first calling a commissioned officer for permission. [9]

At 6:30 am on October 23, 1983 Ismalal Ascari, an Iranian operative of Hezbollah, drove his yellow Mercedes truck past the two Marine sentries on duty and into the lobby of the Marine barracks in Beirut, Lebanon. The sentries were powerless to stop him because they were forbidden to have live ammunition.

According to one survivor, Ascari was smiling as he drove past. The truck, loaded with explosives equal to 12,000 pounds of TNT, collapsed the Marine barracks killing 241 servicemen and injuring 60 others. It was the worst single day death toll for the Marines since the Battle of Iwo Jima in 1945 during World War II.[10] The U.S. made no retaliation against Iran or Hezbollah. Why not? Within six months 259 Americans were killed in two acts of war committed by a nationally financed army of another country. Was Hezbollah's war against us a mystery?

Well, it wasn't as much a mystery as it was "our own fault" according to our media who reported to us that America was interfering in a civil war just like we did in Vietnam.[11] America was wrong again. We supported the Christian side of the government who our press called "warlords and mafia dons".[12] However, the Islamic armies protected the Commodore Hotel where the western media had their offices and sent a strong message to them by murdering numerous western reporters for investigating Islamic connections to terror in Lebanon.[13] Strangely enough, the overall news content Americans got was that the U.S. was helping the "wrong side".

The Christians and Israelis seemed to be preventing the Muslims from ascending to their rightful position. By the way, a similar message is stated in the *Quran*[14] and you can read the detailed explanation for it on page five of the notes for "Al Fatihah" found at the back of *The Muslim Prayer Book* by Maulana Muhammad Ali. Here it says that the Jews incur God's wrath and the Christians deceive the world about Jesus.[15] It also teaches that the birth of Muhammad brought the kingdom of god to earth calling all Muslims to find their true place in the struggle to subdue all nations under Islamic rule.[16] Isn't that fascist?

So America stood in the way of the Islamic takeover of Israel and the Lebanese democracy that day in 1985.[17] While the two teen holy warriors preached to me on the streets of Bent Jbeil, America remained the great obstacle to Islamic fascism ascending. As a result, the war against the United States continued.

As for me, my life was verbally threatened three times. Then, one night in Lebanon, an Israeli soldier shot a 30-caliber machine gun at my car ...and missed. On another occasion by the alertness of my translator, I escaped kidnapping. On still another I narrowly missed being blown up by a car bomb. Any one of these incidents could have ended my life. Instead, I lived and spent more than a year gathering news in Shiite dominated South Lebanon face to face with those who promised to destroy us.

Before then I spent a full year researching the Lebanese conflict that included a trip to Beirut and an interview with the Lebanese President who persuaded both U.S. Presidents Eisenhower and Regan to send the Marines to Lebanon. When I returned from Beirut in January 1983, I suspected that a war that began in the 7th Century was declared against America in the 20th Century. I was right. The enemy attacked America twice that same year and many more times in the years to come.

September 11, 2001 exposed numerous weaknesses in our security that were obviously probed and tested by our enemies before they attacked. Our intelligence community was caught flat-footed. According to the *9/11 Commission Report*, America was at war without knowing it.[18] What's up with that? How could we not know it? In the two decades before 9/11 there were 84 Islamic paramilitary and terror attacks against the United States that killed 1215 Americans. That 's one attack on Americans every 3 months continuously for 20 years. [19] What's the big mystery? We were at war, sure enough.

Why were we so unwilling to publicly identify the enemy and their strategy? Did we really not know? Was our media unable to see the truth? This book shows that we were tricked by our enemies, and deceived by ourselves. My fellow Americans, let's wake up and smell the coffee!

If America short circuits her armed forces from achieving victory; if our lifestyles put us to sleep; if we make impossible rules of engagement by ridiculous laws, there will be no defending America from the disaster that looms on the horizon. Tyranny will win.

In ancient history the watchman on the city wall sounded the alarm and gave the report of what he saw coming. Today, we the people of America must wake up, expose the enemy where he hides and make ourselves victorious in the war against our land.

Part I

America, Israel and Lebanon

Chapter 1
Caution, Fatal If Swallowed

"Education is a weapon whose effect depends on who has it in his hand and at whom it is aimed." _____ Joseph Stalin[20]

I stared down the gun barrel pointed straight at my brain. The large silencer on the front of it told me nobody would hear the shots. Instead, it would sound something like free speech, and the bullets weren't meant to kill me, only to poison my reason.

So went my undergraduate experience at the University of Wisconsin in Madison. Luckily I took Mark Twain's advice to never let my schooling interfere with my education. Seriously, though, I'm grateful for the educational opportunity I had there. Receiving my BA was an honor and proved to be only part of the preparation for life I gleaned during those years. The chaotic situation I lived through in Madison taught me how to find truth in the midst of fear and disorder later in my career when real guns were pointed at me in the Middle East.

Madison, Wisconsin is a special place. It's not only the capital city with the picturesque state legislature in the center, but the home of the main campus of the University of Wisconsin System that has 26 campuses across the state.

The city is built on a strip of land between two big lakes and the university campus occupies one and a half miles of unobstructed lake front property along Lake Mendota. With 45,000 students and faculty and another 16,000 employees,[21] one in five residents of Madison was directly involved with the university.

No cars were allowed along the lakefront, only a walking path stretched from the armory past the lakeshore dormitories to Picnic Point, a forest and game preserve. For that matter the entire campus was like a forest preserve with thick groves of maple, oak, poplar and pine trees interspersed with sidewalks and academic buildings rising up over the treetops.

Before I got my own apartment on the east side of Madison I lived in Kronshage Hall in the lakeshore dormitories. In the fall after the leaves were off the trees I looked out my window at night across the four miles of Lake Mendota to the twinkling lights of the town of Mendota

1

on the other side. It was a peaceful experience…but all that was about to change.

Like most students I didn't have much spending money, so I joined a private lunchroom co-operative in early 1970. As students, we volunteered work and paid pennies a day for a home cooked meal. Washing pots and pans the first week after joining I met a friendly guy in his 30's who I assumed was a graduate student. So, I asked him what he was studying. To my surprise he wasn't enrolled in the university at all but explained that he attended classes for free by just dressing like everybody else and walking into the lecture halls. Bragging that political science was his favorite subject area, he explained that he didn't repeat a class and stuck mostly to larger lectures. Then, he rattled off an impressive list of classes he'd "audited".

Wow! Taking classes for free, now that made sense. But soon it struck me that without my name on the roster I couldn't get credit, so I really didn't have time to devote to extra classes even if they were *free*. Worse yet, within two weeks my part-time job squeezed out the food co-op and I was back to bag lunches. The possibility of making up my volunteer time on weekends was out because I worked full time those two days for the Dane County Highway Department.

Every Saturday and Sunday morning I got up no later than 7:00 a.m., ate breakfast, packed a bag lunch and rode my Raleigh super-course bike five miles from my flat on Riverside Drive along the Yaraha River to the county's main garage. I had my twenty-minute ride time down pat.

I crossed from Riverside Drive to a through street and turned left on East Gotham. Avoiding the capital square I buzzed out onto University Avenue where I cut left at North Park Street. A mile out North Park I swung a half-right onto Fish Hatchery Road and shifted into high gear for the next mile and a half to the giant Dane County garage where I arrived at 7:50 a.m. There I worked as a dispatcher and pumped gas and cleaned windshields for all the police and ambulance vehicles on weekend duty.

Since I worked in the state capital I met all kinds of interesting police detectives and homicide investigators on their breaks. I even met a detective who worked on the famous Ed Gein case that later served as the factual basis for the characters of psychopathic murderers Norman Bates in the movie *Psycho* and Buffalo Bill in the movie *Silence of the*

Lambs.[22]

The detective told me how they traced the disappearance of a local woman in Plainfield, Wisconsin to a man named, Edward Gein, and searched his farm where they found the body of the missing woman decapitated and gutted like a deer carcass. But inside Gein's farmhouse was an inventory of dead people's parts that included an armchair made of human skin, female genitalia in a shoebox, a belt made of nipples, a human head, four noses and a heart. Most grizzly of all was a suit of human skin sewn together from victims.[23]

"How do you sleep after seeing that stuff?" I asked the detective.

"Your mind develops a defense that makes it possible," he replied. "Not everybody can do it."

No kidding, I thought. Yet those conversations with the police and the homicide detectives on their breaks brought me in contact with a scary side of reality. My imagination observed these events through the eyes of the hunters. Every day they applied both their crime science and their instincts stalking predators, evil people who lived among us waiting to pounce on the innocent and the unsuspecting.

Talking to the detectives I learned that evil is real and that it has no boundaries except those provided by the vigilant. Evil stalks like a lion seeking to devour. It knows how to smile and wears many faces. Evil speaks lies to gain advantage over the unsuspecting, but the goal is always the same…steal, kill, and destroy. This lesson in reality complete with eyewitness testimony helped me on my Middle East assignment ten years later. But right then, I was about to learn more.

Later on in the spring of 1970 protest riots broke out at the campus and turned ugly shutting classes down for days at a time. Fires were started and stores in the downtown area were badly damaged. The cops would show up for gas at the county garage in riot gear driving old cars equipped with steel grating welded over the body and replacing the windows. One Saturday two cars of police held a briefing in my office before heading into the riots.

They spread out a group of large black and white photos across my desk and briefed each other on key figures in the photos. These were the known organizers and leaders. Before I could stop myself I blurted out, "I know that guy," and pointed to my fellow pot washer from the food co-op that was pictured in three of the photos on the desk.

"What do you know about him?" one of the policemen asked.

"He goes to classes at the university, but doesn't have the money to pay for them, I answered. "He just goes and sits in the lectures."

"Do you know what classes?" the policeman asked. And before I could answer another policeman in the briefing sneered, "Let me guess, political science?"

"Just give him a chance to talk," the first policeman commanded the second and turned back to me. At that point I realized I was under a police spotlight being questioned. I looked back at the cop who answered for me.

"Yea, you're right," I said. "He likes political science. How'd you know?"

"He does more than like political science," the second cop said. But at that the first cop looked at the second in a manner that clearly said *shut up*.

"Can you remember anything else he told you?" asked the one in charge.

"Well, he told me I could go with him to crash classes anytime I wanted," I answered. "And, oh yes, his father lives in South America."

"Bolivia?" the policeman asked. "Yea, how'd you know?" I replied.

"We think his father is part of the Communist Party in Bolivia," continued the officer. "The man you met attends university classes to make contacts. We think he has sources of money from outside the United States as well. Do you still have contact with him?"

"No," I answered. "I haven't seen him since I quit going to the food co-op months ago."

"That's all the better for you," the policeman told me. "Apparently, he's a trained organizer."

"Trained communists at the university," I said quietly.

"Unfortunately, yes," replied the officer in charge. "Our Marxist friends in the Kremlin have successfully made their way into our universities and they're using our free speech environment to get to our young people."

While I filled their cars the police finished their briefing and headed into the city to help control the riots. Before they left I couldn't resist what was churning inside me, "How bad is it?" I asked.

"Oh, it's bad," answered the officer who questioned me. "Bad enough that Marxists are accepted on the faculty and held in esteem at the University of Wisconsin."

I walked from the gas pumps into my little office and sat in silence thinking about the university environment and reflecting on how I'd come in contact with this organizer. I found myself in a conversation with him in less than two days after joining a lunch co-op.

He was intelligent, friendly and just an ordinary guy like me. Almost an older brother type, someone had trained him well because he knew that most students were short of money and would jump at the chance to beat the system. Attending classes for free was like sneaking into the movies or shoplifting a bottle of scotch from a liquor store. From there it was just another step into the riots. And to help students make that all-important undergraduate step, on-campus training was available for free at the student union. No, really, I'm not kidding.

I found out about it through my friend, David, who I met in the dormitory my first year. As winter ended in early 1970, David invited me to a meeting at 8:00 p.m. in the student union. There, two older type students had their own room and were teaching a class to other students on how to act in the upcoming riots that would be held in the spring when the weather got warmer.

They taught us how to breathe when tear-gassed by using wet handkerchiefs as bandanas and how to break the hold of an arresting policeman. They taught how to throw projectiles at the police (referring to them as *the pigs*) protecting ourselves behind the first line of protesters and why it was most effective to aim at the officers' faces and knees. But not every class was as openly radical as these workshops. A student could get his Marxism in accredited lectures.

Sociology professor Maurice Zeitlin taught one of the classes that actually could be attended for free if a student who paid for the class invited you. As you might guess, my friend David invited me. He was one of the few and the proud who actually signed up for this popular class before it filled up during the first hours of registration.

Zeitlin was somewhat of a campus cult hero, the cult of Cuban communist revolutionary, Che Guevara. At the University of Wisconsin this was actually a designer look that included Che t-shirts, and army greens with black berets and Che goatee beards. The only thing missing were autographed Che backpacks sold at the university bookstore. To sport the Che look about campus meant that you were in the face of the imperialist United States and for the socialist revolution that would transform America and the world.

What made professor Zeitlin a celebrity was his published interview with the communist revolutionary shortly after Castro took over in Cuba. Soon after Castro announced his allegiance to Moscow, Zeitlin rushed to Havana and interviewed Che Guevara who was Castro's 2nd in command.[24] Then in 1967 Che went to Bolivia to foment a socialist revolution there. (Hmmm, Bolivia sounded familiar.) But Che was captured and executed by the Bolivian government in October 1967.[25]

Che's diary was taken along with him and *Ramparts* magazine published it and circulated it worldwide.[26] Zeitlin cheered the Cuban Revolution writing for *Ramparts* [27] and turned out to be a Che groupie. "No social justice is possible without a vision like Che's,"[28] Zeitlin would say about the man who helped bring totalitarian dictatorship to Cuba.

An evangelist for Marxism, professor Zeitlin let his students invite others about the campus to attend his lectures. "Ok, ok, I'll go," I told David. And we arrived at the class after walking through a cold winter day in Madison. The place was packed with sixty students and I had to stand along with about twenty others in a room with a capacity of about forty.

There was no place to hang our coats and the air in the room was rebreathed. About 15 students promptly lit up cigarettes ignoring the no smoking signs on the walls and a blue haze filled the room as they struck their blow against authority. It was a politically correct statement for revolutionaries to smoke. And Zeitlin said nothing against the smokers but talked in a rapid streak like he'd been drinking coffee all morning on an empty stomach.

He spoke in terms of concepts that were layered in his premises. However, from the classes that I attended with David I would summarize it this way: America oppressed the world and real freedom and social justice will break out in the Western Hemisphere if the great evil engine of American Capitalism ceased to exist. All this would happen when Americans understood and lived out socialism. It was good to get outside and breathe fresh air again.

But the open air at the University of Wisconsin was no retreat from classes in a Marxist worldview. At least once a week in the spring there was some type of "free speech" declaration going on in the mall area outside the main library. Listening there I learned penetrating analysis of world politics and economy. I learned that America is the great perpetrator of worldwide injustice through its international corporations. Instead of exporting jobs and development, our military industrial complex sucked resources and enslaved populations.

And even though Russian Premier Nikita Khrushchev threatened to bury America and later installed nuclear missiles ninety miles off our east coast,[29] I learned there was no real nuclear threat from the Soviets. It was only their fear of our naked aggression that drove them to build nuclear weapons. -----Of course, I slept better after hearing that. -----

I also learned American foreign policy was driven by uncontrolled corporate greed for profits; any good that we claimed to do was tainted with evil motives. For instance, our military actions in Vietnam were criminal and actually meant to squash the aspirations for freedom of an oppressed population so that we could reinforce their servitude to our imperialist agenda. Did you get all that?

Above all, America was bad. Even the Declaration of Independence was actually a clever deception meant to give a small band of rich white men their own nation. The only real solution was a new order of authority where greed was unable to control the distribution of wealth. The best and final solution, then, was a new socialist world order. *Who will be in charge of that?* I wondered.

In addition to the bullhorns and microphones of protest every spring, there were the picket lines of students outside the classrooms on strike against the war, the President, the military, and the university. After braving the pushing, shoving and verbal harassment to cross the picket lines and attend a class, at any moment pepper gas could drift gently inside on a spring breeze. Taking lecture notes is a pain when you're noxious and blinded by tear gas, but I surmised it was still a small price to pay for a quality education at a distinguished university.

Of the forty courses I took at the University of Wisconsin studying for my BA, there were eight that stood out, but not because of their excellence. They were the courses where my professors *did not* make politically slanted and cynical remarks.[30] To be fair, I'm sure there were others I've forgotten about. But, according to my best recollection, I was subjected with regularity to political opinion in at least half of my classes. And the climate of academic intimidation reached into all areas.

One Catholic student I knew, Maureen, passed her final Biology exam with an "A". But when she wrote a one-sentence note to her professor that she believed in creation rather than evolution, he summoned her to his office and threatened to fail her unless she recant to his satisfaction her belief in God as Creator and agree with "scientific evidence." Apparently, his mission teaching Biology included attacking students of the Christian faith. Outrageous? Yes. Unlike Maureen who sat patiently through the class, mastered the material and aced the exams, her professor felt his dominion and power threatened by an idea.

He shared the same fears of Joseph Stalin who said, "Ideas are far more powerful than guns." [31] And one idea terrified that professor of biology. After all, just imagine what manner of rebellion might break out at the University of Wisconsin if an "A" student of an atheist professor was allowed to believe in the Creator. Never mind the United States Declaration of Independence, she had to be stopped! She was punished for not learning the material. He lowered her grade.

Right now you might be thinking, *Oh come on, that was over thirty years ago. It was nothing more than a freak incident from a time of unrest?*

Not so, today it's worse. According to best selling author and scholar, David Horowitz, student indoctrination and intimidation in American universities is an accepted practice. In his book *Indoctrination U.,* published in 2006, Horowitz demonstrates academic abuse of students as an accepted practice nationwide by teachers in both high school and college.

Most telling were the hearings at Temple University in Philadelphia where student after student came forward with accounts of radical political agitation and in-class harassment. Every student interviewed said they kept quiet for fear of reprisals from their professors.[32]

In another case a student at Palisades High School in Palisades, California was thrown out of class for saying that Saddam Hussein had gassed the Kurds; a fact his teacher said was false.[33] The student was right, but the incident left a nagging question. Why throw any kid out of class for giving a wrong answer? That's not education. But it sure serves the goal to indoctrinate students and abuse them for disagreement.

Going back to 1970 is exactly the point because that's when many universities changed direction. The thirty years of radical discourse and political correctness that followed produced entire areas of curriculum on campuses based on socialist assumptions. So while socialism failed all over the world and communist nations embraced free markets,[34]

American universities embraced socialism. Go figure. And according to Horowitz, those socialist agendas *require abuse* as a means of enforcement.[35]

So much so that the student governments in 160 universities across America passed "The Academic Bill of Rights" to fight academic abuse saying that students have a right to learn free of political harassment and academic reprisals.

But it finally took the exposure of University of Colorado professor Ward Churchill to bring the magnitude of the problem to the attention of the American public in 2006. Professor Churchill was recorded and later publicly exposed for teaching his students that the victims in the twin towers who died on 9/11 were little Adolph Eichmanns. Churchill taught his students that the professionals in the World Trade Center were Nazi mass murderers who deserved to die.[36] In the twisted Marxist mind of Professor Churchill the professionals profiting in world trade were evil, and he approved of their deaths at the hands of Islamic psychopaths.

The University of Colorado investigation found Churchill guilty of gross misconduct as well as falsification, plagiarism and fabrication. In other words, he was a lying phony.[37] In their report, however, The University of Colorado said they hired him in full knowledge of his political viewpoint and his unqualified academic status while later promoting him to full professor.[38] So if Churchill didn't deceive them, what was he doing as a full professor at the University of Colorado? Answer: They wanted him for what he was, but they fired him because he embarrassed them at their own game.

From Pennsylvania to Wisconsin to Colorado to California students are taught to "believe" in political agendas put forth in numerous academic classes where disagreement means lower grades and public humiliation.[39] Why?

For that answer we have to turn back to that champion of the socialist utopia of Russia, Joseph Stalin, who said, "Education is a weapon whose effects depend on who holds it in his hands and at whom it is aimed."[40] Is the picture becoming clearer?

In the early 1970's the University of Wisconsin offered students a smorgasbord of socialist indoctrination that would make Stalin proud. Marxist professors taught their worldview in the classrooms. Protest organizers preached the spiritual laws of the new socialist world order in free speech gatherings outside. Behind closed doors in the student union graduate students coached the undergraduates in how to riot and maim policemen. And friendly trained communist revolutionaries from Latin America attended classes for free staying close by to coach students in organizing a revolt. But wait, it got worse.

On May 4, 1970 only a few days remained in the spring semester. Five hundred and fifteen miles away from Madison, Wisconsin 14-year-old Mary Ann Vecchio[41] joined her friends experiencing the more adventurous life she sought when she ran away from her home in Opa-laka, Florida. For her the action was on the Kent State University campus that day where anti-war protests were continuing. She joined in but within minutes found herself kneeling at the side of Jeffrey Miller who was shot dead in front of her by the Ohio National Guard.[42] A photojournalism student named John Filo was at the protest and snapped her picture capturing her anguish.

Days earlier demonstrators raged out of control and torched the ROTC building on the Kent State campus causing the Ohio governor to call up the guard to restore order. When demonstrators directly targeted the guardsmen with rocks, they responded with tear gas. Then suddenly, a volley of live ammunition was fired and four people fell dead. John Filo's photo hit the wires nationwide and campuses erupted in protests.[43]

The story was covered in the *Daily Cardinal*, the University of Wisconsin's campus newspaper. Working at the paper during these days was 22-year-old Leo Burt who met a young writer named David Fine. Burt introduced Fine to the Armstrong brothers who were already responsible for three bombings in Wisconsin, one of them an ordinance factory in Baraboo.[44] In July the four of them began planning to write a front-page story of their own.

Physicist and researcher Robert Fassnacht went to his lab located in the basement level of Sterling Hall at the University of Wisconsin and worked all night and into the early morning August 24, 1970 to finish up loose ends before leaving on the family vacation. He never made it.

At 3:42 a.m. the Armstrong brothers, Fine and Burt detonated a 2000 pound car bomb of ammonium nitrate and jet fuel that gutted Sterling Hall, damaged 26 other buildings and was heard miles away. Their target was the Army Math Research Center. They missed. But Robert Fassnacht died in the explosion and was survived by his wife, a three-year-old son and twin baby girls. The bombers all made the FBI's

Ten Most Wanted list.[45]

Two days after the bombing the *Wisconsin State Journal* published an article about UW students arming themselves for further action. The president of the student government, Michael Jaliman, told the newspaper that students were stockpiling weapons and would "probably" carry out further attacks in order to remove ROTC (Army or Navy Officer Training) units from the campus.[46] Then in a statement meant to further terrorize ROTC students with fear of being killed, the Wisconsin Socialist Party said that Americans who supported the Vietnam War should not be surprised at the Sterling Hall bombing.[47] In response, the Navy moved their weekly drill practice inside the locked doors of the Camp Randall Sports Center next to the football stadium.

The Reserve Officer Training Course (ROTC) is a competitive examination process that awards a few outstanding high school graduates across the country with full scholarships to top universities. A student on a Navy scholarship had to successfully complete the military classes in addition to maintaining a good grade average in all his other course studies while graduating in four years. Afterwards, they served as a commissioned officer on active duty for five years in return for their education. Apparently, winning an academic scholarship from the Army or the Navy made you a moving target for the socialist revolutionaries.

It seemed the University of Wisconsin had finally reaped the whirlwind of the radical socialist revolution it embraced. In the fall attendance dropped dramatically as thousands of parents and students began to realize how dangerous the environment had become.

I was in the north woods of Wisconsin at the time and was advised of the threats against the lives of those in ROTC units. I was entering my 3rd year of NROTC (Naval officer training) and the conversation I had one evening after a fishing trip jolted my world even more.

Colonel Wright was a family friend who had just returned from a year of combat duty with the U.S. Air Force in Vietnam. He had an MS in physics and 20 years experience as an Air Force pilot. As we sat out and enjoyed the late August evening at Lake Adelaide, we talked about what had happened just days before. "The University of Wisconsin is a dangerous place," he told me. "Are you going back?"

"Yea, I am. I think I can get a full scholarship from the Navy this year," I said. "But I've got a question for you, Colonel. What do you think is really going on?" He answered abruptly and without speculation.

"Kent State and the University of Wisconsin in Madison are two top schools where mathematical research for national defense is conducted," he began. "That's why they were the top targets for anti-defense riots."

"So, you think this is coordinated?"

"Absolutely," he answered. "Our enemy has a coordinated media strategy in America complete with rhetorical symbolism. It's part of an aggressive military strategy to gain headlines, manipulate the media and sway public opinion. Our enemies can't defeat us in the field, but they can defeat us through public opinion and the manipulation of our media in America."[48]

And that's exactly what they did according to Stanislav Lunev, Russia's highest-ranking military defector to the West. The Kremlin used undercover operatives and front organizations to fund every antiwar movement in America. By 1970 their budget for antiwar propaganda in the United States exceeded $1 billion, enough money to buy 125,000 thirty-second Super Bowl ads that year. And by targeting the universities they not only steered our public opinion but also trained the next generation of Americans in Marxism. "It was a hugely successful campaign and well worth the cost," said Lunev.

There was a cold nip in the air. Summer was over and college students across the nation returned to their campuses. Colonel Wright was prophetic, of course. Within months the United States was pulling out of Vietnam. In the years that followed millions died in the socialist killing fields after the communist takeover. A takeover that American Marxist historian Eugene Genovese said he welcomed.[49]

Upon returning, the commander of my Navy ROTC unit at the U.W. nominated me for a full scholarship, the Navy approved and I accepted. Then, the Navy took charge of my education and changed my entire curriculum from liberal arts to engineering. They paid all tuition, furnished me with textbooks, provided all penalties for my revised enrollment and began paying me fifty dollars a month.

I was delighted. My new classes included Chemistry, Naval Science, 2nd level Calculus, and Computer Science completing the Navy's required 17 credits per semester. But God didn't give me the talent to be an engineer, and within one semester I was on academic probation and promptly summoned to appear before Lt. Commander Kyle, a graduate of The United States Naval Academy in Annapolis, Maryland who was in charge of the 2ⁿᵈ classmen (Junior year students).

"Sit down, Mr. McGregor," he commanded.

I obeyed quietly as he stared at me silently across his desk for a moment then spoke again. "I'll be brief, midshipman. Your academic record is unacceptable to the United States Navy and we're paying for your schooling. Do I make myself clear?"

"Yes, sir," I answered.

"Do you want to keep your scholarship?" he asked.

"Yes, sir," I answered.

"You're going to have to prove that," he challenged. "Because if you don't want to succeed, I'll see that you get out of this program."

I sat in silence as Commander Kyle's bedside manner sunk in.

"We'll see if you've got what it takes to be a Navy officer," he continued. "Personally, I don't think you do. Maybe you'll prove me wrong. Who knows?" Then he began to smirk. "I understand you applied to go to The Naval Academy once."

"Yes, sir," I said.

"You'd have never made it," he said, and paused for effect. "Well, you have to get your grades up to stay in this program. Any questions?"

"No, sir," I said.

"Dismissed."

With that I left his office and quickly walked out the front door of the NROTC building at 1610 University Avenue. *Nice guy*, I thought. The meeting had taken all of three minutes, and I was shaking in my loafers. I've always wondered if Commander Kyle's put downs were meant to motivate me. I'll never know. I got my grades up and managed to get within six months of my commission, but a sudden illness disqualified me from Navy service in my senior year.

However, I learned a very valuable lesson about the U.S. military. They hold themselves accountable for protecting a nation. Failure, and poor preparation mean losing in combat, and that was not an option for a U.S. Navy officer. Mr. Kyle simply told me the way it was.

Two years later in 1972 President Nixon unleashed American firepower to end the Vietnam War. Air Force B52's bombed the North Vietnamese capital city of Hanoi by night and Navy fighters destroyed their missile defenses by day. Realizing they soon would be ruling over rubble, the North Vietnamese delegation promptly returned to Paris and signed the treaty.[50] But that was still two years in the future.

It was late fall in 1970 as I walked back down University Avenue about five minutes and turned left at Charter Street. Then, for some unknown reason, I walked past Chamberlain Hall and stood in front of what was left of Sterling Hall after the bombing. The building was a charred and pot marked shell. There were no windows, only holes, and entire sections inside were gutted. It was eerie, silent, and sad.

The university leaders were shocked that such an act happened. They might have benefited from a little military training themselves. Perhaps they could have recognized the rhetoric and language of an enemy on their own campus. Our early released prisoners of war from North Vietnam had told their story of torture to the press the year before in August 1969.

It didn't take a genius to recognize that the protest organizers in Madison used the same anti-American slogans as the North Vietnamese prison guards who beat and tortured captured American pilots on the other side of the world in the infamous torture chamber named "The Hanoi Hilton."[51] Why didn't the U.W. administrators connect the dots?

What was the big mystery? An enemy always probes for weakness before attacking. The University of Wisconsin had been dancing with the devil. All manors of rebellious rage and rhetoric took place there. Sterling Hall was merely another rhetorical symbol permitted by the University of Wisconsin, a school where the student government President supported armed terror against ROTC students.

The rhetoric of agitation and protest had dissolved into the rhetoric of war and threat. Finally, an act of war was committed and someone died. As I stared at the bombed out hulk of Sterling Hall, it was a premonition of events to come in my own life.

In the mid 1980's I would be staring at many such buildings in Lebanon, a little country about 135 miles long on the east coast of the Mediterranean Sea directly north of Israel. And the events that would take me to Lebanon as a reporter and television producer had already started as I stood staring at Sterling Hall that very day.

During that fall semester at the U.W. in 1970 events on the other side of the world were taking place that would change the politics in that little nation that traced its ancient past to the Phoenician city-states that flourished in maritime trading 3000 years ago. In 1970 Lebanon was the only democracy in the Arab World. It's high educational standards and free enterprise developed a wealthy, pristine, beautiful nation of hilltop villages, recreational beaches and snowcapped mountain resorts.

The capital city of Lebanon was Beirut, often referred to as the "Paris of the Middle East". Somewhat of a mini Las Vegas with beautiful hotels, casinos and nightclubs, Beirut was also a shopper's dream town where the latest European fashions and the world's finest goods could be purchased at prices of a bargain hunter's fantasy. Under priced Mercedes, BMW's, fine Persian rugs, hand made furnishings and tailor made designer clothes were all part of the atmosphere of Beirut. One man was about to change that. His name was Yassir Arafat.

In the Middle East September 1970 would become known as, "Black September," a month that set in motion the loss of 100,000 Lebanese lives and the destruction of the only Arab democracy, Lebanon.

But the actual events of Black September did not take place in Lebanon. Instead, the name refers to the events that took place in the country of Jordan when an armed militia called the Palestine Liberation Organization (PLO), under the command of Yassir Arafat, tried to overthrow the government and kill the king.[52] (I discuss the details of this in the chapter, *Six Days That Changed The World.*) When the Jordanian Army defeated Arafat's anarchistic militia the PLO retreated into neighboring Lebanon and proceeded to destroy that nation.

Yassir Arafat, himself, was a made up image, a poster child. In full living color he represented the Arab media's ad against America and Israel. When *Time Magazine* put him on their cover in December 1968,[53] he sported sunglasses, five days growth of beard and a checkered headscarf called a kafeeya. This was his trademark along with a holstered pistol and pressed olive drab army fatigues with shoulder epaulets. "The others are not using this style. I have my own style," bragged Arafat.[54]

But Arafat's real style was that of a thug. The head of his mother's clan, Amin al- Husseini, the Grand Mufti of Jerusalem, recruited Yassir Arafat when he was a teenage gang leader in Cairo. An ally of Adolf Hitler, Husseini was listed by the United Nations as a war criminal, yet he escaped the WW II war crimes trials in Nuremberg, Germany and fled to Egypt.[55] There he mentored Yassir Arafat in a "liberation theology" that included killing Jews and destroying countries.[56]

Having failed in Jordan, Arafat later applied his skills to Lebanon where his Soviet sponsored and armed PLO controlled entire sections of that nation. Rape, murder, kidnapping, mutilation and extortion of the

Lebanese were everyday occurrences in those PLO sectors.[57]

In Madison when the weather turned cold numerous students sported the PLO look as a statement of solidarity with Yassir Arafat wearing checkered kafeeyas as scarves under green army surplus jackets. Of course, the students in Madison didn't know about Arafat's mentor the Mufti, Amin al- Husseini. Arafat boasted of that connection later in 1985.[58] However, in 1965 the prominent Jewish historian, Joseph Schechtman, published his 14th book *The Mufti and The Fuehrer* that made a scholarly investigation of the sinister connection between Hitler and the Arab Middle East. So, the documentation had been public for at least five years.[59]

In the meantime Arafat remained an image, a sketch, a symbol fashioned for the western media. Dressed in fatigue jacket, pistol on hip, scruffy bearded in checkered kafeeya…he was Che Guevara meets desert liberator. While in truth, he was nothing more than a street gang leader trained by a Nazi war criminal. But dressed up with his sunglasses spouting freedom-fighter-rhetoric, at 5' 4" he cut a swashbuckling image for Americans willing to believe such nonsense.

Yet while Yassir Arafat pranced across the world stage, he didn't realize the Soviet Military manipulated him. The Russian KGB placed a Palestinian agent inside PLO headquarters as an aid to Arafat's most trusted advisor, his chief of intelligence. So, Arafat's militia in Lebanon became just another part of the Soviet Union's use of the Muslims in the Middle East. Then, beginning in 1970 the Russian military supplied arms and Arabic speaking advisors to train the Muslim militias in Lebanon.

More confident and encouraged after his talks with Moscow in 1972 the Lebanese Shiite leader, Moussa al Sadr, called for the Islamic takeover of Lebanon saying, "If our demands are not met, we will take them by force; if this country is not given, it must be taken." So, there it was. The Kremlin successfully divided the Lebanese democracy setting Muslims against Christians. When the Lebanese Civil War began three years later in 1975, Russia supplied the Islamic militias through Syria.

But Communism was doomed to failure. Based upon socialism that led to its bankruptcy, only 75 years passed from the Russian Revolution to the downfall of the Soviet Empire.[60] Nevertheless, leading universities in the United States seemed very comfortable embracing socialism and the rhetoric of our enemies who tortured our prisoners of war.

Such a gullible climate deserved another lie, and a secret organization that Yassir Arafat belonged to saw their opportunity. In 1963 The Muslim Brotherhood (Al Ikhwan) founded the Muslim Student Association in the United States. Two years later Joseph Schechtman revealed the Nazi connection, but the game was already afoot.

Islam teaches the Doctrine of Deceit known as *Kithman* and the Doctrine of Lying named *Taqiya*.[61] Jihad, Islamic war against unbelievers, teaches the non-Muslim world must be deceived giving Islam the advantage to conquer the trusting and unsuspecting.[62]

"We Muslims have been ordered to do brainwashing," said the imam recorded undercover at Green Lane Mosque.[63] In 1963 aspects of Islam came to America presenting a media profile and an academic presence to set us up for a fall.

At the time I couldn't know the Lebanese war zone was in my future. I graduated with my B.A. in 1973 and moved away from Madison. Yet, even with the chaos, danger and socialism, I believe I was in the right place at the right time. Call it destiny if you like because when I journeyed to Lebanon ten years later, I felt well prepared. The University of Wisconsin contributed greatly, but my life took a turn that opened a door leaving an ominous decision staring me in the face.

A decade passed between the year I graduated from the University of Wisconsin and when I left for the Middle East war zone. I worked steadily towards that moment. Yet, when it arrived, I still asked myself, *"Are you really going to do this?"*

Chapter 2
Discovering The Jihad

My heart was pounding as I hung up the phone. My t-shirt was wet with sweat. It was two in the afternoon on a hot June day in Virginia Beach and I'd been awake 34 hours packing all night. Everything I could move was in the living room in boxes. The rest I was leaving behind or giving away, including my car. It was the moving company that just called telling me their truck was in route to my apartment for pick up.

Within hours I'd be leaving Norfolk International for Israel. I sat down. Sweat dripped slowly down my face as I stared at the six-foot pile of boxes directly in front of me and stopped to think, *what happened that brought me to this point?* While I waited for the truck, I reviewed the highlight reel. I didn't know what was coming. At that moment I couldn't possibly anticipate that I'd soon be face to face with terrorism.

So, my mind flashed back and the videotape played peacefully in my imagination. The faces of my friends were clear in the sunshine of the crisp fall air and I heard their voices as we left Calvary Church early Sunday afternoon, November 4th, 1979; the day these events began.

The next day, Monday was a day like most others. Turning on the CBS Evening News I listened in astonishment as Walter Cronkite unfolded the story about a group of armed Iranian students that stormed the American embassy in Tehran on Sunday, November 4th and were holding 63 Americans hostage. Like many Americans I thought, *what the hell's going on here!*

Not only was this a violation of international law, historically, America had reacted with military force to any such threatening actions against its embassies. This was not to be as President Jimmy Carter's administration sought to play it cool and wait out the new Iranian government of Ayatollah Khomeini.

I could see it clearly in my imagination. During those weeks Iran learned how to play with America. They learned our values and measured our reactions to their actions. They learned how to use and manipulate us according to our emotions. They learned that our respect for life could be used to gain international attention to their cause. They would kidnap and demand. We would put them on TV. They would preach their hatred. We would listen and broadcast it to the world. They were on the offense running their plays. We were on the defense stunned and staggering backwards.

As the days turned into weeks the American people watched in disbelief and mounting anger while their government appeared helpless, unable to do anything to take back their embassy or gain the release of the hostages. Instead, night after night, Americans watched as the three television networks sought to outdo each other in their coverage of the ongoing story.

Driven by competition and profit, the U.S. media played right into Khomeini's hands. He was good for ratings! On November 8th just four days after the embassy takeover, ABC introduced a new nightly ½ hour news show called *Nightline* that was dedicated solely to the coverage of the *Iranian Hostage Crisis*. This was exactly what Khomeini wanted. Just imagine; the American media actually gave the Iranian Revolution its own show on American television!

The American audience got a daily dosage of what the kidnappers holding the embassy thought of us. We got videotaped lectures from Khomeini, himself, who defined America as a morally degenerate nation, the "Enemies of Islam," the "Great Satan" of the world who sponsored the "Little Satan," Israel. The Ayatollah said the United States was responsible for the oppression of the Islamic people of the world. And through the crisis, he demonstrated to Muslim terrorists how to successfully attack America.

Like so many Americans, I looked at this gray-bearded-black-robed-turban-headed-hate-preacher as a weirdo who captured the world stage largely as a result of our American television networks giving him airtime. He was good for their ratings. After all, ABC bet the success of their new show on, *I wonder what the Ayatollah is doing tonight?* So, the United States watched television while the Iranian terrorists learned.

"I was amazed," said Touraj, an Iranian soldier from the Khomeini guard. "Our media strategy worked better than we ever imagined. The American reporters believed whatever we told them. And believe me, Khomeini was a lot worse than the Shah ever was. He killed a lot more people." [64]

A month later during the Christmas holidays my roommate, Gordon, invited me to his parent's house for a special dinner celebration. He wanted to introduce me to his uncle Wesley. Now, my roommate had a kind heart and a sense of humor that loved to catch you off guard. Nonetheless, I was thrilled to be going to a big family celebration at Christmastime. My roommate's father ran an office cleaning business, and the family home was a white house on the most peaceful street in Illinois.

We walked up the front porch steps into the vestibule, took off our winter coats and were welcomed into a room full of 12 smiling people. A gentile smiling medium built man in his mid forties stepped towards us. "Let me introduce you to my Uncle Wes," Gordon said. "Perhaps you two will find some common interests. Uncle Wes is the White House Correspondent of United Press International." I glanced back at Gordon and realized he was smirking. *Gotcha*, his smile said. That evening I got tutoring time that must have been the envy of a thousand other up-and-coming reporters.

I questioned Uncle Wesley about his understanding of President Carter, as well as world events. He questioned me on my future aspirations, and I told him I wanted to be an international correspondent. As the evening went on it became evident to me that I needed years of experience, schooling and some good breaks to fulfill such aspirations. My first break came two months later in the spring of 1980.

The host of a series of television programs being made at Channel 38 in Chicago took a liking to me and invited me along to observe the five nights of recording. At the station I met a fascinating guest participating in the programs, an archeologist who specialized in the Middle East. For two nights as we rode the Northwestern Commuter in and out of the Chicago Loop together, he made these ancient civilizations come alive.

I remember his bright blue eyes sparkled with life as he sat opposite from me engrossed in giving me a midnight mini lecture on the double-decker commuter car. Suddenly my imagination was 3500 years in the past. His vivid explanation of the Codes of Hammurabi of Babylon compared with the Laws of Moses of the Hebrews made me realize that regarding some aspects of history, a thousand years was truly as one day. [65]

As the videotape played in my imagination those two late night commutes finally fell into place with an *ah-ha, now I see it.* Those two train rides with the archeologist showed me that Israel and the Middle East never left the world stage. The ancient times were today's news, and I was going to be involved in history.

The next scene that flashed through my mind made me laugh. When I entered graduate school later that fall, I volunteered Friday nights participating in the studio recording of a weekly news summary program broadcast Sundays on the local cable system. I think our audience was measured once at 100,000 people. It was never clear how we got so many to watch us instead of those *big network guns* on their Sunday talking head programs. Our program was filled with local talent on their first gig, so I think they all wrote to their families and relatives telling them to watch.

My big responsibility was in a non-descript spot. I was the teleprompter operator. It was the lowliest and most dead-end job in the production. I scotch taped the news copy read by on-camera talent to a five-foot long electric belt that passed in a loop under a small non-broadcast 7-11 security style black and white camera. The electric belt worked on a light dimmer switch and moved faster or slower as I twisted the knob.

The signal from this camera was connected to a device that hung on the front of the studio cameras. As the on-camera talent read their lines they looked directly into the broadcast camera. The talent never had to look down or turn a page. It gave the very slick illusion to the audience that the newsreader was telling the news from memory, but woe to the man operating the machine when a newsreader lost their spot.

"What the hell do you think you're doing!" the producer yelled at me kicking open the studio door. The on-camera talent who lost his place and froze up was right next to him screaming. "Who do you think you are sabotaging me? I can't believe it. You deliberately tried to make me look bad."

"What are you talking about?" I replied. "When you stopped, I stopped. When you started, I started. Why would I sabotage you, anyway?" The two of them unloaded their tension and rage on me for another five minutes until the executive producer calmly walked in and said to get started with a retake. There was no justice for me that night. I learned that television was a mean place where 800-pound-gorilla-nobodies saw their raw ambitions and fears come to the surface. Truth was easily changed to make people look good. *Whew, how did I ever survive?* I reflected.

The answer flashed quickly to mind. Friday after Friday night for the next six months I scotch taped news copy to the teleprompter belt, turned it on and secretly read the copy to myself before the studio production began. I asked the executive producer if I could research and write a story for his approval. And within a year I was reading my own stories on-camera. Many of those stories concerned some aspect of news in the Middle East so I began tracking the story lines through five newspapers each week. I read the *Times of London, The Jerusalem Post, The International Herald Tribune, The Chicago Tribune* and the *New York Times*. Another break was about to come my way.

The executive producer expressed interest in the Lebanese Civil War where The Palestine Liberation Organization (PLO) was playing a major role. A militia led by Yassir Arafat, the PLO had 40,000 non- Lebanese soldiers living in Lebanon. According to my producer everybody was saying the same line. The PLO were the underdogs and the "so-called" Christian militias were oppressing Muslims. "See if you can find another angle," he said to me. "I know you're busy with studies, but if you find something good, you can cover it."

Within a week I found an organization in Washington, D.C. called the Lebanese Information Center. They were dedicated to telling the press about the Christian perspective on the civil war in Lebanon. We needed each other. Their success with the press in D.C. was limited, and I was looking for their story. So, I drove to Washington to meet a man named Gus, a spokesmen at the center. He was very gracious and spoke excellent English. I made some interesting discoveries.

The correspondents in Beirut from the major networks and newspapers of the Western press lived in the Commodore Hotel, which was owned by a Palestinian. The Palestinian Army (PLO) protected the reporters so long as they played along and didn't ask too many questions. The phone lines were dependable in war torn Beirut because the hotel owner paid off his *friends* who controlled the central telephone build-ing.[66] So, the hotel was protected, the phone lines were good and the bar at the Commodore stayed open. Little surprise that the news in the English-speaking world from Beirut favored the Palestinian cause.

Gus said the Lebanese Christian students at George Washington University were having a dinner meeting that week and he would get me an invitation. "You'll get to interview some students who can open your eyes," he promised. "I think this will give you a new angle on your story." Wow, no man ever spoke more understated words.

As I entered the room where the dinner was held, I noticed easels placed about with huge black and white photos. Looking more closely at the photos I saw gruesome scenes of mutilated children, dead bodies in the streets, and decapitated people tied to chairs in living rooms. It was a holocaust display of massacred Lebanese Christian towns.

Gory photos from the Christian town of Chekka in Northern Lebanon close to Arafat's PLO stronghold in Tripoli were shown. But the largest display came from a town named Damour, a seaside suburb to the south of Beirut where 583 people perished in one night at the hands of the PLO January 20th, 1976. The town was pillaged, the women raped, the church desecrated, and the cemetery destroyed. A person claiming to be an eyewitness said children were shot in the streets at point blank range.

That night I interviewed five male students whose comments I edited into a montage. They told of being kidnapped, beaten, and tortured by PLO soldiers for being Christian. One told of a friend whose body was cut into pieces and returned to his family in a box after they paid a ransom. Two of the young men told me of women they knew who were kidnapped and repeatedly raped by PLO soldiers. From that evening it became clear that the news we got of the underdog PLO fighting off "Christian oppression" had been carefully shaped for our consumption in America.

I went back one more time for another day of interviews with a Catholic Priest / historian and another shadowy figure that had worked in the pentagon and was directly involved in "defense counseling" of the Christian militias. Simply put, he was a gunrunner to the Phalangists militia (the leading Christian militia) that supported President elect Bashir Gemeyal, who was assassinated in September 1982 just two months before my interviews.

Bashir Gemeyal was 35 years old when he was elected President of Lebanon on August 23rd, 1982. A handsome young family man, many Lebanese compared him to President John Kennedy, the glamorous young American President assassinated in 1963. Like President Kennedy, Bashir Gemeyal was known for his passionate speeches and quick wit. In one famous line from a speech he referred to his own nation of Lebanon metaphorically as a "farm" forever caught in the age of castles. After Bashir was assassinated he became a mythical figure, a hope for Lebanon that vanished as a vapor.

During these times my work pleased my executive producer with some noteworthy material, but most importantly, I won the trust of the Lebanese Information Center who lined me up to interview Ex-President of Lebanon, Camille Chamoun. (President for the six years 1952-1958) He was the patriarch of Christian political leaders and one of the most powerful men in Lebanon. He was coming to America to meet with President Reagan.

I returned to Washington, D.C. on a cold winter day late in 1982. The air had the crisp smell of new snow I was familiar with from living in a Chicago suburb. A young bodyguard met us in the lobby of the Dolly Madison Hotel and took my cameraman and me to a room where we were allowed to set up our lights and the two chairs for the interview. In about ten minutes I was introduced to the President's son, Danny Chamoun. He volunteered to talk on camera and gave a pleasant interview. Afterwards, he explained that his father would only talk for a few minutes due to his age and the long trip.

Camille Chamoun entered the room dressed in a charcoal black three-piece suit and sat calmly in the chair opposite me as my cameraman put the miniature Sony lavaliere microphone on his red silk tie. Danny Chamoun sat closely by off-camera while I interviewed the soft-spoken ex-President of Lebanon. He talked about his relation to President Eisenhower and how the U.S. Marines had helped stabilize Lebanon in 1958 during the Pan Arab Movement begun by President Nasser of Egypt. We quickly moved on to discuss the current situation involving the Israeli Army's invasion of Lebanon earlier that summer.

He explained the inability of the Lebanese government to control the PLO's "state-within-the-state" and spoke sadly of the destruction the PLO's lawlessness brought upon Lebanon. "Have you ever been to Lebanon?" he asked in a very fatherly manor. When I answered, "No," he challenged me. "You must go and spend at least a year there," he said. "Then, you will understand."[67]

With that Danny Chamoun ended the interview. As the President left the room Danny Chamoun looked back at me, "We have more than enough journalists in Lebanon, he said with a smile, "He took a liking to you because my father doesn't usually invite journalists to visit

Lebanon."

Call it prophetic if you like. But a few weeks later in January of 1983 I left on a 10-day trip to Beirut along with a team of doctors to meet with the Lebanese Minister of Health. When we stepped off the plane at Beirut International, we all breathed a sigh of relief. After 26 hours of travel without sleep, we wanted a bath and a nap. As we came through customs three taxis from the government met us. Each of our drivers was hand picked for their experience and trustworthiness. Unknown to us at the time our arrival had been publicly announced on the radio the day before making us already at risk on the meanest streets in the world.

My cameraman, Dino, was more relaxed and outgoing than me and quickly struck up a conversation with our driver. "Hello, do you speak any English?" he asked him. To which the driver held up the palm of his hand and twisted his wrist so as to indicate a little, maybe so-so. "What's your name?" Dino shot back. "Halil," he answered, gesturing that he was driving us to our hotel to eat late breakfast. Dino fell into form as he and Halil gestured and spoke in half sentences. I was tuning them out when something caught my ear. "Bashir," said Halil pointing to himself and motioning with his hands on the wheel.

"You drove for Bashir?" Dino replied and looked my way with a nudge in the ribs. Even a sleepless night and jet lag faded quickly as I chimed in, "You drove for Bashir Gemeyal?"

Halil answered nodding *yes* as we came around a corner and into one of the most chaotic traffic jams I ever saw. It looked like the Chicago Loop at rush hour with no traffic lights. In the next 60 seconds I saw a piece of driving that still leaves me at a loss for words. Halil wove through traffic, changed lanes, honked his horn, cut off cars, shifted gears like a racecar driver and never reduced speed. In another minute we popped out of the entangled mass onto a somewhat normal street. He navigated one block against one-way traffic the wrong way, made a hard 90-degree turn and flawlessly joined into another lane going the right way. Dino and I just looked at each other and laughed.

In minutes Halil drove the car up a steep corner and into the compact parking lot of the Alexandre Hotel in the Ashrafieh area of Beirut. We checked in to the main desk and left our television gear in a private locked room. The bags went upstairs with a bellman and Dino and I went straight for the late breakfast especially prepared for our team. We tore pita bread and dipped it into a yogurt cheese called "lebni" that was served with drizzled olive oil and sprinkled on top with fresh mint. On other pita bread we spread butter with marmalade and ate hard-boiled eggs and oil cured black olives that were placed on individual plates between us. I drank fresh orange juice and the waiter suggested some hot chocolate for Dino who didn't like coffee. We were almost finished with breakfast when the rest of the team arrived in the other two taxis.

Halil turned out to be telling the truth about his driving for Bashir Gemeyal. Halil was actually Bashir Gemeyal's private driver.

At three o'clock that afternoon the Prime Minister's son welcomed us in a meeting at the biggest hospital in Beirut. A secretary served Turkish coffee to everyone but my little demitasse cup got the dregs of the pot. I was sipping murky sludge that was sticking in my mouth like wet sand. You just don't gag and spit out your coffee on the table in front of the Prime Minister's son. It was a very uncomfortable moment as I calmly took a napkin up to my mouth and pretended to cough as I spit the mud into the napkin and moved the napkin to the table. Trying not to turn green slowly my hand reached out to the assorted soft drinks provided within arms reach. 7up never tasted so good.

My eyes were burning from lack of sleep when we called it a day around 9:00 p.m. Beirut time that night. Dino and I were both zonked at about 11:00 when rifle fire broke out on a rooftop close by. We both were up instantly as Dino went to the window and tried to see. Neither of us turned on a light. Neither of us could see anything. It was close enough to hear the firefight, but far enough away to feel safe. Well, maybe safe was not a good word. At any rate, we got back to sleep, but not for long. Rooftop roosters from neighboring buildings began crowing at 3:00 in the morning. By 7:00 a.m. the sun was up and both of us were ready for some breakfast.

January in Beirut was like Southern California where 70 degree sky blue sunny days encouraged people to tend their flowers. At night a cool breeze wafted in off the Mediterranean Sea requiring a sweater and windbreaker. Gnarled traffic jams made horn honking a driver's art while twenty-year-old Mercedes flatbed trucks excreted bursts of nasty black diesel smoke briefly engulfing cars behind them. Outside the hotel the daylong ritual of beeping and bursting smoke was in full swing. Dust was everywhere.

Having invaded Lebanon six months earlier in June 1982, the Israeli Army stayed in force south of Beirut. A battalion of U.S.

Marines was outside Beirut International with French and Italian forces controlling other sectors of the city. Making our way from meeting to meeting the team's three cars passed through checkpoints every time we moved between sectors. At first Dino's instincts were to use the camera and document our passage through the checkpoints. The first time we tried it, we nearly lost our camera to a not-so-friendly Italian trooper who warned Dino by pointing his rifle directly at him.

An American citizen originally from Beirut our team leader, Elias, broke up the boring days of meetings with a little tourism. "Today we are going to the Dog River," he announced to the team one morning at breakfast. "There I'm going to give you a little ancient history lesson on Lebanon." This brought some grumbling because some doctors felt it a waste of their time. Holding serve, Elias insisted that nobody wanted to insult our Lebanese host by not taking an interest in their history. So, we piled into the cars heading eleven miles north of the city.

Prior conquerors left monuments to themselves at the mouth of the Dog River. Over 3000 years before, Ramses the Great of Egypt made the first signed peace treaty of world history with the Hittites in 1258 BC naming the Dog River as the border between the two empires. The Babylonians, the Assyrians, the Romans, even the French and the British have all left markers at the Dog River signifying their rulership of the territory known as Lebanon. Fifteen miles further north up the coast laid the ancient ruins of Gebal (Byblos), the oldest city of the Phoenicians referred to by the prophet Ezekiel in the Bible.[68]

That morning in Lebanon, the ancients came alive. I was in the land the archeologist lectured to me about three years before on the commuter train. A thousand years of history was as one day. Here I was in this ancient place with a team of compassionate men of great skill trying to reach out to a broken land and people. At the time none of us except Elias realized how soon the tentacles of evil embracing Lebanon would reach out to America. "Those Marines are going to be massacred," Elias whispered to me alone in confidence. "They're sitting ducks. America just doesn't understand what they're dealing with in Lebanon."

The next morning Gus from the Information Center in Washington, D.C. joined us. He flew to Beirut joining us especially for this day. After meetings in the morning, we went south of the city into the Israeli Army sector to visit the ghost town of Damour and hospitals in the city of Tyre.

Gus had lost two entire families of cousins who were trapped inside their houses in Damour and massacred room to room. For the first time in six years he was returning to look upon the two houses and grieve the passing of so many lost. For him the day was an epiphany.

Directly down the coastal highway going south adorning a high hill with an unobstructed view of the deep blue Mediterranean Sea sat Damour. Six years before almost to the day of our visit the PLO army had surrounded the town in the night with 16,000 soldiers armed with fully automatic weapons, trucks, armored vehicles and machine guns. Tired of using more austere outposts, the PLO army looked with bitter envy on the beautiful pristine Christian village and decided that Damour would become their operational base complete with housing. They simply had to massacre the inhabitants and move in. And that's exactly what they did January 23rd, 1976.[69] An eyewitness, Father Labaky recalled:

> The attack took place from the mountain behind. It was an apocalypse. They were coming, thousands and thousands, shouting 'Allahu Akbar! God is great! Let us attack them for the Arabs, let us offer a holocaust to Mohammad.' And they were slaughtering everyone in their path, men, women and children.[70]

As Halil turned left off the coast road and drove our car up the main street of Damour to the town square where the community center had been, I noticed the coat of arms of the PLO painted large onto the side of the building that occupied the main focal point of town. The emblem showed two fists holding crossed rifles and a hand grenade superimposed on a map of present-day Israel.

The church was desecrated, the graveyard overturned, and houses ransacked. When they invaded six months earlier the Israeli army routed the PLO from Damour in short order. By the time we arrived that January afternoon, Damour was a ghost town. Closely observed by an Israeli APC (armored personnel carrier) with a machine gun, we walked the main streets of Damour in the bright cloudless day.

The next evening I would be just north of Beirut in the suburban port of Juneih, a stronghold of the Christian Lebanese Forces. There I

29

would have an interview with the spokesman of the Lebanese Christian militias, Fadi Hayyak. A lawyer and historian appointed to his post by former President Bashir Gemeyal, Hayyak explained details that cleared the picture up even further. (I go into this meeting in depth in chapter 11.) But this day we were headed deeper into the past. After leaving Damour we traveled further south to the city of Tyre for more meetings. It was another city whose history went back to ancient times.

In 332 BC Alexander the Great conquered the Phoenician city-state of Tyre by building a causeway connecting the mainland part of the city to the island fortress that protected the harbor and the citadel. As the sun melted like a golden ball into the Mediterranean that day in 1983, Dino and I walked down the 2300-year-old causeway and under the Arch of Conquest built by Alexander's army. *How could it be?* I thought. *How can my modern civilization in America be directly connected to this ancient part of the world?*

But connected we were. Two thousand, seven hundred years ago the prophet Habakkuk warned:

> The violence you have done to Lebanon will over-whelm you,…for you have shed man's blood; you have destroyed lands and cities and everyone in them.[71]

That evening as I walked the causeway of ancient history and passed under the Arch of Alexander the Great, I couldn't help but wonder. *The picture of who was doing the violence to Lebanon was not so truthful.*

Yes, it was plain to see Beirut car bombs were a weekly feature on the nightly news. In addition, the major news networks presented the cruel injustice of our time; the mighty Israeli Army with tanks and jets had routed the "underdog" Palestinian Liberation soldiers from their bases in Lebanon and their control of two-thirds of Beirut. The "so-called" Christian militias were to blame for the massacre of helpless Palestinians. And General Ariel Sharon, commander of the Israeli Army in Lebanon, was guilty of turning his back to permit such unprovoked killings.[72] But this was not what I found to be true.

I found a Christian community in Lebanon fighting for their very lives against hoards of Muslim armies armed to the teeth. Virulent

Islamic hatred of Israel had encouraged artillery shelling of Northern Israeli towns. With Israeli citizens living in bomb shelters, the Israeli invasion of Lebanon liberated towns in both nations of PLO oppression. Still, the Arab world blamed Israel as the perpetrators of the bloodletting in Lebanon.[73] When in actuality, the PLO killed more than 50,000 Lebanese Christians, for which the Christian militias took their revenge at Sabra and Shatila.[74]

But with the PLO out of Lebanon, a real clue of the conflict came a year later after the Israeli Army pulled out of Beirut. United Muslim militias overran sixty Christian villages in the Shouf Mountains leaving 1000 dead and 50,000 Christian people homeless.[75] It was as Camille Chamoun said. The PLO had been a catalyst that united the Muslims to "Islamize" Lebanon.[76]

Where was the balance in the American press on these issues? Without reporters stating the conclusion specifically, the body of news content did it for them. Ever so clearly we got the picture that the Israelis and the Christians were the real bad guys of the Middle East. *The storyline seems upside down,* I thought. Was the Western media living in the Commodore Hotel influenced by an Islamic agenda?

Halil performed his road magic as we headed north from Tyre towards Beirut with the Mediterranean Sea on my left. The last red rays of daylight dissolved into thick black darkness on the coast road and I was lost in thought. *This is an old fashioned Muslim jihad against Christians and Jews.*

"Worldwide Movers," said the man through my screen door. With that the video images in my mind abruptly turned off. I was less than three hours away from the start of my adventure into history.

Chapter 3
Where Wise Men Fear To Go

One month had passed since I interviewed with the general manager of Middle East Television, a company with offices in Beirut, Jerusalem, and the beautiful Mediterranean Island of Cyprus, Greece. *How can I go wrong?* I thought. "Mr. McGregor, I reviewed your work and it's my pleasure to congratulate you and offer you a job as an associate producer," he told me. *Great!* I thought.

"We have a new position opening up," he continued. "We're assigning you to Northern Israel and South Lebanon. You'll be living in the far north of Israel in a town named Kiryat Shemona on the Lebanon border." A moment of silence followed as I realized the only time I'd heard of Kiryat Shemona was last summer when terrible rocket attacks on the town led to Israel's invasion of Lebanon. "Thank you," I said and asked. "How soon do I leave?"

This job was a step up from being a reporter and carried good benefits like a housing allowance, my own company car, and a modest expense account. The moving van had just hauled my stuff away so I went upstairs and put on a clean pair of Levis and a fresh shirt. Grabbing my last cup of coffee that I would ever drink from my faithful old coffee maker, I dragged my two suitcases from upstairs into the empty living room. The taxi pulled up minutes later and I was on my way to Norfolk International coffee cup in hand. Shortly after tipping the cab driver and wheeling my bags in the door of the terminal, I met Nate, a multi-tasking-mid-level manager assigned to accompany me on the trip.

From Norfolk we checked our bags through to Israel and boarded our early evening flight to New York's Kennedy Airport where we connected with a TWA jumbo jet headed for Tel Aviv by way of Paris. By now I was running on adrenalin and caffeine and there was no way I was going to fall asleep before I boarded the plane for Israel. Nate on the other hand was perfectly calm and charged me with waking him up when the plane boarded from our waiting area at Kennedy International. *Lucky for you I can't sleep,* I thought and told Nate, "Sure, no problem. I'll wake you up."

I read a newspaper in the waiting area for over an hour and a half while Nate slept peacefully in the seat next to me. What seemed so strange to me was that we were the only people in the waiting area and still no plane had pulled up. I looked at my watch and realized the flight was supposed to leave in less than twenty minutes. "Hey, Nate, wake up," I said and nudged him. "Is our flight leaving at 7:50 p.m.?" I asked. "Yea, why?" he shot back still half awake. "Well, why isn't anybody else here in the waiting area?" I continued.

Suddenly Nate was awake, looking at his watch and back at me with eyes like saucers. "Gate change!" he exclaimed grabbing his windbreaker as both of us were off and running down the corridors of Kennedy International. We looked up our flight at the first wall of monitors we came to and continued in a jog that worked us both into a sweat by the time we arrived at the assigned gate.

The waiting area was empty as we ran up to the desk out of breath. The TWA jumbo jet had already pulled back from the gate and was fifty yards out onto the tarmac. Whatever Nate said worked as he pleaded with the flight attendant who stood by the desk of the empty waiting area. She picked up the phone, presumably speaking a few words to the pilot then turned to us, "Come with me," she said.

In two minutes we were actually out on the tarmac and going up in a lift to the plane's side door. A stewardess greeted us and sealed the cabin door behind, but as we boarded the plane the captain made known his irritation with the incident and announced, "Ladies and gentlemen we apologize for the delay but we are just now being joined by two very late passengers." All we could do was smile and try to act like 350 people weren't really staring at us.

First class was to the left and I looked lustfully in that direction before turning my head back into reality and getting a smiling nod from the flight attendant that said, *Well? Let's go.* To our right was the business class that continued back for about fifteen rows. *Nice wide seats here,* I mused. Then came the tourist class or "sardine can" section where our seats were located another twenty rows back. This is the part of the plane with three seats next to the window on each side and another five seats crammed elbow to elbow in the middle.

Nate's seat was alone on the aisle three rows up from mine. No such luck for me. My seat was smack dab in the center of the long-legs-forbidden middle section. It wasn't that the seat was too small, but its location squeezed a passenger into such a spot that you needed a shoehorn to wedge yourself between the other passengers in the row. And this flight was packed to the gills. As I looked at the one open seat in the middle of the row I thought, *can I make it to Paris without using the restroom?*

Smack dab in the middle of five seats there were two passengers on my right and two on my left with seven hours of traveling together just beginning. It was a forced kind of social setting that leaves you uneasy. From their conversations directed at each other it was clear the two on my right were traveling together and so were the two on my left. So, where did that leave me for the next six and a half hours?

Fortunately, the couple to my left was more social and sometime after dinner we introduced ourselves. They were Israelis from the suburb of Herzliyya, a few miles further north up the coast from Israel's largest city, Tel Aviv. To my delight they both spoke English fluently and explained that part of their family lived in New Jersey. They had two children and were returning to Israel after spending three months in America.

"Are you going on vacation to Israel?" the wife asked.

"No," I answered. "I'm going to live there."

"Oh, are you making Aliyah?" she asked with a polite smile referring to the term for a new immigrant moving to Israel.

"No," I answered. "I'm going to Israel to work in television news."

"Oh," she replied pleasantly. "Are you going to live in Tel Aviv or Jerusalem?"

"Neither, I'm going to live in Kiryat Shemona," I said. With that she switched to Hebrew and talked to her husband for about 30 seconds.

"Why are you going to live in Kiryat Shemona?" she asked with a little frown. Doesn't your company have a bureau in Jerusalem or Tel Aviv?"

"They have a bureau in Jerusalem," I answered. "But my assignment is Northern Israel and South Lebanon."

"Lebanon!" she shot back, and switched back to talking Hebrew with her husband for another 30 seconds. "My husband is in the army and he just fought in Lebanon last summer," she continued again in English. "Stay out of Lebanon. You'll get yourself killed there."

"Lebanon is a very dangerous place," her husband added quickly.

"I was a tank commander in that war last summer and my unit went all the way up to Beirut. It's a very unstable country and filled with all kinds of factions. One town is friendly and throws rice to welcome you while the next town tries to kill you. I don't advise it. Maybe you can get a different assignment from your bureau."

"I don't think that will be possible," I replied. "I signed a two year contract and that is where I've been assigned."

"Then you must be very careful," she instructed.

"You must never stop watching," he told me. "Always be very careful."

With that we moved on to other topics and in a few hours I learned that he had fought in every war since 1967. Always as a tank commander and now in his forties, he'd lost two tanks and three crewmen. He'd been wounded three times but always returned to serve again. They lived half the year in Israel and half in America, but it was easy to tell that Israel would always be their home. I'm sure they expected to read about me in the newspapers or perhaps see my face on the television as another American reporter who was killed or kidnapped in Lebanon.

Our seat assignments changed between Paris and Tel Aviv so I made arrangements to sit next to Nate. My legs enjoyed the aisle seat he gave me, but I missed talking to the tank commander. I never forgot the conversation.

Hours later I passed through customs and walked out into the lobby of Ben Gurion Airport in Tel Aviv, Israel. There, I was stopped at the sight of a small statue of another soldier whose exploits made history and stunned the free world. He was known simply as "Colonel Yoni".

Yoni Netanyahu was an Israeli commando with his nation's highest decorations. After the 1973 Arab Israeli War "Colonel Yoni" was promoted to Commander of the Sayaret Matkal, (called The Unit) Israel's elite counter terrorism commandos, whose motto is "Who Dares Wins". One of their duties was hostage rescue outside of Israel's borders. So, on July 1, 1976 the impossible mission of the "Entebbe Rescue" was placed at his feet.[77]

Days before an Air France jet was high jacked by Arab and German gunman and flown to Entebbe, Uganda in Africa. Protected by Uganda's Muslim President Idi Amin, the high jackers demanded the release of fifty other Arab terrorists or they would kill all 106 Jewish passengers aboard. In a daring secret rescue led by Colonel Yoni "The

Unit" flew 3000 miles undetected by radar and landed on the Entebbe airfield at midnight July 4, 1976. Disguised as a Ugandan military group, the Israeli commandos took the terminal, killed the terrorists and freed all the hostages. The only soldier lost by the Israelis was Yoni who died from his wounds on the flight home to Israel.[78]

Until then virtually unknown outside the Israeli army, Yoni's name became famous overnight throughout Israel and much of the world. The small statue of "Colonel Yoni" in Ben Gurion Airport in Tel Aviv makes a simple promise: *We care this much.* But "The Raid on Entebbe" made a much bigger statement on the world stage. In the U.S. the news broke on our Independence Day. And it set an example that said, "Israelis come after their own." I thought, *Colonel Yoni set the example for the free world to follow.*

"Well, gentlemen, welcome to Israel," said the General Manager to Nate and me as we continued dragging ourselves forward. "You two are looking pretty good for traveling all night."

"Looks can be deceiving," I answered and got a goodhearted laugh in return.

With that we loaded into the manager's Peugeot 605 sedan and made out for Northern Israel traveling up the coast past Herzliyya and Natanya to Hadera where we headed east toward the center of the country then turned left heading north again over a ridge and down into the plains of Megiddo.

A capital city of the ancient Canaanites dating back 5000 years to before the conquest of Canaan by the Israeli general Joshua, today Megiddo is a spectacularly excavated archeological site. When king Ahab of Israel reinforced his cities in 870 BC, a tunnel 230 feet long was dug through solid rock and connected to a shaft descending 100 feet to fresh water springs; thus securing the city's water supply from a siege. In recent times archeologists verifying ancient historical accounts rediscovered those tunnels.[79] And so it was that we left the airport in Tel Aviv, a city not 100 years old, and within one hour turned a corner and passed another city 5000 years old. A thousand years were as a day.

"If that's Tel Megiddo over there," said John, the general manager, gesturing to the right. "Do you guys know where we are?"

"The Plains of Armageddon," answered Nate confidently. "The Valley of Decision," I whispered to myself thinking how appropriate the name was for me right then.

"Very good," John said. And a silent pause followed that no one wanted to interrupt. The silence spoke to all of us as we began to look toward the horizons as if to take in the expanse. It goes farther than the eye can see, a triangular shaped plain 36 miles long and 15 miles wide marked roughly by Mount Tabor on the N.E., Mount Gilboa on the S., and Mount Carmel on the N.W. It takes at least a half hour to drive through it lengthwise.

On the eve of battle against the Turkish Army in 1799 Napoleon stood atop Mount Megiddo. Looking out over the enormous Valley of Armageddon, the marshal declared, "All the armies of the world could maneuver their forces on this vast plain."

One thousand eight hundred years earlier the Apostle John predicted that the armies of the world someday would do just that: "

> And He gathered them together in a place called in
> the Hebrew tongue, "Har Megiddon"[80]

But four hundred years before John's vision the Prophet Joel said something similar as he looked into the future and saw:

> Multitudes, multitudes in the Valley of Decision.[81]

Yet even more astounding are the words of the prophet Ezekiel whose book was written 200 years earlier than Joel. Ezekiel's heavenly visions of Israel looked out across 26 centuries of history that had not yet happened. In the first few chapters of his book written shortly before the Babylonians conquered Israel in 597 BC, Ezekiel predicted the fall of Jerusalem and the captivity of the people to Babylon.

But in the latter chapters he unfolds another eerie vision of a non-existent nation, a ghostly beast of dry bones arising from the dust to live again. In that vision the people of Israel are living peacefully in their own land when the combined armies of Russia, Persia, Libya, Germany and Turkey attack them.[82] Thus, the great campaign of Armageddon begins and continues for three and a half years.[83]

> In future years you will invade a land that has
> recovered from war, whose people were gathered

from many nations to the mountains of Israel, which
had long been desolate. They had been brought from
the nations, and now all of them live in safety.[84]

For 2000 years there was no Israel. The territory was called
Palestine after it was conquered by the Roman armies and renamed.
Ezekiel's prophecy remained impossible because Israel didn't exist and
the Jewish people were not controlling the land. In the national bestseller,
The Innocents Abroad published in 1869 by Mark Twain, the famous
American author harshly criticized the Arabs of Palestine for their total
neglect. After visiting Jerusalem and traveling extensively over Palestine,
he rebuked 1800 years of Arab negligence:

> Jerusalem is mournful, dreary and lifeless. I would
> not desire to live here. It is a hopeless, dreary,
> heartbroken land... Palestine sits in sackcloth and
> ashes.[85]

But after WWII the victorious western powers had crushed
the anti Jewish Nazi armies of Hitler, and the United Nations voted to
reestablish the ancient nation of Israel. Jewish people were gathered in
from many countries and immigrated to Israel to build a nation. And so,
the dry bones Ezekiel spoke of 2545 years before in his vision rose up
from the dust of history and the modern Israel of today walked back onto
the world stage.

When you think about it, this is an absolutely incredible event
in history. A people went into exile, were dispersed, and survived for
2,000 years. Without a national homeland they came back from nations
across the globe and re-established their nation and their language on
the same ancient territory that disappeared two millennia before. It is a
miraculous, singular event.

As we drove through the valley of the Plains of Armageddon, I
think all of us sensed the weight of destiny. A thousand years were as
a day. And in the most real sense, two and a half days had passed on
the heavenly clock. Israel had done far more than shake off the dust.
These dry bones had flesh. We were in the midst of a teeming modern
first world civilization that breathed and danced and celebrated life. The
Jewish people were back in the land and they were thriving.

In less than forty years these persecuted peoples who survived the Nazi death camps had built a nation of new towns and cities. The desert was in bloom from irrigation. Fish were harvested on trout farms supplied with the cold waters from the snows of Mount Hermon. Apple orchards covered the hills of Metulla; forests covered the previously barren mountains outside Jerusalem, while vineyards drank in the sun on hillsides everywhere. Universities were built, restaurants and cafes lined the busy streets, and symphonies were conducted in concert halls of Haifa, Tel Aviv and Jerusalem.

The country survived four wars in thirty-five years and only grew stronger. Surely her Arab neighbors looked upon her prosperity with envy. *But no way Russia wants a fight with Israel,* I thought. *And they'd have to be idiots to make an alliance with the Iranians.* But Ezekiel was batting 1000 and time can change politics faster than we imagine. As the archeologists continued to dig and prove the truth of ancient writings, the words of the prophets spoken in three books 2500 years before were coming true in the news. *The time of decision for mankind is running out,* I reflected.

Forty minutes later we left the vast expanse of the Plains of Armageddon and drove past Mt Tabor. As we continued up the North Road I was wondering, *where are we on the timeline before the Campaign of Armageddon begins?* We were somewhere inbetween the re-establishment of Israel and the attack of the Russian alliance. I am absolutely certain that the rest of it will come true. Now, it's only the matter of a few years.

"I'm going to stop up here as we come to the top of this next set of hills," said John." I think you'll like the view." We went around a curve and the road cut through a thirty-foot hill where the manager stopped the car and pulled onto the shoulder. In front of us was a breathtaking view of the Sea of Galilee. Bluish gray against the brown hills in the afternoon sun, it appeared as though unchanged for two thousand years. Thirteen miles long and eight miles wide the Sea of Galilee is actually a fresh water lake fed by underground springs and the Jordan River flowing down from the streams off Mount Hermon in the far north.

"In about thirty minutes we'll be at the far north end of the lake on the hills above Capernaum," said John. "There's a restaurant up there that was started by a retired city bus driver from Chicago. It's got great burgers and fresh rainbow trout. Can you guys hold out?"

"Lead on," replied Nate. "I'll save more sightseeing for another time," I agreed. And with that we were off. We drove through the city of Tiberius built on the Western side of the lake and wound our way up from below sea level by the lakeshore to the hills above the north end. There we stopped at the "Rose of Galilee" restaurant and met Yehuda, the owner who was in his late fifties. During dinner he asked if we were interested in seeing the pristine excavations of Chorazin, one of the cities mentioned by Jesus in his lament for Israel.

Nate and I turned him down. I hadn't slept but one or two hours in two days, and Nate was ready to turn in early too. We left the Rose of Galilee and headed up the North Road again for Kiryat Shemona. "I've got you both booked at the North Hotel," said John. "It's not the Holiday Inn but the sheets are clean and breakfast is included."

No words were more welcome. It had been "a large day" On the plane flight I was introduced first hand to the kind of character it took to live in Israel. On the way out of the airport I was reminded of the price they were willing to pay for each other. The road through the Valley of Armageddon and by the Sea of Galilee showed me that mankind is caught in the very real tick-tock of history from which it cannot escape. And each of us must come to grips with what we will do in the steady march of events that are weaving their way through history. So it was 2000 years before for a group of fishermen who lived in small towns by the Sea of Galilee.

I reflected on the surrounding landscape and realized that besides Tiberius, there were no large towns, only small villages of one or two hundred people. Then it occurred to me; Jesus emptied the towns when he taught. The crowds numbered ten to twenty thousand at a time. Where did they all come from unless nobody stayed home when Jesus was preaching? Little wonder, radical Christianity was happening in Galilee. Lives were being transformed.

> The blind receive sight, the lame walk, those who
> have leprosy are cured, the deaf hear, the dead are
> raised and the good news is preached to the poor.[86]

The sun was setting fast. In the twilight I reflected on the drama of the history and the land where I was. By the time we entered the south end of Kiryat Shemona via the main highway, it was almost dark. I was

41

nodding off in the car, but a surprise was waiting for me that would keep me up another hour.

Chapter 4
Danger, Rats!

The North Hotel is what you might call a two star hotel. It was bare-bones-clean, no bellmen, no waiters, and absolutely no luxury. It was the best place in Kiryat Shemona at the time. John dropped us both off at the front of the North Hotel and left us to carry our own bags in to the check-in desk. Nate was traveling light because he was staying one more day in Kiryat Shemona before heading south to visit the Jerusalem Bureau Chief for a couple days and then returning to the U.S. We carried three bags between us as we walked up the steps through the front doors and into the lobby. The first thing I noticed was a very common looking polished stone tile floor and the check-in desk straight in front of us.

Then my eyes were immediately drawn to the right as I looked and saw television lights set up around a couch. And sitting on the couch in the midst of the lights surrounded by reporters and cameramen was the Prime Minister of Israel, Yitzhak Shamir, dressed in a short sleeve shirt. I was at a loss for words.

There was no fanfare out front of the hotel, no bodyguards at the door, no limo in the parking lot, and nobody in the hotel lobby seemed to be making the slightest fuss. Turning back to the hotel clerk I asked, "Is the Prime Minister staying in the hotel too?" She answered, "No," and continued to explain quietly that he had come up for the day to meet with the Mayors of Israel's two northern most towns of Metulla and Kiryat Shemona.

He had come over to the North Hotel lobby to talk to the press because there wasn't enough space in the mayor's office for the interview and the television lights. I couldn't help myself and moved closer to the group gathered only ten feet from where I stood. It was a chance of a lifetime, and this was my territory.

As I listened I learned that before Shamir's visit there had been numerous reports about the demand for Israel to withdraw all troops from Lebanon. Naturally it made the northern towns like Kiryat Shemona nervous about further rocket attacks out of Lebanon. If the army wasn't there to create a safety sector, they feared the rockets would fall on their towns again.

Prime Minister Shamir went to the north to confront the rumors. He explained that no timetables for a withdrawal had been established. In addition, he said that the Israelis meant to coordinate any withdrawal with a transfer of responsibility to General Lahad and the South Lebanon Army.[87] General Lahad was also part of my territory; in fact his office was within walking distance of my office in Lebanon.

Within a few minutes Shamir finished, briskly arose from the couch and walked out of the lobby to a common-looking four door Mercedes, sat in the back seat with another person and rode off into the night.

The entire scene took no more than 10 minutes. At that point I was too tired to bother with unpacking. So after I checked in, I took my overnight kit with me to my room and left my bags downstairs behind the front desk. I figured if the Prime Minister of Israel can sit here in the lobby with just his driver and talk to the press in his shirtsleeves, my bags were safe till morning.

After breakfast I spoke to the desk clerk and tried to find out what else I could about Shamir's visit. I marveled once again at the nonchalance of the entire scene. The Prime Minister of Israel was the equivalent of our President in America. Yet there he sat the night before calmly speaking to the press on a couch with an open collar. Some one passing the hotel on the outside would not even know anything special was happening inside.

What a contrast to the U.S.A., I thought. If the President were in the lobby of the hotel I was checking into, I wouldn't be able to get in the door until he left. Limos and security would be stacked tree deep outside and the roads would be cordoned off so no cars could pass by. Not so in Israel, particularly in the North when the Prime Minister or the Defense Minister came for a visit, citizens got the impression that he was just the same as them. It was like he was the neighbor from down the street, a very pleasant touch.

The climate in Kiryat Shemona was also pleasant and never really harsh. Similar to Arizona, it was dry and hot in the summer but seldom over 100 degrees and never much below sixty-five in the winter months when the rains came. It was somewhat dreary in the winter as every third day brought rain. The cold got to you because the buildings didn't have central heat. Whether you were inside or outside, the temperature was the same. Most houses used kerosene space heaters that left a wet film on the interior walls and smelled from the fumes, but the fuel was cheap compared to electricity. I longed for a good wood fireplace during the winter months.

Nine months of the year there was no rain just clear blue cloudless skies. A little drip irrigation worked wonders. So much so that the main streets of Kiryat Shemona were lined with roses, shrubs and trees. The Israelis had made the Negev Desert bloom in the South with miles of black plastic hoses that dripped water onto the roots of whatever crops they planted. Northern Galilee was the same. Miles of fields displayed the same picture. Wells with pumps and pressure tanks by the sides of the fields supplied miles of black hoses watering rows of healthy crops on lands that were previously swamps and prairies.

The rose bushes lined the streets of Kiryat Shemona and bloomed twelve months of the year. As you traveled the highway up the middle of the town looking to your left going north you could see that the town extended up the base of the mountain to the west.

A series of roads parallel to the North Highway below had tight switchback turns at each end as they twisted serpentine ascending the base of the mountain creating different plateaus in the rows of houses. The sides of these winding roads were terraced with limestone walls that were themselves cut with perpendicular lines of staircases climbing up the mountainside to each level of houses. It was a picturesque and peaceful neighborhood setting that featured the contrasting colors of the green shrubs, pastel flowers, limestone terraces and steps ascending and descending in a crisscrossing pattern.

But Kiryat Shemona was not a place for the faint of heart. At the base of a mountain and four miles from the Lebanon border, the city was named for seven men who gave their lives defending the high ground at Tel Hay two miles to the north.

The Lebanon frontier hangs 2300 feet above the town and directly over the mountain ridge to the west. For over three decades small Lebanese border towns seething with anti-Jewish hatred served as a base to send Katyusha rockets down on the peaceful Israeli streets.

There were few public restrooms in Kiryat Shemona and some people urinated in plain view. Rats were a common sight by garbage bins. Viral diarrhea was easy to catch from the drinking water and deadly food poisoning awaited you at many of the *friendly* little restaurants. In

45

short, a person could die early in Kiryat Shemona. Many did. It was my goal not to become one of those statistics.

But each day brought a new challenge and especially those first few days as I was trying to get situated into an apartment. I was introduced right away to Terry, our personal banker at the Israeli Discount Bank in the town center. I opened an account that was twenty years ahead of its time. My Visa card was a check and debit card attached to my personal account. Since all my spending was on a company account, I hardly ever wrote a check. *Great idea!* I thought. (That was 1984.)

Terry was from London, England and had a delightfully upbeat personality. He journeyed to Israel on a summer vacation after completing college at Oxford. During that summer while working on a kibbutz he met and married an Israeli girl. According to Terry his father used to joke, "So why did I put you through college, Terry? Ah yes, so you could pick oranges on a farm in Israel?"

But Terry was a great contact and within two days he introduced me to Gigo, a Romanian immigrant who had a primo top floor 3-bedroom apartment with a picture window on the main drag in the middle of town. I rented Gigo's apartment for $200 a month with six months up front. That was a break because usually apartments were rented with 12 months advance rent required up front. I even got Gigo to put in a new showerhead so I could actually stand up in the shower American style rather than the uncomfortable European style that required someone to sit in the tub with the showerhead on a hose in your hand.

I was happy. I could look out my picture window south down the main street of town and see trees and rose bushes. What I didn't realize was that when the Israeli army battalion on duty changed the guard, they did it in the middle of the night. The first time it happened I sat straight up in bed as my entire apartment building shook as the huge flatbed trucks carrying tanks piggyback rolled down out of the Lebanon mountains past my front door downshifting and roaring their engines in the middle of the night on into the morning light. I never quite got the schedule down, so it was always a surprise and always a sleepless night.

But after I first moved in, the change of units in Lebanon was the least of my worries. Gigo left all his belongings boxed in the living room for the first month. There was no dining area and the boxes were piled up to the ceiling covering the light switch so I entered into pitch-black darkness unable to find a light.

Worse yet, Gigo had taken the screens off the windows permitting the rats from the streets to get inside my apartment. They dug themselves a home in the boxes after he moved out and before I moved in. When I entered the pitch-black living room the first time the rats screeched at me in chorus so loud that I thought I'd entered a house haunted by banshees. I froze in my steps for about thirty seconds until my mind could identify this sound I'd never heard.

It was an evil sound and something told me to carefully back out the door and concede the territory for that night. I was wise to do so because I learned these rats would attack humans when cornered, and I had them cornered. It took me two weeks to trap and kill them. Thirteen full size brown healthy rats, each one as mean as a coiled viper. I enjoyed watching them die as I drown them one at a time inside the box trap in my kitchen sink. It taught me a lesson about that part of the world. Killing evil animals was a way of life.

For the first week as the rat population was dwindling, I stayed on at the North Hotel where I got to know Shoshana, the desk clerk that had the day shift. She was outgoing and spoke English well. Like most Israelis she was interested in the news and asked me what I saw as I moved in and out of Lebanon each day. We had a few cups of coffee at the cafes and she showed me around town the few times we were both off duty. One time that stuck in my mind was when we passed a scarred place in the pavement on a side street in front of a school.

"You see those streaks in the pavement?" she asked pointing at a shell burst.

"Yes," I replied recognizing the scars left from exploded shrapnel. It was a sight I'd seen all over the streets and buildings of Beirut.

"That's where my teacher died," she said matter-of-factly. "As the Katyusha rockets were falling she came back out of the bomb shelter because she thought one of us was missing. We found her dead here."

"Was someone missing?" I asked somewhat stunned.

"No, she actually miscounted," Shoshana, continued. "But she was a brave woman. She never hesitated for herself when she felt a child had been left outside. She told us not to leave the shelter and she went right back out to look even while the bombs were falling. That's where she died, right there. She gave her life to protect us."

As we went back to the café and finished a piece of cake and coffee I thought to myself; *how would Americans react if our towns were shelled?* Who of us in America grew up experiencing what Shoshana did? Perhaps that's why the press and the public in America were so quick to criticize Israel.

It wasn't our children who were rushed to bomb shelters in the midst of their school days. None of our children saw their teacher dead in the street from shrapnel wounds. Our families were not waking up in the black of night to exploding shells and running with children in their arms to a bomb shelter. No, none of those trials for Americans, but we reserved the right to criticize the Israelis for invading Lebanon. *Seems hypocritical and out of touch,* I thought. But, the Arab viewpoint said Israel deserved it.[88]

Then, I reminded myself that the American press had lived in the Commodore Hotel in Beirut, protected by the Palestinian militia and careful not to ask too many hard questions of their protectors. When the Israeli Army invaded Lebanon, their worldview was challenged. As long as Jews remained a victimized race, the Western press could take their side. But now, Israel was a nation with an army and an air force. Now Israel played a different role. No longer the victim, they could assert themselves against their enemies with might and power. So the Western press drifted anti-Semitic without being challenged. They had to find a new underdog to cheer for.[89]

I had been in Israel only a few months. Yet, as I moved in and out of Lebanon daily by passing through the Israeli Army checkpoint, I discovered a different balance to the ongoing story of the conflict between these two nations. It was time to look up a mentor in Jerusalem and use him as a sounding board. "Uncle Wes" was still with the United Press International but no longer assigned to the White House. He was the Jerusalem Bureau Chief of that organization. I got through to him on the telephone and invited him to dinner. We ate at a well-known place named, "Fink's," close to Yehuda Street, the walking mall of cafes and sweet shops in the heart of Jerusalem.

I told him my impressions were different than most and asked if I was somehow drifting off course. He looked at me intently and reminded me of how far I'd come and gave me a challenge, "You are the only reporter in the world who can move in and out of Lebanon and Israel 24 hours a day 7 days a week. You are going to see more than press briefings and prepared statements. You don't have to go in a press pool under Israeli supervision, so trust your impressions. You're in a very unique position."

He was right, of course. American news reporters in the Middle East worked from facilities provided by other nations. Those countries "headquartered" the foreign press in their buildings, fed them news and supervised their mobility. This often led to a "pack mentality" in reporting.

My situation was completely different. I was an English-speaking news correspondent and producer for METV, the only independent television station located in the Middle East. I say independent because the other broadcast stations in the Middle East were government owned. For instance, there was Jordan TV, Syria TV, Israel TV, Egypt TV, Greek TV and so forth. We were not state owned. Instead, we had our own facilities in three nations and sent broadcasts into seven countries. And we got mail from viewers throughout the Middle East.

Our employees came from all over the world…Greece, Switzerland, Israel, England, New Zealand, Wales, Cyprus, Lebanon, Egypt, South Africa, and America. Speaking two languages was minimal. Reading, writing and speaking three to six languages was more common.

As the METV producer I drove from Kiryat Shemona, Israel across the border to an office on a mountaintop overlooking the Litani River Gorge six miles deep inside radical Shiite dominated South Lebanon. In the course of my work I interviewed people from 27 different nations.

There were no restraints on my mobility. So yes, my job was quite unique, and with it came serious dangers. Present a threat to any armed checkpoint in the war zone and they'd shoot you. Lebanese, Israeli, Muslim or Christian, it didn't matter. For me it might all have ended suddenly one night.

As my car raced through the blackness of Lebanon towards an Israeli guard post on their northern frontier, a 50-caliber machine gun shot two bursts directly across my windshield. I stopped in time. In the months that followed I was threatened, shot at, hospitalized and arrested. But in spite of all that, there were some really good times.

Chapter 5
Hidden Joys

Crossing from Israel into South Lebanon was not a complicated process for me. The Israeli army set up a gate and built a by-pass road that only army vehicles were allowed to use. Except, I was allowed to use the same gate. In fact, I actually had one up on the army units. I used the gate at will 24 hours a day 7 days a week.

For two years my company had an office in Kiryat Shemona and another office in a mobile trailer in Lebanon. During that time we proved ourselves trustworthy to Israel because we never tried to outmaneuver the Israeli censors, instead, we actually asked for their guidelines. While I heard some comments from other networks criticizing this approach as a "sell out", in the long run it was wisdom.

Once I won the trust of the Israelis, it was amazing the latitude they gave me. I filled out a little yellow chit like every one else, but the vehicle inspectors would wave me past the lines of army vehicles in convoys stacked up waiting to cross. They actually became defensive over me and asked when to expect me on my return. I developed a reputation for being brave and stupid both.

It was like the tank commander's wife told me on the plane flight from America. No Israeli desired to go into Lebanon, in fact, they hated going and only did it because it was their military duty. But for someone like myself to go in and out at all hours every day, to the Israelis, well, that was just plain crazy. But they also recognized that it was brave. And there is something about an act of courage that soldiers admire. So, I was always recognized with a respectful nod, a wave, and on a few occasions, even a salute.

It was kind of strange, really. I respected the Israeli soldiers for their daring and professionalism. And they respected me for my bravery and dedication to go matter-of-factly in harm's way day after day into the pit of hell they called Lebanon.

As one of those many days north of the Israeli frontier came to an end, I was seated with Rafiq, my interpreter, sipping coffee on the porch of his parents' house in Dier Mimas, South Lebanon.

"Do you realize you are already a marked man?" asked Rafiq.

"No. I didn't realize that." I replied. "What makes you think so?"

"One of my friends was at the souk (an open air market) in Bent Jbeil last week and overheard two people talking about you," Rafiq answered.

"Hmm, Bent Jbeil," I reflected. "You don't say?" And my mind flashed back to the first time I was in the large Shiite town. Two Israeli F-16's popped up over the mountains at low altitude flying up from the south suddenly swooping in on Bent Jbeil. My feet stuck to the pavement and my heart pounded with fear as their engines screamed at tree top height like two huge angry birds of death. Both banked into a turn that sent streaks of smoke peeling off their wing tips as they circled the town and their engines shook the air. In seconds both descended toward the houses and made what looked to be a bombing run yet without dropping bombs. "Just looking for rats," I said to myself.

"Are you hearing what I'm telling you?" asked Rafiq.

"Oh yes," I replied. "I'm just reflecting on how dangerous the rats are in this part of the world."

"Ah, not only the rats," replied Rafiq with a smile that read my thoughts. "The scorpions and the vipers as well, we have many varieties of deadly animals in the South of Lebanon."

"So what does your intuition tell you?" I asked.

"It tells me the word is out in some Muslim areas," Rafiq answered. "They may be trying to kidnap or kill you."

"What for?" I asked.

"For being an Israeli spy," said Rafiq. "They see your car has an Israeli license plate and you use a two way radio. To them that makes you a spy."

"Hmm, sort of a James Bond image," I joked trying to lighten the mood.

"Don't be too proud of yourself," Rafiq cautioned. "To people who've been taught to hate the Jews and the Americans, killing you would bring them status."

"So, what do you suggest?" I asked.

"Let's go in a different direction," he advised. "Suppose we go north and stay out of the south for a few days. I know of a school in the Beqaa Valley that would make a great feature. You interested?"

"OK, sounds good to me," I replied. "When do we go?"

"Give me a couple days to get the details together," he concluded.

"OK by me," I said. "I've got some reports to catch up on, tomorrow. I'll meet you back here in two days at 8:00 a.m." With that we finished our coffee and snacks. The sun had gone down and I was off duty the rest of the night. I headed back to Kiryat Shemona.

Six months prior to my arrival in Israel the trailer that made up our facility in Lebanon was blown up by a car bomb one Sunday afternoon. Nobody was there so nobody was hurt. But for a time we had no office in Lebanon. So, an official from the town of Marjayoun offered us an old Lebanese Army building that had suffered a direct hit from Palestinian shelling. The building was almost rubble but the location was breathtaking on top of one of the highest hills in the town with a direct line of sight to Beaufort Castle. Built by French crusaders it sat atop a 1400-foot sheer cliff on the other side of the Litani River Gorge.

Living in Marjayoun at the time was an America missionary whose background was in construction. He took the bombed out army building and transformed it into a beautiful modern facility with furnished offices, overnight sleeping accommodations, showers and cooking facilities inside and a lush green lawn with rose bushes on the outside. He also built an auxiliary power plant with a battery backup that tripped a six-cylinder diesel generator whenever the power went out. Gates with cement anchors protected the two approach roads and an exterior wall with a mechanical iron gate protected the entrance. It was a pleasure to drive to my office in Lebanon.

Two days later I wound my way back up the two lane blacktop roads through the army gate and crossed the Valley of the Springs between the Shiite Muslim village of El Khiam and the Christian village of Dier Mimas (named in honor of the 3rd Century Christian martyr, Mimas) where Rafiq lived. At 8:00 a.m. the clouds still hung over Dier Mimas obscuring it from view. The road in front of me looked like a windy black ladder climbing into the unknown.

I arrived in the thick fog at Rafiq's house and sat down to join him and his father for breakfast. We ate fresh eggs deep-fried in olive oil, and spread our pita bread with orange marmalade. The cups of Turkish coffee his mother served were never clogged with the mud that settled at the bottom of the pot because Rafiq's mother poured the finished product through a paper filter before pouring it into our cups.

Rafiq's family owned an olive orchard so every two years they harvested the olives. The workers spread out plastic sheets under the trees and beat the olives off the branches until the plastic sheets were totally covered. The olives they cured for eating were hand cracked with a large flat stone. This crack permitted the brine water to cure the olive throughout making it tender and savory. The rest of the olives were taken to a facility with a stone press that squeezed out the oil. Except for the use of plastic sheets the process hadn't changed for 5000 years.

The olive oil was fresh from their harvest, the eggs were collected that morning and the coffee was clean and laced with a touch of sugar and cardamom spice. The smell of the cold wet air from outside mingled with warm smoky air from the wood fire inside the kitchen stove and filled the house. As the warm rays of sun burned off the fog, we sipped the coffee and my taste buds savored the richness of ordinary cuisine from the most humble of dwellings.

It was easy to understand why these people lived in the same towns for hundreds of years. The flavors were full, the stress non-existent, family and friends were just down the street and they could walk to church twice a week. Work was a means to an end. The drive to become rich that obsesses most Americans made no sense in this setting. As Americans worked two jobs and isolated themselves from their own families, these ever so humble people were actually living a richer life style, a lifestyle whose taste was as vibrant as the incomparable flavor of their homegrown olive oil.

"It will take us an hour and a little extra to get to the school," Rafiq told me which meant that we were traveling one third the length of the country; you can drive from one end of Lebanon to the next in three hours. I had arranged to switch cars with one of our Lebanese workers. We made our journey in a 1975 red Mercedes 280c with a four speed that had black and silver Lebanese plates.

An hour and fifteen minutes later we rounded a bend in the road and came upon a peaceful grove of trees. Turning to the right we entered through a gate and found the Schneller School compound all across our view. Started by German Christian missionaries in the 1860's in Jerusalem, it was moved north to the Beqaa Valley of Lebanon during WWII because the Nazi influence in the Jerusalem Arab community put the children's lives in danger.

The school's buildings were pristine and uniformly finished with cut limestone exteriors and red shutters on the windows. We spent two full days there and did stories on orphan children from all three religious communities of Lebanon, Muslim, Christian and Druze (a reformed Shiite Muslim sect representing eight percent of the Lebanese population).[90]

All during the years of Lebanese Civil War (1975-1982) and the battles between the Israeli and Syrian Armies in 1982, the school escaped without a scratch. Though entire towns around were bombed and shelled, there in the midst of that grove of trees the buildings were untouched as if a giant plastic bulletproof bubble covered the compound. By contrast alone it was an amazing story. I wondered why nobody else had covered it before me. I guess it wasn't worth leaving the aged whiskey at the Commodore Hotel in Beirut to discover something good about Lebanese Christians. It didn't fit the editorial viewpoint.

And many other things in South Lebanon didn't fit the editorial viewpoint of the Western Media either. For instance, the mayor of the far northern Israeli village of Metulla invited the mayors of the towns of South Lebanon to a cultural exchange and down home celebration. Held at the junior high auditorium in Metulla, two hundred adults and children from Lebanon joined another hundred from Israel for dinner and skits performed on stage. I attended the evening's festivities and was surprised to find that instead of tension there was a sense of warmth and fun. It was like an indoor church picnic! The sad reality was that Israelis could not go north into Lebanon for the same type of festival because factions would kill the Lebanese town mayors who dared to host such an event. They would be accused of collaborating with the enemy.

But the door remained open for Lebanese kids to come south. So the Israelis opened a summer camp along the Mediterranean Sea beaches of Ashkelon in southern Israel. Lebanese boys and girls came in 2-week shifts accompanied by supervising counselors from their own towns. It was two-weeks-all-expense-paid summer beach fun with Israel as the host country. Chartered tour busses picked up about sixty kids at a time at the Northern Israeli-Lebanon border crossing known as, "The Good Fence." From there they traveled three hours south to the camps on the beaches of Ashkelon.

This was a story the American public needed to know. I thought, *this shows who really wants peace and friendship between Israel and Lebanon, the parents and their children.* So, I tried to pass this story on to other TV stations in the U.S.---- nobody seemed interested.

Back north in Lebanon another community exchange project involved fresh water, a precious and scarce resource in that area of the world. Israeli civil engineers were sent north of the border to assist in water purification and rebuilding projects in some of the war torn areas of South Lebanon. Israel not only shared their money and resources but their clean water as well.

Traveling from town to town in South Lebanon with a mixed group of Israeli and Lebanese we heard from mayor to mayor what they thought of the co-operative project. Some of the mayors used it as an opportunity to bad mouth Israel. Later, talking to a top ranking Israeli officer in the North Command, I asked about this attitude and he replied, "Let them talk and say whatever they want. We don't require them to like us. We just hope that some day they learn to stop hating us."

Then, as summer ended and the long hot days were met by cooler nights in Lebanon, the time to harvest grapes arrived. A good crop always had to reach their maximum size before the rains arrived in the late fall. All wine makers know that water before the harvest can make a good year a bad one because the concentrated juice inside the grape is diluted. In Rom, a village twenty-five miles north of Israel in the Lebanese mountains, the harvest was about to begin.

We drove north from our office building in Marjayoun on winding mountain roads for over an hour to attend the all day celebration. As we drove to the growing area of the town we stopped and beheld. Built all in stone with red tile roofs, the picturesque homes and vineyard chateaus were atop the mountainsides. In front of us on immaculately terraced hills extending a thousand feet up were the manicured vineyards as far as you could see. Afternoon sun drenched the mountainside as we watched people in the distance walking comfortably erect under wine trusses three meters high. This was their wine country.

The judging of the crops from the competing vineyards followed a morning of games for children. Roasted chicken with a garlic dipping sauce famous to Lebanon was served for lunch with home fried potatoes and private wines or distilled spirits from the region. When night arrived people came from the surrounding villages for the grand finale, a banquet dinner, with live music and dancing.

The banquet dinner offered an entree choice of beef or chicken, but there were so many traditional salads and other dishes of cuisine specific to the region that a visitor could not possibly be bored. Everything was fresh and numerous plates of variety filled the middle of each table. There were grape leaves stuffed with rice and ground beef, parsley and wheat salad called tabouli, different dips for pita bread made from yogurt, chick peas, sesame seed paste and fresh eggplants as well as tomato sauce, garlic sauce, and a light yogurt sauce laced with mint.

Throughout the dinner bottles of mineral water and liquor called "Arak" were continually brought to the tables. This distilled spirit most famous and popular in Lebanon was 100 proof, clear like vodka and flavored with anis. A double shot poured into a glass was mixed with mineral water making a milky looking substance with a refreshing taste that packed quite a wallop. As the waiters cleared the tables and the music began in earnest so did the drinking and eventually the walloping.

But the Arak and food created energy for dancing. And the people danced and danced in styles and varieties from slow to fast. The bands played western music and popular songs, but eventually the women who knew a little belly and hip dancing began to show off to the delight of the men. Earlier in the day we were warned to consider staying overnight because the dancing festivities went into the dawn, but we weren't warned about how wide open the dancing would get.

As the women competed with hip movements some became more openly erotic than others. To our amazement there was a traditional dance where the man got on his knees in front of the woman's erotic hip movements. "Oh my goodness!" said my cameraman's wife as she went speechless staring at the fertility dance going on directly next to her at our table. As I looked around I noticed numerous couples going through the same gyrations that would make any soft porn moviemaker proud. I felt as though we had fallen into the ancient fertility rites of Baal, the Canaanite god of sex. But then, why should I have been surprised, I was in the ancient land of Canaan at the harvest festival.

At approximately 1:00 a.m. we thanked our hosts and made out for Marjayoun and eventually entered Israel around 3:00 that morning. As we drove the twisted blacktop roads winding through the mountains we had to climb above the cloud cover that had drifted in above the villages. We broke through the heavy mist and saw a sky filled with stars too many to count and a slice of moon casting a silver light over the clouds beneath us making them glow from above. The streetlights of the mountaintop villages twinkled from underneath the cotton texture of clouds with red, yellow and bluish hues.

We could see village after village twinkling up from underneath separated by waves of clouds and appearing like separate islands in a silvery white sea. Like Bashir Gemeyal had said, there they were, fiefdom after fiefdom worlds apart and caught forever in the age of castles. Something told me this was a moment of peace to remember because minutes later we descended from the heavenly view to the earthly dangers that were boiling inside the caldron of Lebanon.

Part II

Events that Made Today's Jihad

Chapter 6
Enter The Iranians

It was a beautiful spring morning in 1985. The cloudless sky above the mountains brought clear air in off the Mediterranean Sea. The sun had already burned off the early morning fog that usually obscured the blacktop streets of Marjayoun. This strategic South Lebanon mountain village occupied a perch 1200 feet above the Litani River gorge and controlled all the roads below. From my office I looked directly across the gorge to the ruins of Beaufort Castle atop the mountain that was exclusively Shiite Muslim territory. I had no idea of what was about to happen.

It was near the end of the first year of my contract as producer for Middle East Television. From our offices in Beirut, Jerusalem, Marjayoun and Metulla we produced television news programs broadcasting in both English and Arabic across seven countries of the Middle East. As part of the English department I worked as a correspondent in both Lebanon and Israel. This morning my cameraman and I were heading further south to the large Muslim town of Bent Jbeil.

South Lebanon was the bottom third of the country and almost exclusively Shiite Muslim in population. I was an American working on a two-year contract occupying an office in a Christian village in the heart of Shiite dominated territory. To say I was kidnap bait was an understatement.

The Israeli army patrolled this sector, and every week some of their soldiers were wounded or killed. I crossed the border from Israel into Lebanon through a sector held by the South Lebanese Army. Since I had a pass from each side I traveled by myself 24 hours a day 7 days a week in and out through the Israeli Army Gate. Some called me crazy, but I was the only correspondent in the world who was doing it. As a result, I was about to be thrown into a story years ahead of its time.

That morning my cameraman, Mark, and I drove down the mountain ridgeline from Marjayoun through the towns of Qlaya, Dier Mimas and Kifar Kila and continued along the Lebanon-Israeli frontier past Aytarun where we curved west and then south into Bent Jbeil that was surrounded on all sides by high hills. We were going after "evergreen" video footage that we could use in all manner of stories. The town itself was very colorful with traffic, mosques, shops and a big open-air market called the souk. Traditionally, the market was a place of truce where sides in conflict could meet for commerce.

My bet proved good. We got plenty of attention, some smiles and also some of the most vicious glares I've ever seen. We were recognized yet the tradition of truce held strong. We got great video but as we were preparing to leave two young men that tailed us for some time finally approached. As a friendly gesture, I smiled and asked if they spoke English.

One stepped forward and said clearly in English, "We want to talk with you."

"On camera?" I asked.

"No, no camera, no camera!" he said raising his voice and then asked, "Are you working with the Israelis?"

"No," I replied.

"Are you an American reporter?" he asked.

"Yes, I'm an American," I said.

"Well, I hate Americans," he shot back and continued to rant for another minute telling me how Israel and America were evil. But his final statements were chilling.

"Some day we will come to America and make you pay." he raged. "We are the holy warriors of god, and some day we will come to America and kill you Americans. You'll see! You'll see!" With that they walked away.

This wasn't the first time I'd heard anti-American hatred in the Arab community. The Middle East is full of it. But it was the first time I encountered two teenage *soldiers of god* that promised to come to America and wage war. This was the first clue.

Shortly after this incident I was invited by an Israeli Army spokesman to attend a briefing northeast of Marjayoun in the village of Hasbaya. The South Lebanon Army had a small detachment close by that patrolled the sector. We drove along the Hasbani River winding through ancient olive orchards to the base of Mount Hermon where the town is situated. An 800-year-old Crusader fortress occupies the center of town with the original gigantic wooden gate that still opens on its hinges. A horse and rider could enter through the gate without dismounting.

Only two other reporters attended the briefing, both of them from Eastern European countries. It seemed strange to me that there were so few reporters, but I was actually happy at being able to ask numerous questions without having to compete with twenty other reporters. This was more my style. I disliked going in the press pools being escorted around with forty cameramen and reporters.

The Israeli Army spokesman explained that their intelligence had discovered a network of 1500 terrorists in South Lebanon. They were living in the Shiite communities and being trained by Iranian operatives. We were also told that the weapon of choice might be suicide car bombs and on any given day some of these could be circulating on the roads searching for targets.

This was part of the Khomeini doctrine of the Iranian Revolution of 1979. South Lebanon Shiite Muslims had a direct connection to Iran where theology changed in the late 1970's sanctioning suicide as a means to achieve martyrdom.[91] Hezbollah taught a new doctrine in the mosques, suicide for political gain became the highest form of personal religious devotion and guaranteed entrance into paradise.[92]

The briefing went on to explain that Lebanese forces were going to patrol larger areas of the security zone created by the Israeli Defense Forces (IDF) in Southern Lebanon. This would be accomplished by the South Lebanese Army (SLA) commanded by General Antoine Lahad. The rest of the briefing was spent visiting two SLA outposts.

I followed up this briefing with my own visit to the SLA headquarters in Marjayoun a day later where I met Dr. Sakar, the information director. On his office wall was a very large detailed map of Lebanon. He caught me studying it.

"What do you see there?" he asked.

"A map of Lebanon," I replied.

"That's the Lebanon we are trying to restore," he said. His remark referred to the history of civil war beginning ten years earlier that splintered Lebanon into sectors controlled by militias rather than one unified country.

As our conversation continued Dr. Sakar verified what the Israeli Army briefing said about the makeup and size of the SLA. It was an army of 3000 volunteers made up of Muslim and Christian men recruited from the local towns of South Lebanon.

I remember that he sparred with me about what I thought about

Israel and *Lebanon for the Lebanese.* I can only conclude that I must have passed his screening because he smiled at one point and said, "Ok. If you like, I'll arrange an exclusive interview for you with General Lahad. Can you be here at 2:00 p.m. tomorrow afternoon?" Of course I agreed, and returned to his office promptly the next day.

General Antoine Lahad was in his mid fifties and had retired from the regular Lebanese Army. Then in 1984, ex-President Camille Chamoun persuaded him to take the new assignment in South Lebanon. The General explained that the goal of the SLA was to make it possible for the Lebanese to secure their own borders and bring about the complete withdrawal of Israeli forces.

His passion for Lebanon was moving. And he indicated he was willing to co-operate with the Israelis so long as they were willing to return the sovereignty of Lebanon to the Lebanese. That was General Lahad's way of saying the terrorist network Iran was building in towns like Bint Jbeil was not welcome. He knew the Iranians believed that Israel shouldn't exist. So if they succeeded in controlling South Lebanon they would set up a state within the state. With supplies and help from Syria, Hezbollah and the Iranians would use South Lebanon as a base to attack Israel. The result would mean continued destruction to Lebanon.

In the general's view Lebanon for the Lebanese meant calling on the citizens of South Lebanon to exercise proper control over their own territory thus removing any motivation for Israeli forces to remain in South Lebanon. Lahad's passion was to reunite South Lebanon into the whole of Lebanon and that required a negotiated settlement with Israel and factions inside Lebanon. [93] It was an unpopular political position in an Arab world whose media publicly favors the destruction of Israel.

Lahad's position was the only realistic solution, and it left me asking if the Arab world really wanted peace with Israel --- obviously not. Why they didn't was another piece of the puzzle I soon came to understand, and today's Western Civilization needs that next clue to survive.

Meanwhile, on the other side of the border the Israeli government informed the press of a dramatic change. Their army would be pulling back to the Litani River in South Lebanon. This would put the northernmost towns in Israel within range of rocket attacks. So, days after the announcement Defense Minister Yitzhak Rabin made a personal visit to the mayors of Metulla and Kiryat Shemona.

He went there to reassure the people that the Army would still be able to protect the Northern Israeli villages from rocket attacks. I went to this meeting in Metulla where Rabin said that if Lebanese villages sheltered groups that sent rockets into Israeli towns, the suffering in Lebanon would be tremendous. His prophetic statement came twenty years before its fulfillment in the summer of 2006. [94]

The rockets didn't fall on Israel in 1985 because Hezbollah couldn't get the weaponry while Israel maintained a security zone in South Lebanon. But the Iranian operatives inside Lebanon began another tactic and things got ugly. In Beirut they kidnapped prominent Americans to get media attention and in South Lebanon suicide bombers blew themselves up in cars and on foot. I was right in the middle of it.

Out the northern end of Marjayoun and down the hill from my office at the bend of a narrow road in the Valley of the Springs sat the Voice of Hope radio station run by Christian missionaries. They were signing off the air at midnight when two Islamic suicide bombers cut through the wire and opened fire killing the security guard by the entrance gate.

To open the locked door one bomber blew himself up at the entrance to the building severing his lower body and scattering his upper remains all over the outside entrance. With the door opened the other entered the station and murdered the operator inside, but not before the operator told what was happening and bid farewell. Then, the second bomber saw he couldn't escape and blew himself up inside the radio station. It was a cowardly act that demonstrated nothing more than Islamic hatred of Christianity.

That's the way it was. Death was never far away. Not long after the Voice of Hope attack I decided to go to my office in Lebanon on a beautiful Sunday morning. My car's engine revved as I downshifted around a curve climbing up the mountain road from my apartment in Kiryat Shemona to Metulla located on the Israeli side of the border by the Lebanon frontier.

Normally cracking with activity, my two-way radio was quiet because the camera crews working in Lebanon returned to Israel Saturday night and took Sundays off. Taking advantage of the break, I was driving across the border from Israel to a quiet office in Marjayoun, Lebanon to complete my report for the week of March 10, 1985.

As I headed up the road to the Israeli army gate where I usually crossed over into Lebanon, a small troop convoy of three trucks and a few jeeps lined up in front of me filling out their paperwork. Written names and identification numbers accounted for every Israeli soldier in the trucks before they crossed into Lebanon. I would be waiting at least half an hour. So, I turned my car around and headed for lunch.

A few minutes later I pulled up and parked in front of the Arazim Hotel in Metulla. It was an historic site where Major Hadaad of the Lebanese Army held a secret late night rendezvous nine years before with leaders of the Israeli Army in 1976. Following this meeting Hadaad founded what became the South Lebanese Army. Then, after Major Hadaad died of cancer, General Lahad took over.

Composed of Christians and Muslims from the areas that it controlled, the SLA shared a common enemy with Israel. Yassir Arafat and the PLO occupied and oppressed the South Lebanese villages and terrorized Northern Israel with random rocket attacks. By forming the SLA in 1976 Major Hadaad hoped to reestablish Lebanese sovereignty and prevent an Israeli invasion of Lebanon.

Located next to the border fence on the Israeli side, the Arazim Hotel had a direct line of sight into the Valley of the Springs on the Lebanese side of the border. It was a peaceful scene with the Shiite village of El Khiam on one side of the valley and the three Christian villages of Dier Mimas, Qlaya and Marjayoun ascending the mountain ridge on the other side.

"Hello, how are you, today?" the Israeli waitress asked.

"Fine, how are you?" I replied.

"OK," she said. "Beef or chicken?"

"Chicken," I replied.

"Soup or salad?" she asked.

"I'll have both, please." And with that she turned and went about her business. It wasn't that she was unfriendly or couldn't speak English well. That was just the nature of service in Israel, perfunctory.

In short order she brought me some vegetable soup and fresh baked bread. I poured a glass of sparkling mineral water from the bottle on the table, buttered a piece of fresh bread and began to eat my soup. The Israeli troop trucks had passed through the border and were driving right to left across the Valley of the Springs just a few hundred yards beyond the border fence inside Lebanon.

A small pickup truck descended the mountain road just south of

Dier Mimas and approached the lead Israeli jeep moving the opposite direction toward the Shiite village of El Khiam. The officer in the lead jeep motioned the truck to the side of the road. It obeyed but suddenly pulled back on the road next to a passing troop truck.

BOOOOM!! The pickup morphed into a huge ball of orange flame and black smoke. Two children outside the hotel dove face down to the street and scrambled for shelter. Windows shattered in houses across the street and the hotel shook from the blast. The entire top of the troop truck disappeared leaving a twisted piece of frame with two tires and the rear axle facing upwards like the hind legs and severed torso of a large dead animal.

Immediately, I left my table at the restaurant and went to the border fence. There I watched in silence as soldiers ran to help from other trucks in the convoy. One soldier tore his shirt off as he was running down the road to aid a surviving soldier who was standing straight up in the road with his clothes on fire. The first soldier reached the second, wrapped his shirt over him and smothered the flames.

Jumping out of the lead jeep another soldier ran back toward the mangled troop truck. From a dead run he slid onto his side embracing a fallen soldier lying in the road. Then, he stood back up and screamed in anguish as he raised both his arms to heaven crying out for his dead friend. The burned soldier standing in the road collapsed but the shirtless soldier who extinguished the flames never left his side.

Israeli helicopters began arriving evacuating the living and the dead. When I finally left the fence all that remained was a squad of soldiers picking up body parts. Among those parts they found pieces of an unidentified woman.

Israel closed the army crossing for the next few hours so I went to our Metulla office and filed my report with our Jerusalem news bureau. Afterwards, I stopped by the Israeli Discount Bank in Kiryat Shemona and spoke briefly to my banker who was a good source for information. I told him what happened and he immediately went into action. Within a matter of hours he had further highlights for me. Twelve Israeli soldiers died and fourteen others were wounded.

He also said that shortly after the truck bomb exploded a facility inside Lebanon broadcast a prerecorded videotape message of the truck bomber, a teenage Shiite woman associated with Hezbollah. An Israeli listening post monitored the transmission that contained the usual suicide message.

She said Allah called her to be a *fida'i,* (holy warrior on a one-way mission) who welcomed death. She wanted her death to serve as a light to all *jihadis* in the *harb,* (an endless war) to overcome *unbelievers* and *apostates* until all submitted to the *peace* of Islam.

Hezbollah played their hand openly. Virtually the same age as the two teenage boys in Bent Jbeil, she was the missing link. Her video recording used the same words in Arabic as the two boys used when they spoke to me in English, holy warriors on a mission. Her calling was obviously suicide in Lebanon. But the two boys bragged to me about their mission in America indicating someone already had made arrangements for their immigration. Then it struck me. *Their calling is suicide in America!* Now the pieces fit the puzzle. The war was coming to America.

Although this incident occurred more than twenty years ago, in today's news we read and hear the same language used by Sheik Nasrallah, Osama bin Laden, Mahmoud Ahmadinejad, Ali Khomeini and Muslim protesters in the streets of Britain and America. An entire section of language and doctrine in this religion is dedicated to violent conquest of those who don't see it their way.

Beginning by dividing all mankind into two areas, there are those at *peace* inside submission to Islam and those of the *harb,* all people outside Islam. Those outside Islam are in a continuous state of war against Allah and Muhammed. This revelation says that Islam is destined to inherit the earth by persuasion and by force. Lands must be absorbed, and for 1400 years non-Islamic nations where the Christian faith is practiced have stood in the way of this destiny.

This is the *jihad,* the ongoing struggle to bring submission upon the *unbelievers* and the *apostates* worldwide. Unbelievers are those who don't believe in Islam and apostates are those who once believed but have fallen away to another path.

"The summit of Islam is jihad!" proclaimed the Imam.[95] Sadly, according to this theology, all who wage violence reach higher status and gain paradise if they die as warrior *jihadis* in such conflicts. The greatest of these are the one-mission warriors, *fida'in,* like the teenage truck bomber. By dramatic acts of death the *fida'in* wage psychological war to force people outside Islam into submission through fear and terror.

The truck bomber's statement spoke of the "ongoing struggle."

That's it, I thought. *That's what's missing. The Arabs don't want peace because the war isn't over.* Though cease-fires existed, the war never ended. Israel must be destroyed, Lebanon had to come under Islamic dominion, and America, The Great Satan, had to be pulled down. So, the 1400-year-old Islamic war of world conquest looked west and set their ambitions on the thriving civilization known as The United States of America.

Today, the Islamic faithful are encouraged to move to non-Islamic nations, live peacefully and wait for the opportune time to take over those nations by politics and violence. "You have to live like a state within the state until you take over," said the teacher at Green Lane Mosque in Britain January 2007.[96]

We might ask what makes it so important for Americans to reflect back on this? Here we are today talking about a Middle East democracy in Lebanon that crumbled 30 years ago. What's that to us? It's a loud voice crying out from the darkness of tyranny, "Beware!" It speaks today about the very survival of our American civilization.

Our reporters, our networks and our newspapers were in Beirut but saw the Lebanese Christian militias as holding back the progress of democracy for Muslims. That's the oldest doubletalk in the Islamic playbook! Remember? Everybody outside Islam holds the Muslims back from ascending to their rightful place at the top of all civilizations. The entire world outside Islam is at war against Allah constantly offending the Muslims and holding them back. That's the fundamental premise of 1400 years of Islamic jihads.[97]

However, in Beirut the American media was headquartered in the Commodore Hotel that was owned by a Palestinian and protected by the PLO. Their telephone lines worked and the hotel owner, Youseff Nazal, poured aged scotch whiskey for western reporters like it was water. "Communications, safety and booze---what more could a reporter ask for?" [98]

Yet, it was outright dangerous for western reporters to disagree with the Islamic viewpoint. CBS correspondent, Larry Pintak, said that was death. "Several European reporters who were investigating PLO ties with European terrorist groups were killed or disappeared."[99] And history proved the Muslims weren't seeking to rise in the Lebanese democracy. Instead, they sought the *conquest of democracy,* and the creation of a Muslim controlled government in Lebanon.

How did we miss the obvious? We missed it through our naïveté. We missed it through our Americanized viewpoint. We missed it through the editorial slant in our media. We missed it because we didn't understand the basic concepts of an Islamic jihad that is 1400 years old.[100]

They simply outwitted us by using our values against us. They planned their media campaign years earlier and worded it with symbolism that played right into the sympathies of American reporters. Phrases like--freedom from oppression...revolutionary struggle...refugees from our homeland...freedom fighters--- all had two meanings. Designed to trick the western media into agreement, the Arab media knew it meant making Islamic nations.

One thing is for sure. Because we missed the truth in Lebanon, we welcomed the jihad warriors to our shores in America. Remember, the Christians were the oppressors, so the downtrodden were welcomed to America. And who were they? Why, the oppressed Muslims of course. So, the U.S. staked its civilization on a false premise.[101]

For instance, just seven years later Mohammed Hammoud, a Shiite Muslim from Lebanon, stifled his impulse to laugh in the faces of the U.S. immigration officials that asked him to step into a private interview room in 1992. Hezbollah recruits before him had already run this gauntlet and told him exactly what would happen when they caught him with his fake tourist visa. He was trained to tell one of a number of stories that worked for gaining political asylum for Lebanese Muslims. Everything went exactly as he rehearsed it.

He explained to the interviewers that he fled south from the Hezbollah recruiters around Beirut, but was kidnapped by the South Lebanese Army that was sponsored by Israel. They kept him in jail where they interrogated him, roughed him up and eventually released him back in the Beirut area. Now he had nowhere to go because he was marked as an Israeli sympathizer. Everything was a lie, but immigration swallowed the bait hook, line and sinker.

Within hours he and his cousins were granted political asylum and released on the streets of New York City. From there they headed to Charlotte, North Carolina to join their Hezbollah cell.[102] When the FBI eventually broke up the cell for interstate cigarette smuggling, charts and maps were found of other cell groups across the United States. So far, Hezbollah's operational strategy inside America has been to stay beneath the radar of law enforcement while they find weaknesses in our defenses.[103] If Hezbollah stays out of the news, then Americans will continue to believe they're not in danger.

Islam's continuing war against Christendom has entered a new phase, a phase that requires alertness and endurance from every freedom-loving American citizen if we hope to survive as free people. Western Civilization is the greatest obstacle standing in the way of victory in this struggle that has endured fourteen centuries. And today, nations like America, Israel, and Great Britain are clearly pictured in the crosshairs of the riflescope of that worldwide jihad.

After calling in my report on the Valley of the Springs truck bombing that March afternoon in 1985, I left Metulla in Northern Israel that night and made the run to our Jerusalem News Bureau down the Jordan Valley Road that snaked through ancient Jericho.

The next day I did an insert on the English News presenting my eyewitness account of the Hezbollah attack. After recording our program at the Jerusalem Capital Studios, I drove back north to my apartment in Kiryat Shemona the next afternoon. The preceding days were a whirlwind, yet within a short time I discovered there were even more hazards than bombs and bullets in Lebanon. However, the suffering I was about to endure gave me a whole new insight.

Chapter 7
Six Days That Changed The World

Ijuggled assignments from our Jerusalem News Bureau with other stories I investigated in South Lebanon. Meanwhile, my duties as the department head for productions at the Middle East Television station in Marjayoun continued as usual making for some long days. In Lebanon there were no Pizza Huts, Burger Kings, Wendy's or McDonald's. If you didn't pack a lunch the only alternative was finding a local restaurant. I made the mistake of eating on the fly at one such street corner shop and within hours found myself in the hospital with food poisoning. I was violently ill with diarrhea and vomiting making me rapidly dehydrated and somewhat incoherent.

An Israeli Army doctor educated at Harvard Medical School attended to me in the emergency room of the Marjayoun hospital in South Lebanon. Can you imagine, all the way on the other side of the world and an English-speaking doctor educated in America treated me, amazing. I later found out that he was on assignment in the Israeli patrolled sector attending to virtually every serious case admitted to that Lebanese hospital during the weeks of his duty.

It was a great news story, but local people pleaded with me not to do it. They explained that they wouldn't be able to use the hospital after my story aired. Worse yet, they would be marked as traitors to the Arab world and assassins would be sent to kill their families. *How could this be?* I wondered. Then, I found the answer.

When speaking of Israeli leaders such as the Prime Minister, Arab news anchors referred to them as, "the liar, Shimon Peres" or "the mass murderer, Ariel Sharon". They depicted the Israeli Army as marauding rapists and pillagers and presented the Israeli people as an evil and wicked civilization. This twisted viewpoint aired every night of the week on the Arab news stations in Lebanon, Syria, Jordan and Iraq. No wonder the people were terrified. It was the worst example of public agenda setting by the media that I've ever experienced. Since death lurked around every turn for these people, I kept them off the television.

For me, those first two days in the hospital were bad. I couldn't eat and had to be fed intravenously. But as the first night approached around sunset a stunning Lebanese woman walked into my room. She had long jet-black hair and wore designer blue jeans and a cream colored sweater that accented her tan skin.

"Hello," she said in perfect English with a slight accent. "My name is Brigitte. I'm the hospital supervisor's assistant, but I'm the only one around here who speaks English fluently, so if you need anything call for me."

"Thank you," I replied. "Is the Israeli doctor coming to see me tomorrow?"

"No," she answered. "His duty ended today so he went back to Israel. But he left specific instructions for your medicines and your diet. You are to remain in the hospital for at least four more days. Do you have anyone to cook meals for you?"

"No," I answered.

"Then, my family and I will cook your meals and bring them to you," she said.

And that was that. She did exactly as she promised. Her sixty-five year old mother cooked my meals and walked one mile back and forth to the hospital three times a day until I was released. But later that first night my ordinary hospital stay turned into somewhat of an adventure.

In the middle of the night I woke up to strange munching sounds and paper rustling. A large Lebanese prairie varmint had crept into my room. I fumbled for the light hoping to scare it away, but when the light went on I didn't find a varmint, instead I found a man dressed in pajamas sitting upright in the next bed eating sunflower seeds out of a paper bag. The rodent-like munching sounds in the darkness were the man's front teeth cracking the hulls off the seeds. I looked at my watch…2:30 a.m. He smiled at me with seed husks stuck to his lips and teeth. Disgusted, I got out of bed and headed for the bathroom wheeling the i-v stand still in my hand.

The mountain mist drifted through the dimly lighted hallway looking like a murder scene from some horror movie. I opened the door to the bathroom. No toilet, no washbowl, just a porcelain hole in the floor with a single faucet next to it and a three foot piece of green garden hose attached to the faucet. *Ah, the new spray flush model,* I thought.

A single twenty-watt light bulb hung from the ceiling on a black cord. Behind the hole in the floor the toilet paper was attached to the wall threaded through the cardboard center by a piece of wire coat hanger whose ends were stuck into two holes chipped into the cement wall. *So, this is the glamorous lifestyle of the correspondent,* I mused.

As I returned to my room I noticed an armed South Lebanese Army soldier seated outside the room next to mine. While guarding his prisoners he continuously clicked the safety of his AK-47 rifle on and off to keep himself awake. Click, it went off as I stood in front of him. To my surprise he greeted me with English. I explained my complaint about the munching using hand motions and he spoke to my roommate in Arabic. Pretty soon we were all laughing and I went back to sleep.

When I left the hospital I spent another week recuperating at the house of a missionary living in Marjayoun. Given ten days free from work, my predicament afforded an opportunity unlike any other. During my time off I read *Moshe Dayan's: Story Of My Life,* the autobiography of Israel's Defense Minister and legendary one-eyed general. On this perfect location in Lebanon I researched events surrounding Black September and the PLO's occupation of South Lebanon. By discussing my readings with residents from Marjayoun and Dier Mimas who lived through those difficult years, I verified my findings.

Black September took place in Jordan, Israel's neighbor to the west. There, Yassir Arafat's Palestinian militia tried to overthrow the government and kill the king.[104] After their defeat by the Jordanian Army, the Palestinian militia fled into Lebanon setting in motion events that caused the loss of 100,000 Lebanese lives and the destruction of the only Arab democracy.

However, the real key to understanding the Middle East happened three years earlier in June 1967 when the united Arab armies suffered a Biblical scale defeat by the Israeli Army. Ever since known as The Six Day War, its results changed history dramatically. If you don't understand this piece of the recent past, you cannot understand the Middle East, and you cannot see clearly through the fog of Arab propaganda to help secure America's future against Islamic fascism. The results of The Six Day War shape today's world events. Virtually all the Islamic arguments presented against Israel, America and Western Civilization are founded in the results of the Six Day War.

How Events Unfolded

The Russians figured that Israel's special relationship with the United States made its Muslim enemies natural friends of the Soviet Union. So, beginning in 1955 the Soviets allied themselves with Egypt's President Nasser hoping to establish a Marxist movement in the heart of Islam that would conquer the Middle East. The Russians poured arms and military advisors into Egypt who responded by leading the Arab states in three wars against Israel.

By 1967 the Arab states of Egypt, Iraq and Syria were client states of the U.S.S.R., the old Soviet empire. They purchased all their military hardware --- guns, tanks, bullets, warplanes and bombs --- from Russia. Together with Jordan these three countries formed an alliance and made plans to attack and destroy Israel once and for all time in June 1967.

But the Israel Defense Forces surprised the Arab world with a lightning preemptive strike known as the Six Day War. Israeli intelligence services had tapped the military communications lines of the Arab armies and intercepted their plans and their codes in advance. As the Arab forces gathered to attack, Israel struck first catching their foes concentrated in mass on the ground and inflicting devastating losses.

The map of the Middle East changed in less than a week as Israel took and occupied portions of Egypt, Jordan and Syria.[105] Conventional inter-state warfare had failed for the Arabs in 1948, 1956 and again in 1967, only this time the embarrassment to the Arab world was devastating. They found themselves crushed in Biblical style. Although drastically outnumbered, Israel defeated the united Arab armies of four countries in six days and captured significant portions of their lands.

It started on May 14, 1967 when Israeli intelligence observed Egypt moving its military forces into the Sinai Peninsula on Israel's southern border.[106] In the following days 1000 tanks, 200 warplanes and 80,000 troops moved into attack position as Israeli civil defense in Tel Aviv prepared 40,000 beds for the expected casualties.[107] Then, on May 22nd Egypt closed the Straits of Tiran cutting off all shipping into Israel's southern port of Eilat on the Red Sea. This act of war by Egypt was a demonstration to the Arab world to join together against Israel who would be too weak to defeat the united Arab armies.[108]

Egyptian President Nasser's attempt to rally the Arab countries succeeded. On May 30th Jordan signed an alliance with Egypt and Syria while Iraq joined four days later.[109]

Isolated and completely surrounded, on June 1st Israel called the legendary-one-eyed General Moshe Dayan out of retirement and appointed him Minister of Defense.[110] On June 3rd Israeli intelligence presented Dayan with the information that Egypt was going to attack in force from the Sinai joined by a Kuwaiti armored brigade.

Only days before Jordan had placed her military forces under Egyptian command to coordinate a simultaneous invasion of Israel from the west. And while one Iraqi battalion was en route to Gaza on Israel's southern border, four Iraqi infantry brigades with supporting tanks were alerted and preparing to cross into Jordan as part of the western invasion front. The united Arab armies would attack on Egypt's command.

Most ominous was the intercepted communiqué the day before from the commander of the Egyptian forces in the Sinai saying:

> The eyes of the world are upon you in your most glorious war against Israeli imperialist aggression on the soil of your fatherland...your holy war for the recapture of the rights of the Arab nation... Reconquer anew the robbed land of Palestine by the grace of God and of justice, by the power of your weapons and the unity of your faith.[111]

With her forces vastly outnumbered 25 to 1, U.S. President Lyndon Johnson told Israel that America's support was based on Israel "not firing the first shot." Sadly, this meant waiting to be victimized by the overwhelming odds.[112] Unwilling to take that chance, Israel didn't wait to see how devastating the united Arab armies' first strike might be. Instead, at 7:45 a.m. June 5, 1967, Israel attacked by surprise. 183 Israeli jets attacked Egypt in the first wave and 164 more Israeli jets attacked in a second wave at 9:34 a.m. Syria responded at noon with 12 warplanes followed 10 minutes later by Jordan and Iraq. But they were met in the air by the third wave of Israeli jets that launched at 12:15 p.m.

By late afternoon on the first day of the war Israel lost 19 airplanes and 11 pilots, but the united Arab air forces were devastated. The Egyptians had lost 304 planes before noon and by sundown the entire Jordanian air force was destroyed down to the last aircraft. Syria lost 53 and Iraq lost 10 more. In all a total of 454 aircraft of the four united

Arab air forces were destroyed by Israel before sunset June 5th. Only 130 combined Egyptian, Iraqi, and Syrian warplanes remained to defend the armies and the cities of those four Arab nations.

In effect, as June 6th dawned on the second day of the war, Israel controlled the skies of the Middle East.[113] With her 300 fighter jets supporting the armored infantry, the Israeli Defense Forces crushed the Egyptian Army, captured the entire Sinai Peninsula and reopened the Straits of Tiran by nightfall. Meanwhile, Israeli paratroopers fought the Jordanian Army all night capturing the last Jordanian Legion positions surrounding Jerusalem.

But as Israeli forces closed the circle around Jerusalem on June 6th at 2:00 a.m. Syrian artillery started pounding Israeli settlements in the north with 265 cannons firing 40 tons of shells per minute into the Galilee region of Israel.[114] Yet, General Dayan refused to open a third front choosing instead to threaten Egypt the next day with invasion by land and air.

The road to Cairo was open. Egypt had lost 85 percent of its war machine in two days --- 304 warplanes, 350 tanks, 480 artillery pieces, 10,000 vehicles and 15,000 soldiers dead.[115] Two more day of fighting might leave Egypt paying Israeli taxes for years to come.

Jordan's position was even worse. With their air force destroyed the day before, King Hussein commandeered a jeep in the late afternoon on June 6th and drove to the front. There he observed his army in pieces and watched helplessly as Israeli jets bombed tanks, trucks and soldiers before his own eyes.

Hussein cabled President Nasser in Egypt saying: "…if it continues there can be only one outcome: you and the Arab nation will lose this bastion, together with all its forces…"[116] -------Notice how this communiqué uses the language, "the Arab Nation," when referring to the different Arab countries and their armies. It's significant because this is an Islamic term referring to the Islamic countries of the world as one nation-------

But even though Egypt was at a point of surrender, they lied to their Syrian allies in the north and told them that they had defeated the Israeli army and were advancing on Tel Aviv. Acting on the misinformation, Syria responded and attacked Israel with infantry and tanks, yet what followed was another Biblical scene.

The initial Syrian probe lost 100 soldiers dead and nearly a dozen tanks as Israeli armed civilians poured out from bomb shelters underneath Kibbutz Dan and stalled the advance. Then the main Syrian thrust got confused and couldn't find the rally point while their Soviet tanks proved too big for the bridges crossing the Jordan River. In the meantime, a squadron of Israeli jets arrived on the scene and bombed the Syrian positions, so the rest of the invading forces ignored their orders to move out.

With their attack stalled, Syrian command returned the favor to Cairo and lied to them saying that they were advancing rapidly and would soon succeed in conquering the Galilee regions of Northern Israel.[117]

While the united Arab armies were deceiving each other, Israeli paratrooper were about to accomplish a feat that would rally all Israel, crush the morale of the Arabs and stun the world. On the morning of June 7th Israeli forces captured Jerusalem's Old City and the Western Wall of King Solomon's 3000-year-old temple.[118] A brief emotional phrase came across the radio from General Gur commanding the paratroopers to General Narkiss. "The Temple Mount is in our hands," said Gur.[119] Within a few hours his words were broadcast across the earth.

Since the destruction of Jerusalem by the Roman Legions in 70 AD, for nearly two thousand years Jews the world over consoled each other with the words, "next year in Jerusalem." It's a phrase of hope that says that some day, perhaps next year, the Jews scattered across the world will return to worship in Jerusalem. On the morning of June 7, 1967 those words came true.

Photos went out worldwide across wire services displaying Defense Minister Moshe Dayan, Chief of Staff Rabin and General Narkiss walking calmly together in the morning sun through the Old City streets of Jerusalem. Other pictures showed Israeli paratroopers weeping with their hands touching the 3000-year-old wall of Solomon's temple. While the song *Jerusalem of Gold* blared from every transistor radio in Israel, another eerie sound filled the air in the Old City.

Standing before the temple wall a single victorious paratrooper was blowing a shofar,[120] the ceremonial ram's horn that Joshua's troops blew 3500 years earlier to destroy the walls of Jericho. The ancient sounding of the shofar in front of the army signaled to God that Israel was going into battle against overwhelming odds. In the Biblical accounts something was released in the spiritual realm that meant confusion, fear and destruction for the enemies of Israel.[121] As the paratrooper blew the shofar in front of the temple wall the morning of June 7th, whether the Arab armies were listening or not didn't matter. Their doom was already certain.

Only minutes before the shofar sounded yet still unknown to the Egyptian Army, a small group of nine Israeli tanks had captured the Mitla Pass in the Sinai Dessert cutting off the path of retreat for 30,000 Egyptian troops and 300 of their tanks. On June 7th the retreating Egyptian Army went through a meat grinder as Israeli warplanes pounded them from above. Then, from in front and behind on the ground Israeli tanks broke Egyptian formations and destroyed them in every direction they moved.

So, on the evening of June 8th Egypt accepted a cease-fire.[122] Jordan followed suit and Israeli intelligence intercepted another Egyptian communiqué from President Nasser. This time it went to President Atassi of Syria telling him to go along with the cease-fire.

For two days the Syrians had shelled Israeli villages and kib-butzim (collective farm towns) in the north, and Defense Minister Dayan decided it was time to make a statement before the Syrian President could make up his mind. At 2:00 a.m. June 9th the decision was made to attack. Beginning at 9:45 Israeli jets attacked Syrian positions, but the battle uphill by Israeli tanks was a different story. The Syrians destroyed twenty-four of twenty-six Israeli tanks before the road south of Quneitra was secured.[123]

The first day of battle to take the Golan Heights from Syria continued in like manor with Israeli infantry casualties exceeding those of the Syrian Army whose defensive positions withstood the bombardment from Israel's air force. Fighting 900 feet uphill against fortified emplacements, Israeli assault troops threw their bodies over barbed wire allowing those behind to run through the wire into hand-to-hand fighting.

The battle lasted all night with entire platoons of soldiers lost on both sides until Israeli troops were too exhausted to continue as dawn broke over the Golan. A counter attack in the early morning by Syrian forces might have pushed Israeli forces off the Golan Heights. Instead, the Syrian counter attack never came.

Inexplicably before mid-morning on the last day of the war, June 10th, the Syrian Army began blowing up their bunkers. The national radio channel announced prematurely that the strategic town of Quneitra had fallen to Israel only forty-five miles outside Damascus opening the road for invasion of the Syrian capital. Fearing the worst, both the army and their tanks withdrew completely from the Golan Heights and fell back to defend Damascus from invasion.

Then, in a very clever move, the Israeli Broadcasting System recorded and rebroadcast the Syrian's false news report in its original form on an Arabic speaking channel announcing the fall of the Golan Heights. As rumors of Israel's possible use of secret nuclear weapons circulated within the Syrian military, 7000 soldiers fled their posts seeking shelter in Lebanon and Jordan.

United together only days before as they outnumbered Israel 25 to 1 surrounding them with 465,000 troops,[124] the Arab armies awaited the "go order" to invade from three directions, crush the Israeli Defense Forces, and end the existence of the state of Israel. This was what the world expected to see.

Instead, the tables turned on the Arabs in less than a week. All they anticipated doing to Israel was now within Israel's hands to do to them. With Arab armies and air forces in ruin the routes of invasion lay open for Israeli forces to advance on the capital cities of three Arab nations simultaneously. If Israel had nuclear weapons[125] and wanted to use them, there was nothing to stop her air force from reducing Damascus, Cairo and Amman to cinders on the evening of June 10th.

Israeli Chief of Staff Rabin advised at least taking Damascus, and a Golani battalion commander agreed later that Damascus would have fallen. But Defense Minister Dayan said, "no." Israel had won. The nation was saved. Her enemies were defeated and their military forces incapacitated.

The Arabs showed the world their desire to conquer and destroy Israel. Yet, when faced with the opportunity to return the favor, Israel showed no such appetites. Moshe Dayan informed the United Nations that as of 6:00 p.m. June 10, 1967, a cease-fire was in effect. [126]

So as the cities of her enemies lay open to invasion, Prime Minister to be, Golda Meir proclaimed the restraint shown on the ground as Israel's public policy June 11th in New York saying: "The last thing that Israelis want is to win wars. We don't want wars. We want peace above all else."[127]

Further demonstrating good faith and consistency, within ten days of the war's conclusion on June 19th the Israeli Cabinet passed the motion to return captured lands for signed peace treaties that recognized Israel's right to exist. And five months later on November 22, 1967 UN

Resolution 242 included Israel's offer as part of an overall peace plan for the Middle East.[128] That offer stands to this day.

However, three months after the June cease-fire on September 1, 1967, the Arab countries decided at the Khartoum Summit to regain their lost territory by war alone.[129] So, negotiated settlements through the U.N. were a façade to deceive America and buy time, and according to Egypt's President Nasser, it would require about three years to rearm before another war could be launched. In the meantime, a guerilla war of attrition against Israel was the actual policy. This meant there would be another conventional war, but not until Egypt felt ready to attack. Until then, they would lie about the possibilities of peace.[130]

Nasser's estimated three years would turn into six as Egypt had lost 85 percent of all her military equipment and the humiliation to the united Arab armies was astounding. In comparison to Israeli losses the Arabs lost at least 25 times more in every category.[131]

Country losses	Tanks	Planes	Guns	Vehicles	Soldiers killed
Egypt	350	338	480	10,000	15,000
Jordan	179	48	1062	3160	6000
Syria	167	61	470	1200	2500
Iraq	0	23		400	2000
Israel	28	19		100	777
Total Arab losses	696	470	2012	14,820	25,500

In addition to her sweeping military victory, Israel humiliated the Arab armies further by taking 46,000 square miles of land in six days including the Sinai Peninsula, the Golan Heights, Jerusalem and the entire territory west to the Jordan River. Now the Arab armies could no longer conquer Israel in one swift operation. To gain that kind of victory they would first have to reduce the size of Israel to its pre 1967 borders.[132]

Of course, Israel knew this and changed negotiating tactics making the peaceful return of these captured territories a requirement of a signed treaty recognizing Israel's national sovereignty and borders. This forced the Muslim Arabs to forsake a tenant of their religion that forbid peaceful coexistence with non-Muslim nations.[133] In effect, Israel had them. To get their lost territory back the Arab nations had to recognize Israel as a sovereign nation, not an apostate Palestine. The Arab nations had to get out of their Islamic box, risk Allah's disapproval and make peace with Israel.

The Six Day War also brought a new attention to Israel's history because numerous times in her ancient past the nation was faced with similar threats of destruction. And the accounts of those times read like the news of 1967. Smaller Israeli forces routed overwhelming odds. Then, the enemy forces panicked as confusion over false reports, rumors and fears melted their will to fight.[134] It was right out of the Bible:

> Hear, O Israel, today you are going into battle against your enemies. Do not be fainthearted or afraid; do not be terrified or give way to panic before them. For the LORD your God is the one who goes with you to fight for you against your enemies to give you victory.[135]

> The LORD will grant that the enemies who rise up against you will be defeated before you. They will come at you from one direction but flee from you in seven.[136]

> Five of you will chase a hundred, and a hundred of you will chase ten thousand, and your enemies will fall by the sword before you.[137]

Thus, in both ancient and modern times history recorded a similar picture that prompted a question in churches and synagogues worldwide. Was Israel's deliverance and the astounding defeat of her enemies in 1967 a Biblical victory as in her ancient past? And was this victory actually a statement of divine intervention?

In Israel the jubilation was mixed with tears of humility as rabbis referred to an hour of national deliverance from God. And Golda Meir, who became Prime Minister of Israel in 1969, reflected on the victory of 1967 with eloquence and similar thought.

In contrast, the official Arab propaganda after 1967 became *Israel the moral mistake.* Thus, the Muslim governments of the Arab world answered the above questions with disdain saying that it was a preposterous thought to imagine righteousness on Israel's side since Israel did not have the moral right to exist as a nation.[138] And what made the mere existence of an Israeli state a moral failure?

Arab propaganda said the Jews had *stolen their holy land of Palestine* with the help of the United States. That was immoral. The big and strong had beaten up on the weak and defenseless Arabs leaving no other alternative but for them to "fight on for their freedom and self-determination."

So within months, the entire picture of the war was turned inside out by the Arab propaganda machine making Israel the aggressor and oppressor. Israel deserved to be attacked and America was responsible to put their moral error right. As a penance for her sins the least America could do was help the oppressed Palestinians regain their *freedom*, whatever that meant.

With such "freedom" language specifically written to capture the imagination of the western press and consequently the American public, illusions of possible peace were circulated in the best Islamic traditions of *Taqiya*---lying, and *Kithman*---deceit, both accepted practices of the *jihad* against non-Muslims.[139]

For if the war had ended June 10th, how could the war be continuing? After all, it's a simple question of logic. Why would one side continue the war when both sides agreed upon a cease-fire? The answer was within the religion of Islam. So, the Khartoum Conference determined to continue the war against Israel in guerilla style until another conventional united Arab attack could be organized. Notice the following Khartoum Resolutions:

> Article 2: "…The burden of regaining these lands falls on all the Arab States."
> Article 3: "…no peace with Israel, no recognition of Israel, no negotiations with it, and insistence on the rights of the Palestinian people in their own country. (The war continues without end against *Jews holding Palestine*)
> Article 6: "The participants have agreed on the need to adopt the necessary measures to strengthen military preparation to face all eventualities (prepare

for another war)."[140]

Three conclusions and premises were clear from the language. First, all Arab states shared the war together because it was the universal obligation of Islam to restore conquered lands. Second, it was understood that peace could never exist, since only cease-fires were permitted between Islam and infidels. And third, any armistice had to be broken to renew the fighting and fulfill Islam's ultimate destiny to subjugate all non-Muslim peoples of the world.[141]

So as the Six Day War ended, the Arabs changed tactics. They were defeated and humiliated, but they still chose hatred of Israel and refused to entertain the idea of coexistence without continuous war. Therefore, a guerilla war was launched, and a specifically designed and coordinated propaganda campaign was released for western media consumption using the words, "freedom fighters, liberation, self-determination, and struggle against oppression." The American media swallowed the bait hook, line and sinker.

To symbolize this theatrically on a world stage, 250,000 Palestinian people were displaced from *Jewish occupied Palestine* (Israel) and told by their leaders to take refuge in Jordan, Israel's next-door neighbor to the east. This was in spite of the fact that Israel invited these people to remain.[142]

In Jordan the vast oil wealth of the Arab world could have built the displaced Palestinians shining new cities in a matter of months. The Arab Organization of Petroleum Exporting Countries, OPEC, produced 17 million barrels of oil per day in 1967 [143] and Saudi Arabia alone earned $300 million per day in oil revenues.[144] But such actions wouldn't fit the rhetorical image of a people without a country struggling to liberate their homes. It was far more important to the jihad to use these people as a media device for worldwide consumption.

One year later when Yassir Arafat became their popular leader, he took the theatrics up another notch. Appearing in public dressed in pressed olive drab fatigues with epaulettes,[145] he sported a week's growth of beard, a checkered kafia on his head, dark glasses, and a pistol holstered on his hip. He was the new symbol of the "revolutionary freedom fighter" of Palestine, a kind of anarchistic Middle East cowboy with a movie star image.[146] And so he became the poster child for Article 3 of the Khartoum Resolutions, no peace, no coexistence, and evict the

Jews.

The role was perfect for him to play out. His anti-Semitism went back a generation on his mother's side. Though Arafat claimed he was born in Jerusalem at the heart of Palestine, he was actually born in Cairo, Egypt August 24, 1927. Al-Husseini was the family name of his mother whose head clansman was Amin al-Husseini, the Grand Mufti of Jerusalem and personal friend of Adolf Hitler during World War II.[147]

Amin al-Husseini first met with Hitler November 28, 1941 in Berlin. There, he pledged himself to help Germany win the war and exterminate the Jews of Europe and Palestine.[148] The Mufti set up his base office in Berlin from 1942-1944 where he worked feverishly to prevent the escape of Jews from Europe. Testimony at the Nuremberg trials of Nazi war criminals after WW II tied Amin al-Husseini to Hitler, Himmler and Adolf Eichmann in planning the process.

"He wanted to see all of them liquidated," testified Wilhelm Melchers, a Nazi official.[149]

Later, Adolf Eichmann's deputy, Dieter Wisliceny, gave eyewitness testimony about the depth of the Mufti's involvement:

> The Mufti was one of the initiators of the systematic extermination of European Jewry and had been a collaborator and advisor of Eichmann and Himmler in the execution of this plan. He was one of Eichmann's best friends and had constantly incited him to accelerate the extermination measures. I heard him say that accompanied by Eichmann he had visited the gas chamber of Auschwitz.[150]

Yassir Arafat never liked his father, and one can only imagine the exact influence his mother had. But it is clear that he dedicated his life to anti-Semitism and referred to the Mufti, Amin al-Husseini, as his mentor and guide saying, "The PLO is continuing the path set by the Mufti."[151]

In Jordan the displaced Palestinian community followed their leader's anarchistic spirit, and within a year set up a state within the state of Jordan controlled by a conglomerate militia group known as the Palestine Liberation Organization (PLO). The PLO was founded in Cairo in 1964 and established by Egypt's President Nasser to destabilize Jordan, use it as a base of operations, and continue a harassment-style war of attrition against Israel.[152]

Under the PLO umbrella Yassir Arafat led a militia named *Fatah*, an Arabic language acronym that means "conquest by jihad."[153] In 1968 Arafat was appointed chairman of the PLO and Fatah took the leadership role among the militias.

Refusing to recognize Jordan's national sovereignty, these armed PLO thugs seized villages, committed atrocities against citizens and set up armed checkpoints at road intersections thus carving out entire enclaves inside Jordan as they extorted "taxes and donations" at gunpoint from homes and businesses.[154]

Then, using these sections of Jordan as a base of training and operations, the PLO launched cross-border raids against Israeli towns and settlements. The *jihad* was back on with Jordanians paying the price when the PLO hid out in their towns during Israeli retaliations. But this was Nasser's reason for establishing the PLO in the first place.

All throughout 1968 and 1969 Jordan tried to reestablish civil authority. Yet, more than 500 violent clashes were recorded in these two years between Jordanian security forces and the PLO as Jordan's military tried in vain to bring things under control.[155]

Finally, the PLO decided all Jordan should belong to them. When they started a revolt to overthrow the Jordanian government in1970 by launching attempts to assassinate Jordan's King Hussein, he declared martial law. Throughout Black September Jordan's forces mobilized an all out military attack on PLO held Jordanian towns and fought house-to-house crushing the coup. September 1970 was a bloody month in Jordan, but King Hussein's forces eventually saved his country finally defeating the PLO in June 1971.[156]

Beaten but not destroyed, the remaining 15,000 PLO fled into Lebanon and Black September took on a whole new meaning. A shadow of doom spread an evil darkness over this pristine democratic nation with a flourishing Christian community.

There, armed PLO gangs seized homes and took over buildings in towns throughout the south. They strengthened their army with weapons supplied by Russia, and began setting up a state within the state of Lebanon just like they did in Jordan.[157]

Then, in accordance with Article 2 of the Khartoum Resolutions that required all Arabs to help in the reconquest of lost Islamic territories, the PLO set up recruiting offices throughout the Arab world. As multitudes of recruits from other Muslim nations arrived in Lebanon the PLO ranks swelled to 40,000. These recruits joined the PLO's cause to harass and destroy Israel and turn Lebanon into an Islamic state.

Fifteen years earlier the Russians firmly established their anti-west presence in the modern Middle East with the Russian-Egyptian arms agreement of 1955.[158] The Soviets supplied Nasser's Egypt with overwhelming numbers of tanks, arms, supplies and the most modern jets and bombers made by Russia. One year later Egypt started the 1956 War with Israel by closing the Straits of Tiran.[159] Then, in 1958 Iraq joined the pro- Soviet alliance with Nasser after a military coup led by General Kassem murdered the King of Iraq, his entire family and the Prime Minister.

"After the King and Prime Minister of Iraq were murdered, I had to ask President Eisenhower for support to stabilize our country," said Lebanese President Camille Chamoun. "Both Nasser and General Kassem (the pro Soviet general who led the coup in Iraq) were sending hit squads into Lebanon to destabilize our government. They wanted to bring down the democracy and turn it into an Islamic state. President Eisenhower helped us by sending the Marines and within a month or so we stabilized the country."[160]

Twelve years later it was all fitting in to a master plan. What Nasser started inside Lebanon in 1958 the PLO continued in 1970. Yassir Arafat had lived in Egypt nearly thirty years. "Everywhere else I sleep with one eye open, but in Cairo I feel secure," he said.[161] As the international advertising symbol and poster child of the PLO, he continued the Islamic jihad stated in Article 3 of Khartoum in sympathy with Nasser's desire to subjugate Lebanon's democracy into an Islamic state.

"The PLO became a catalyst that gave the diverse Muslims in Lebanon the hope of taking over," Camille Chamoun said. "It was the final element that led to civil war in Lebanon, a civil war aimed mostly at the Christians. Our national Lebanese army was too weak to contain them and later splintered over religious factions."[162]

President Chamoun was right, of course. Throughout 1971 and into 1972 the PLO recruiting offices swelled their ranks in Lebanon as recruits arrived from across the Arab world. These were far more than squads of commandoes from Egypt and Iraq. This time there were thousands upon thousands of armed Muslim militiamen bottled up inside Lebanon looking for a war to fight. It didn't take long.

During the first months after arriving in Lebanon Palestinian hit squads regrouped before launching terror attacks into Israel. One of the most notorious was the 1970 Israeli school bus massacre near Nahariya on the northern coastline of Israel where terrorists killed 12 children and wounded 19 before escaping back into Lebanon. Months later as their final battles against the Jordanian Army ended in defeat in June 1971, 15,000 remaining PLO were escaping into Lebanon.

At this moment Imam Moussa Al-Sadr, the spiritual leader of the Lebanese Shiite Muslim community, saw his opportunity to seize destiny. In many cases the Shiite communities were disrupted by PLO activity that drove them to leave their homes in South Lebanon. But Al-Sadr saw the handwriting on the wall. He knew that this many armed Muslim troops bottled up and spoiling for a fight could be turned into an advantage. So, in 1972 he visited Moscow asking the Soviets for their assistance.[163]

Lebanese Shiite Muslims are part of a geographical arc of that religious denomination that extends from South Lebanon across Iraq and into Iran. In the 16th Century the Safavid Dynasty arose in Iran and made Shiism the official state religion. And travel across the arc by spiritual leaders became a ritual that kept the communities connected throughout the ages. For four hundred years Lebanese Shiite leaders had looked to Iran for direction.

Moussa Al-Sadr was actually born in Iran so his connections there were direct,[164] and his visit to Moscow got him all that he asked for. Not only did the U.S.S.R. send weapons but Russian Military Intelligence also sent Arabic speaking officers into Lebanon where they trained recruits in the PLO base camps of the Bekka Valley from 1972-1975. They also became a presence in the Sabra and Shatila communities south of Beirut where PLO recruits from Libya, Pakistan, Iran, Syria, and Algeria lived [165] along with other international communist revolutionaries and terrorist groups.

For instance, Fusako Shigenobu was the founder of the Japanese Red Army. In 1971 she traveled to Lebanon[166] and stayed in the Sabra and Shatila communities where she allied her organization with the PLO's Charter that called for the destruction of Israel.[167] A few months later she masterminded the infamous LOD Airport attack in Tel Aviv, Israel that killed twenty-six people May 30, 1972.

The delicately balanced Lebanese democracy that accommodated both Muslims and Christians could not cope with the anarchistic mess inside their nation. Clearly a friend of the United States, Lebanon was a target of conquest for the expanding Russian empire. Their military advisors went to Lebanon to help the Muslims conduct a civil war, overthrow the democratic government, and create another pro-Soviet Arab client state. There would be no full recovery for Lebanon after Black September of 1970.

Today's World

The Six Day War of 1967 changed the world in many ways. Hated nonetheless, thereafter the Israeli Army was feared throughout the Middle East. In contrast, the united Muslim armies of the Arab world failed to reconquer *Jewish occupied Palestine* for the third time in twenty years. Even more humiliating than their six-day defeat was their loss of 46,000 square miles of land that gave Israel a new power of persuasion.

Yet the greatest change of the war was the change of national flags flying over the city of Jerusalem. The Israel of the ancient times once lost in the dust of history returned stepping out of that dust with a statement of power into the present day. Israel established itself conclusively for modern times.

Strangely, even though the war took place on the other side of the world, Arabs blamed America for the Israeli victory. In fact, America was blamed for the existence of the state of Israel. But all this was rhetoric that covered up the real story of an endless Islamic jihad that was to come. There was no going back and the Arab world knew it. By 1967 Israel had the capacity to make a nuclear bomb. The Arab states would never reconquer Israel and all that was left to them was rage.

In the next three years the events that followed the results of the Six Day War led to the survival of Jordan's monarchy and the crumbling of Lebanon's democracy. But it was inside Lebanon where the pot would boil the soup of terrorism that eventually spilled across the world. Hit squads, kidnappings, highjacked airplanes and suicide bombers were the future expression of an angry Islamic world unable to reconquer a land named Israel.

After the Six Day War Israel soon gained nuclear weapons. Egypt and Syria tried a land assault once more in 1973 on Israel's holy day of Yom Kippur inflicting heavy losses before Israel turned the tide and surrounded the Egyptian Army in the Sinai Peninsula two weeks later.

President Nixon airlifted everything necessary to Israel to recover their losses and win because it was the Arabs who were in grave danger of pushing Israel too far. President Nixon and the United States knew that Israel had at least twenty nuclear warheads in the closet, and pushed too far, they'd use them.[168] President Sadat of Egypt who led his army against Israel in 1973 signed the Camp David Peace Accords in 1978.[169]

"Never again," shout the Israeli soldiers in training atop the legendary Masada. "Never again," will there be a Jewish Holocaust and "never again" will the land of Israel fall to a foreign conqueror. In 1982 the Israeli's placed nuclear land mines in the Golan Heights to prevent invasion. By the mid 1980's "the Israelis produced hundreds of low yield tactical neutron warheads capable of killing large numbers of enemy troops with minimal property damage."[170] Their missiles can strike targets up to 6000 miles away and their field commanders have nuclear artillery if necessary.

In 1991 as Iraqi scud missiles fell on Israeli cities during Gulf War I, a U.S. satellite observed Israeli mobile missile launchers with nuclear warheads deployed against Iraq.[171] If Tel Aviv fell under nerve gas attack, it may have been the end of Baghdad. Luckily for the world, the Iraqi scud missiles were armed with only TNT.

Today Muslim tactics against Israel are limited to suicide bombers and sporadic small rockets. But they haven't given up because they believe that someday the United States will become an Islamic state or at least be thrown into such chaos and destruction that it will no longer be a factor. "Death to America" is still a rally cry for the Islamic Revolution of 1979 that now seeks a first strike nuclear capacity.[172]

The world changed dramatically in 1967. I remember my mother calling to me from the living room where she was in the midst of watching the evening news on television. The date was June 8, 1967. She had called to me just in time. No sooner did I enter the room than I saw a black and white film of General Moshe Dyan and two other commanders walking in the morning sunshine through the streets of Jerusalem. "Pay attention to this, son," she coached. "This is history. The world will never be the same again."

I was just a boy at the time and it would be years before I understood the meaning of her words. The entire world had been watching to see if Israel could survive against the overwhelming numbers of the united Arab armies. Nobody had expected that Israel would defeat the Arabs in six days in such an overwhelming manner, certainly not the Arabs. My mother was a research librarian not a Bible scholar. Yet, she knew instinctively that the style of Israel's victory was a signal to mankind.

The prophecies of the 2nd Coming of Jesus Christ are tied directly to an existing nation of Israel. Yet, there was no nation of Israel until after WW II when the United Nations voted for the dividing of Palestine and the reestablishment of Israel in 1948. Realistically, as the united Arab armies poised to destroy Israel in 1967, the world expected the Israelis would be defeated and disappear once more into history. They didn't; and the style and magnitude of their victory suggested that the ancient God of the Hebrews knew how to fight modern warfare.

Had God acted in modern history on behalf of His ancient covenant with Abraham?[173] Were a thousand years as a day to God? Circumstances said, "yes." And that meant the world and mankind began ticking towards a final chapter, Armageddon and the 2nd Coming of Christ.[174] For it is over the existence of the state of Israel and on the very soil of an existing nation of Israel that the entire world comes to fight on the Plains of Armageddon.

What are the forces driving our world to such a disastrous conclusion? Certainly part of the answer is found in a 3rd Middle East religion that has refused reformation and sees its destiny to be the conquest and dominion of all nations.[175]

Chapter 8
Why They Fight

It was my first full weekend off in months. As I headed out the door of my apartment in Kiryat Shemona Saturday morning, I had the sense I'd forgotten something. Sure enough, my Motorola was on the kitchen table. It was my lifeline if something went wrong in the war zone.

Hurrying back up the stairs to the 4th floor, I grabbed the radio and flew back down the stairs to my car. In fifteen minutes I'd crossed the border into Lebanon and within half an hour made it to my friend, Brigitte's house in Marjayoun where I had coffee with her and her parents.

Her father was nearly deaf. A few years before PLO artillery shells landed on their home destroying his hearing. It was an odd scene as anything I said Brigitte retold to her father shouting next to one ear. "This is the television correspondent from the hospital, remember?" she screamed. Her father nodded and the conversation continued back and forth for over an hour as she translated my English to Arabic in shouts.

When the PLO invaded South Lebanon this Christian family lost everything: their house, their successful business, their money and their way of life. Brigitte was the only one with a job and it paid almost nothing. Yet when I was in the Marjayoun hospital, this unknown family brought me meals twice a day walking a mile in both directions to help a stranger. Even the random hatred of their enemies had not destroyed their amazing character.

Sometime around noon I left Brigitte's house in Lebanon and drove back through the border fence into Israel. From there I continued driving another three hours south in Israel towards Jerusalem where I was due for dinner at our senior correspondent's house that evening.

Jerusalem is nestled in a cluster of small mountains directly east of Tel Aviv. As I drove up from the coast the air became cooler and the pine trees thicker. I'd been so busy in South Lebanon I hadn't spent time with Peter and Christine in over three months. They lived in a manicured hilltop suburb called Mevaseret Zion that was filled with individual houses of finished limestone exteriors, flower gardens and picturesque red tile roofs.

"This will give me a chance to try out my new tooth," I told Christine. "If you ever need a good dentist, ask for Dr. Mansur in Bethlehem. He's great."

"Oh, I heard about your broken tooth adventure in Bethlehem," she replied. "That reminds me. I'm going to send you to my favorite souvenir shop there tomorrow. I'll give you the directions and you ask for Affiq. Just tell him I sent you. And don't worry, he speaks English very well."

The next day I met Affiq at the souvenir shop in Bethlehem. "Look around, find anything you like and I'll make you a special price," he said. "Did Christine tell you about my brother, Fuad?"

"A little," I replied. "Why don't you tell me what happened?" And with that Affiq launched into the story that had his whole family happy with tears and laughter.

Oldest of the three brothers, Fuad went to college in Jordan where the PLO recruited him on campus. Later he was caught smuggling arms into Israel and imprisoned for 10 years. Miraculously, his sentence was cancelled after three years and he was now home.

Affiq closed the shop for three hours as was customary at noon and we met his younger brother Hatim at their other shop off Manger Square, the main tourist area in Bethlehem. Business was slow so we all went for coffee and later returned to their family home for dinner.

They were Palestinian Muslims living in Israel, but that didn't make a difference to them about me, the American. From day one they adopted me like family and I was always welcomed in their shops or their home with smiles and humor. When I think of a God fearing Muslim family, I'm always reminded of them. Their previous bitterness with Israel seemed washed away by the joy of Fuad's release. To them, Israel had done a noble thing. But they couldn't speak openly of their gratitude to Israel. An Arab assassin would be sent to murder them on the streets of Bethlehem as they walked home from their souvenir shop.

There is a notion in my profession that news is void of religion unless a crime is involved. That's the "western lens" we've used as a matter of habit owing to our American laws calling for the separation of church and state. We avoid religious explanations for news events. As a journalist, however, my purpose was to examine the historical facts and the arguments in order to report truthfully.

In addition, I lived and worked in the war zone where people from three religions were involved in a daily life and death conflict. I didn't want my western lens to become an excuse for avoiding the necessary research. I found that without religious discussion the facts would never be clear. By living and working there, by driving daily between Lebanon and Israel, and by my research, I found the explanation hidden fourteen centuries before our modern time inside the history of a religion.

The Beginnings of Islam

On April 20, 570 AD according to tradition, Muhammad Ibn Abdullah Ibn Abd al-Muttalib was born in the Arabian city of Mecca within a tribe of people named the Quraysh. Arabia at the time was a harsh pagan land known for blood feuds, child marriages and female infanticide because women were regarded as a financial liability.

However, in Mecca the Quraysh tribe prospered commercially accommodating the multitudes of pilgrims who traveled to the shrine at Ka'bah that housed the numerous pagan idols of Arabia.[176] The term *Allah* was used to refer to a god of the region long before Muhammad began to use it in the new monotheistic religion he founded.[177]

Muhammad wasn't known for being either handsome or ugly neither shorter nor taller than other men. Yet, the circumstances that filled his life seemed far from average. He was a poor orphan that married a much older independently wealthy businesswoman.

Wealth didn't elevate Muhammad to the heights he attained, however. Instead, it was his ability to make war that raised him to become the de facto Emperor of Arabia.

At the age of forty Muhammad's religious revelations began in a cave from an unidentified spiritual being who later called himself the angel Gabriel. These annual visits of the angel continued as progressive revelations for the next twenty-three years until Muhammed's death in 632.

But since Muhammad was illiterate, the revelations were recorded by others and later compiled into a book called *The Quran*.[178] Unlike the Bible used by Jews and Christians that had forty authors and was written over a period of 1300 years, the Quran had just one orator, Muhammad, who spoke it for others to write down.

Filling in the Blanks

Since the text and context of Muhammad's revelations were not always clear in the Quran, other books were developed. Chief among these are the *Hadith* and the *Sira*. The *Hadith* is a commentary on the circumstances of revelation and fills in a lot of the gaps by telling stories of what went on during the revelations. The *Sira* is a biography. And the three together make up a collection called the *Sunnah.* Islamic law, known as *Sharia*, is taken and interpreted from these three written sources studied in combination.

The most respected of the Hadith / commentaries were compiled by Ibn Ismail al-Bukhari who lived two hundred years after Muhammad died. Al-Bukhari collected 300,000 sayings that he cross-referenced and distilled down to two thousand sayings. Today, they are published in a nine-volume set and have been translated to English.

Among the biographies / Sira written the most widely used is *The Biography of the Prophet Muhammad* by Ibn Ishaq. He was born one hundred years after Muhammad's first revelation in the year 710 AD and completed his biography approximately 150 years after Muhammad died. However, by this time the tradition was already established that Muhammad's revelations were the absolute will of God, and to insult the prophet was a death offense. So, biographers certainly took this into account and wrote with praise even if the scene described was brutal and gory. The Islamic scholar, Alfred Guillaume, did the most recognized English translation of Ibn Ishaq's book.

The Nation of War

The first decade of the new religion encountered many frustrations including strong rejection by Muhammad's people, the Quraysh. During these early years he carefully developed the military strategy used later to absorb territories and triumph against overwhelming odds. That strategy included immigration, legal change, attacks on civilian travel, and conquest of territory. And one of the greatest achievements that made him successful was deceiving the public by concealing each stage of the strategy until the trap was sprung for the next phase. His breakout year was 622 and by the end of the second decade he'd conquered Arabia by killing and subjugating his competitors.

Chief among these were the Jews and Christians whose monotheistic beliefs were closely related to one another and previously well established for centuries. Islam borrowed many principles from these two religions, for instance: Judaism's history told of their flight from Egypt and how God came down to dwell with his people as they traveled through the Sinai Peninsula on their way to Canaan. Christianity established that God lived inside believers and was present when two or more gathered for worship. Islam used these ideas and created other arguments to challenge the truthfulness of these two belief systems.

But merely finding an argument to challenge religious credibility wasn't sufficient unless a new code of law was introduced that made those differences criminal. That was accomplished in 622 with a written declaration in Medina stating that the followers of Islam throughout the world were *a nation*. Historian Phillip Hitti wrote, "Hitherto it had been a religion within the state...In Medina it passed into something more than a state religion---it became the state."[179]

Thus, any action from communities outside Islam that broke their laws was a violation of their national sovereignty.[180] Since Islam's frontiers extended everywhere, virtually any crime violated their territory, thus placing them in a constant state of war. This became the principle of two worlds, the House of War (*dar al Harb*), those outside Islam not in submission to Allah, and the House of Islam (*dar al Islam*), those believers inside of Islam who have submitted to the authority of Allah.

For those inside the House of Islam the military struggle for world conquest called *jihad* is an obligation. The distinguished scholar, Bernard Lewis, has written more than twenty books on the subject matter. In *The Political Language of Islam* he explains that Islamic law allows only for temporary cease-fires, not peace treaties. Only the final victory of world conquest will end the war and he explains why that process continues today:

> According to Muslim teaching, jihad is...an obligation imposed on all Muslims by God...This obligation is without limit of time or space. It must continue until the whole world has either accepted

the Islamic faith or submitted to the power of the Islamic state.[181]

Centuries before Muhammad had received his first revelation, Judaism and Christianity spread south into Arabia. Entire Jewish communities moved there from Israel in the first century after the Roman armies sacked Jerusalem in 70 AD. The Christian community in Israel also sent missionaries into the region during that same era.

Owing to this, both these monotheistic faiths that came from outside grew in numbers inside Arabia presenting a well-established theological competition to the new religion of Islam. To succeed theologically as a one-God-religion Islam had to create a distinctive difference that would make it the "most desirable" for converts inside Arabia.

Outside Arabia, Christianity was already the big winner having successfully spread by evangelism throughout the entire Middle East for six hundred years. From the middle of those six centuries beginning in 313 AD when the Roman Emperor Constantine converted, Christian thought applied an official influence on the Roman Empire whose legions controlled the Mediterranean World. For Islam to succeed in worldwide conquest they had to start small and develop a proven war strategy that could succeed against superior numbers and strength.

The Competition

In order to understand how Muhammad developed the necessary sharp theological differences to promote Islam in Arabia, some basic background discussion on Judaism and Christianity is helpful. Since both the religions preceded Muhammad by centuries he used them to promote Islam as the newest revelation.

Judaism began over 3500 years ago in the Middle East founded by Abraham and further developed by Moses the writer of five books of law and history known as the *Torah*. It revealed man's relationship to the One True God and developed a great missionary religion to spread knowledge and faith worldwide.[182] For example, their prophet and poet Isaiah wrote God's message saying: "I will give you as a light to the nations, that my salvation may reach to the ends of the earth." [183]

In the 1st Century AD the historian, Philo, wrote that many Egyptian converts to Judaism actually left Egypt [184] fifteen centuries earlier along with the Jewish community that fled from that country in the Exodus (1500 BC).[185] And his contemporary historian, Josephus, praised the international success of Jewish missionaries writing that great numbers of Greeks were converting to their religion as well.[186]

As a further demonstration of the evangelical nature of Judaism the Queen of Ethiopia arrived in Jerusalem on a state visit during the reign of King Solomon (971-931 BC).[187] As a result a Jewish community of Ethiopian converts existed for 3000 years in Africa, and in 1984 and 1991 large numbers of black Ethiopian Jews immigrated to modern day Israel.[188]

In addition, Judaism is considered to be the parent faith of Christianity that began over 2000 years ago inside the nation of Israel, which at the time had been conquered by the Roman Legions and renamed *Palestine*.[189] This conquest brought oppression on the Israelis who looked to the rescue and military triumph of the coming Messiah to overthrow Roman rule with heavenly armies and reestablish Israel:

> The Lord will extend your mighty scepter from
> Zion;You will rule in the midst of your enemies.
> Your troops will be willing on the day of battle.
> Arrayed in holy majesty....[190]

The Spirit of God was also prominent in Judaic history giving special power to leaders to communicate to the people, lead the army, confound enemies, and perform supernatural acts of strength.[191] From the numerous scriptural passages carefully recorded over the centuries of Jewish history, the Trinity or three persons of the One True God were evident in God the Father, God the Messiah, and God the Spirit.

Then, beginning about 30 AD a Jewish commoner in the Galilee region, Jesus of Nazareth, caused great controversy through a ministry of preaching and miraculous healings. Entire towns were emptied as people walked days to see him, to hear his preaching, and to experience healing.

Eyewitnesses claimed that he was the promised Messiah, but Jesus claimed his kingdom was not of this world.[192] This notion clashed directly with the Messiah anticipated by Jewish scholars at the time. That controversy came to a conclusion when Jewish leaders had him arrested and tried for blasphemy. He was turned over to the Roman authorities who crucified him.

Instead, what seemed to be a tragic end turned out to be a miraculous beginning. His followers pointed to many passages of scripture such as those in the book of Isaiah written 700 years before that told of a suffering Messiah who came the first time to be rejected by men and die for their sins:

> ...The punishment that brought us peace was upon
> him,and by his wounds we are healed...
> Yet it was the Lord's will to crush him and cause him
> to suffer. And though the Lord makes his life a guilt
> offering...My righteous servant will justify many,
> and he will bear their iniquities.[193]

Hundreds of Jewish eyewitnesses said and wrote that Jesus rose from the dead and ascended into heaven.[194] Before leaving earth, he had commanded his disciples to go into the entire world and teach all aspects of the new faith just as he had coached them. Thus, Christianity began.

Spanning two thousand years these two faiths of Judaism and Christianity developed a collection of sixty books of law, teachings, history, letters, poetry and prophesies that were compiled into two divisions in a single volume and later called the Bible. By the end of the 1st Century AD, teaching of the thirty-nine Old Testament books and the twenty-seven New Testament books was spreading throughout the Christian churches everywhere.[195]

Because the movement started in Israel the early missionaries of Christianity preached and taught in the network of synagogues throughout the world wherever Judaism had previously spread.[196] Owing to this close relationship in origins and missionary networks, the two religious communities grew side by side in the first centuries after the death of Jesus in 33 AD.

For Christian believers the final instructions of Jesus to his disciples included the promise of a *helper* he would send to all believers following his ascension into heaven. In the division of the Bible called the New Testament, this helper is referred to many times as the Holy Spirit of God. He is the third person of the Trinity (three personal aspects of God) according to Christian belief, and the same Spirit of God referred to in Old Testament history that enabled ordinary people to do extraordinary acts in earlier times.

In Christianity the role of the Spirit of God changed from what it had previously been in Jewish history. Instead of "coming upon" special individuals for various tasks, the Spirit of God "indwelt" all believers giving them a private and personal helper to guide them in truth as they struggled through life.[197]

During the first century after Jesus the ministry of the Holy Spirit to the Christian believers was well documented in teaching and church worship. He was considered to be God's invisible presence in individual lives as well as the guide and helper of church leaders as they sought to chart the course of growth in the expanding community of Christians worldwide.

Though the city of Jerusalem was sacked in 70 AD by the Roman armies causing a dispersion of the Jews to other nations, Christianity flourished and spread throughout Palestine, Syria, Lebanon, Egypt, Greece, Turkey, Iraq, Iran, Africa, Italy and Spain during the next six centuries after the death of Jesus Christ.[198] This was accomplished through missionary travel, preaching, education, giving of finances and the profound public testimony of numerous believers suffering and dying in martyrdom rather than deny the facts of their faith.[199]

The historical data establishing these two faiths in the One True God are important here because they show the nature of their relationship in origins and their shared inspirational literature from 40 different authors [200] long before the emergence of Islam in the 6th Century AD, six hundred years after the death of Jesus and the successful spreading of Christianity.

For instance, the Books of Moses were completed circa 1210-1200 BC predating the completion of the Islamic holy book, *The Quran*, by 1800 years. By approximately 500 BC (1130 years before the Quran) the 39 books that make up the Old Testament were completed and preserved in Hebrew on scrolls.

By the end of the 1st Century AD, the New Testament had been completed predating Islam by 600 years. All original manuscripts that make up the 27 books of the New Testament were preserved in Greek on papyrus, a thin paper-like material made from crushed and flattened stalks of a reed-like plant.[201]

Jewish and Christian communities that worshiped the One True God throughout the world were a result of centuries of successful missionary work, scholarship, education, and financial investment.

Neither the Jewish religious scholars nor the Christian Church leaders recognized the authenticity in Muhammad's revelations that began around 610 AD. This led to the Islamic supposition that both Jews and Christians rejected Islam out of willful disobedience to the commands of Allah.[202] But worshiping the One True God wasn't news to them because the orthodoxy of both the preexisting religions had already been established for centuries. Their increase had profoundly affected the world.

In the case of Christianity three hundred years of brutal persecutions by the Roman Empire ended when Emperor Constantine converted. Afterwards he issued the Edict of Milan in 313 AD recognizing Christianity as an acceptable religion, restoring previously confiscated church property and protecting Christian people from persecution. Then, in 325 AD he summoned all the Empire's bishops to the city of Nicea, and from this council came the Nicean Creed that defines the very foundations of Christian Orthodoxy (true Christian belief) even today, seventeen centuries later. [203]

Three hundred years after the Council of Nicea the secret revelation received in a desert cave by an illiterate man squeezed by an angel seemed somewhat bizarre as the latest news from Almighty God. There can be little wonder why church leaders rejected Muhammad's claims. They didn't pass any of the tests of scripture, history or written eyewitness testimony upon which the church was founded.

Nevertheless, Muhammad managed to capture the loyalty of a few and eventually mold that following into an army that conquered Arabia. The keys to understanding today's news are found in that saga.

I thought of Brigitte's family in Lebanon and Affiq's family in Bethlehem. The PLO recruited Fuad to go to Lebanon and launch artillery against people like Brigitte's family. *What for?* I thought. History manipulated this ancient conflict with events beyond these families, and I needed to discover why that was.

After a few days in Jerusalem with our chief correspondent, I had to return to Northern Israel and get back to work. As I drove north to Kiryat Shemona that late afternoon in my car, I savored the memories of new friends from the Muslim family I met in Bethlehem. To this day I miss them and their wonderful hospitality. They repeated the Arab phrase that their house was my house, and they meant it. It made me wonder about the forces that drove these people to fight each other.

For Fuad from Bethlehem it took the charisma of Yassir Arafat and his representatives on the university campus in Jordan to persuade him against education and to serve Allah by signing up to *liberate Jewish occupied Palestine* and help his brother Muslims overthrow the Lebanese democracy. For Brigitte's family in Marjayoun, the shelling attack on their village fell on them because they worshipped in a church.

Unfortunately, that's the way it's been for 1400 years since Islam spread out of Arabia into ancient Palestine, today's Israel. To understand the principles of that conflict, I had to dig deeper into the past to find out the saga and mystique of the 3rd Middle East religion that claimed to be the "newest and final revelation of God."

Chapter 9
The Newest Revelation

Mohammad gets his Start

When he was twenty-five, before his career as a political / religious leader began, Muhammad met a distant cousin named Khadija bint Khuwaylid, a dignified and wealthy merchant.[204] She hired him as a salesman and sent him on a trading mission to Syria where the Quraysh tradesmen sold their goods to wealthy Damascus business owners.

He accompanied the caravan watching over Khadija's goods as the trade route took them between Medina and the Red Sea on course to Damascus. Some weeks later during the return trip a servant said he saw angels standing next to Muhammad in the blazing hot sun of the Arabian Desert.

Upon arriving back in Mecca Khadija was impressed that Muhammad had doubled her wealth. So even though she was forty and fifteen years older, she proposed marriage.[205] Since this was really out of the ordinary, one humorous account says she had to get the patriarch of her family drunk at the betrothal feast in order to get him to consent to a marriage of such circumstances.[206]

Mohammad's mother and father had both died before he reached the age of six. Enduring such a trauma meant added suffering to the normal difficulties of childhood in ancient Arabia. Perhaps he found Khadija's proposal an exciting experience, maybe overwhelming. Perhaps he was attracted to her for wealth and security. Whatever the case, for the young man raised as an orphan, this was a big step up. He accepted the opportunity and the couple was married.

The next turning point in his career came fifteen years later when Muhammad was forty and he received his first revelation from an unidentified spirit being in the cave of Hira. His retreat to the cave was actually in observance of an Arabian pagan tradition of self-justification called *Tahannuth*:[207]

"...The Apostle would pray in seclusion of Hira every year for a month to practice Tahannuth, as was the custom of the Quraysh in the heathen days.[208]

During one of these annual prayer rituals, a terrifying experience took place that was later described by another of Muhammad's wives, Aisha, and recorded in detail by al-Bukhari in his commentaries as well as in the Quran:

(The Prophet added), "The angel caught me (forcefully) and pressed me so hard that I could not bear it anymore. He then released me and again asked me to read, and I replied, "I do not know how to read," whereupon he caught me again and pressed me a second time till I could not bear it anymore. He then released me and asked me again to read, but again I replied, "I do not know how to read (or, what shall I read?)." Thereupon he caught me for the third time and pressed me and then released me and said, "Read: In the Name of your Lord, Who has created (all that exists). Has created man from a clot. Read: ... and Your Lord is Most Generous...up to... that which he knew not." [209]

Rather than being uplifted in the presence of a holy God, Muhammad returned home and shook with physical torment. Aisha's narrative continues:

Then Allah's Apostle returned with the Inspiration, his neck muscles twitching with terror till he entered upon Khadija and said, "Cover me! Cover me!" They covered him till his fear was over and then he said, "O Khadija, what is wrong with me?" Then he told her everything that had happened and said, "I fear that something may happen to me." [210]

Khadija reassured her husband as best she could. However, it's very possible that she saw this as a great business opportunity. After all, the commerce of the Quraysh in Mecca was based on the worship of many pagan gods and she was a very successful woman of trade and commerce living in Mecca. Having a representative of a god in the family might prove to be very profitable. For this she would have needed an endorsement and went to visit her cousin Waraqa who was a convert to Christianity.

The Islamic version of the story says Waraqa was known as a student of the Old and New Testament scriptures, but had gone blind in his old age. Clearly, Waraqa confused his facts regarding Moses and the manner of prophetic revelations. For according to the accounts of Ibn Ishaq in his biographical text, Waraqa said to Khadija, "…If thou hast spoken to me the truth, O Khadija, there has come unto him (Muhammad) the greatest Namus (meaning Gabriel) who came to Moses afore-time…" [211]

In plain words Khadija's cousin was impressed, but his facts were all wrong. As I mentioned earlier, the *Torah* was completed during Moses' lifetime 1800 years before the Quran and 2000 years before Ibn Ishaq's *Biography of the Life of Muhammad.* Nowhere does it say that the angel Gabriel ever appeared to Moses. On the contrary, the Hebrew Scriptures testify in four places that God spoke to Moses "face to face."[212] Angels were never sent to dictate scripture, and it was well established that God spoke to the prophets in dreams and visions.[213] Christians and Jews had recognized these specifics for centuries.

Even more stunning, the Apostle, Paul of Tarsus, wrote five hundred years earlier to the Christian churches throughout Turkey specifically warning them against any angel appearing to mankind to preach a different message than Christ crucified. "Let him be condemned eternally!" Paul wrote.[214]

For a Christian who studied the Scriptures as Waraqa supposedly did, the news of an angel secretly dictating new scriptures in a cave should have given him serious pause. But it didn't. Perhaps Waraqa was confused in his old age or maybe he never carefully studied the life of Moses in the Torah or Paul's writings in the New Testament. Copies of both documents had been available in Arabia for centuries, and according to the story, Waraqa had studied those documents.

Whatever the case, Waraqa's statement reported by Ibn Ishaq 2000 years after Moses lived was incorrect according to the authoritative accounts of Moses' life that were actually written during his own lifetime.

Nevertheless, according to Ibn Ishaq, Khadija sold the angelic revelation story to her cousin who then endorsed Muhammad as a prophet, but with a warning:

> Allah's messenger asked, "Will they drive me out?"
> Waraqa replied in the affirmative and said, "Anyone
> who came with something similar to what you have
> brought was treated with hostility."[215]

Now, fear of the future added to the emotional trauma brought on by the revelation event in the cave. What could he possibly have to look forward to but rejection?

In all fairness, previously recorded eyewitness testimonies in Judaism and Christianity that described meetings between angelic beings and men were frightening experiences to humans. "Fear not," was almost always part of the angel's greeting because their physical appearance must have shocked and frightened men.

Mohammad acknowledged his deep feeling of inadequacy from the beginning by confessing that he couldn't read; yet, this terrifying being held him responsible for preaching an unpopular message. He was in a double bind. There was nowhere to escape. His joy must have been drained and his fears must have dominated.

Waraqa's endorsement and Khadija's reassurances weren't sufficient help either; instead, Muhammad became suicidal. Fearing he was going out of his mind and becoming demon possessed, he said:

> None of Allah's creatures was more hateful to me
> than an ecstatic poet or a man possessed. I thought,
> *Woe is me, I'm a possessed poet…I will go to the top
> of the mountain and throw myself down that I may
> kill myself and be at rest.* [216]

Nor was his depression a one-time event, instead the suicidal tendencies carried on in waves during an extended period of time. According to Aisha, Muhammad related to her that he attempted suicide many times in the same manner:

And every time he went up the top of a mountain in order to throw himself down, Gabriel would appear before him and say, "O Muhammad! You are indeed Allah's Apostle in truth" whereupon his heart would become quiet and he would calm down and would return home. [217]

Perhaps the suicidal depressions were due in part to the prophet's rejection in his hometown. The Meccans were pagans who worshipped a variety of gods, and they were well aware of the monotheistic religions of Judaism and Christianity that were practiced in the area for six centuries prior.

Multiple gods were part of the culture and the economy of Arabia, so what was the harm in another messenger showing up and proclaiming a new one? Nothing, Khadija was probably counting on it. Normally he would have fit right in, but Muhammad took it a few steps further.

His message ridiculed the other gods, preached hell's damnation on the people's dead ancestors, demanded belief in Allah and called for submission to Muhammad as leader. So in effect, he demanded to be *appointed* President of Arabia while requiring everybody to change his or her religious beliefs to be like his. Anything less and they might all go to hell.[218]

As anyone can imagine, this rocked the boat in Mecca. Allah was a well-known deity already being worshiped in Syria and Arabia at the time. As his new spokesman, Muhammad demanded Allah's immediate promotion to preeminence over all other gods. Following this, Muhammad would naturally assume political leadership of the region.[219] Cousin Waraqa's blind eyes had seen the future clearly. For Mecca's leadership, this was just too big of a pill to swallow and Muhammad would eventually leave town in rejection.

Time to Hit the Road

In the first years Mohammed's preaching began as a simple person-to-person dialogue for a new monotheism that called his people to turn from two popular goddesses, al-Lat and al-Uzza, and accept the god named *Allah* as the one true god.[220] Khadija was the first convert and ten year old Ali bin Abu Talib the second. But the big event that turned on the fiery sermons and tweaked Muhammad's rage came three years later when he arranged for a meeting of all the clans of the Quraysh on a nearby mountain.

During the sermon his uncle, Abu Lahab, heckled back from the crowd that the angel bewitched him.[221] As the crowd jeered, a revelation from Allah told Mohammad both Abu Lahab and his wife would die for the insult.[222] Thus, it was established in the beginning that Mohammad's message was questioned only at grave peril, and insults to the prophet were punishable by death.

So serious is such an offense that even in today's world executioners are dispensed to kill offenders anywhere they may live throughout the world regardless of national laws and borders.[223] Dutch parliamentarian Ayaan Hirsi Ali fled Somalia for the Netherlands and denounced Islam. In her book *The Caged Virgin* she says that Islam is a religion of fear without freedom of speech. She writes that the religion teaches Muhammad is the perfect human being and the one moral source. The Koran is what God said to him and questioning the truth of either source is a death offense.[224]

When such killings followed Muhammad's hilltop sermon to his tribesmen, so did the insults accusing him of lying and demon possession.[225] After a few years of such rejection, Muhammad received a revelation permitting him to vent his rage against such tormenters. The angel told him to wage war against rejecters, but revenge on his Quraysh tribe would have to wait on a more important event. [226]

The Hijra

The Muslims were unhappy and persecuted in Mecca. Twelve years had passed since the revelations to Muhammad began and nine years since the public rebuff by his uncle. In 622 AD "the flight" or *Hijra* from Mecca to Medina took place. By now Muhammad had a plan. To pull it off successfully, he and his followers arranged a pact with the three prominent Jewish tribes living in Medina who had fled to Arabia after the Roman legions sacked Jerusalem centuries earlier in 70 AD.

The pact distinguished between Muslim believers and unbelievers labeling all Muslims as a united community regardless of geography. It also provided for mutual community defense and declared the Quraysh the enemy. But the most telling element of the "Constitution of Medina" was that Muhammad established himself as the *absolute political and religious leader of all Muslims*. He became the head of the religion and the head of the state all rolled into one.[227]

In one swoop he founded a new state in Arabia that was based on increasing the number of Muslims. That's why the Hijra is recognized today as the historical beginning of Islam's success. Thus transformed, the religion within the state instantly morphed into a new state with no boundaries.[228] The expansion of its borders depended on the territory his followers controlled. Even in today's world Muslims are taught that their community is a separate state unto itself.

After all, Mosque and government were one in the same. So apparently, the Hijra also set the precedent among Muslims to create an Islamic state within the sovereign borders of another country; only requirements, the writing of a separate constitution or the changing of existing laws to specifically benefit Islam's followers. The same aggressive philosophy is taught from Arabia today; immigrate, concentrate numbers, change the laws and presto…take control of more geography.

While the Muslims remained a small community in Medina, they represented no threat to local civil authority. Being a sovereign nation unto themselves, however, as the community expanded in followers, they raised their own army. They made their own laws, conquered as they saw fit, and became the regional government wherever they exerted their power.

Financing by Revenge

In the early days when the new state needed money, the solution was obvious to Muhammad. Attack the trade caravans of the Quraysh that journeyed out of Mecca for Damascus. He knew the highway and the caravan schedule all too well from his own trading days.

As the everyday people on the mass transit system of that era, the caravans from Mecca to Syria passed between Medina and the Red Sea without military protection.[229] One night as Muhammad's raiders lay waiting to fall on an unsuspecting caravan at Al-Abwa; the prophet said non-believing women and children were no different than enemy troops in battle. The Al Bukhari commentary states:

> The Prophet passed by me at a place called Al-Abwa or Waddan, and was asked whether it was permissible to attack the pagan warriors at night with the probability of exposing their women and children to danger. The Prophet replied, "They (i.e. women and children) are from them (i.e. pagans)."[230]

Shortly after the Al-Abwa raid in January of 624 AD another raid was sanctioned at Nakhla that established even more precedents combining the religion with warfare. First, the leader of the raid, Abdullah bin Jahsh, said that those who fought with him were "martyrs."[231] Previously, martyrdom known through 600 years of Christianity meant those who suffered death under persecution not as soldiers. Now under Islam, it simply meant fighting on Muhammad's side.

Disguised as pilgrims, Abdullah and his raiders surprised the undefended Quraysh caravan killing as many as they chose. However, since the raid was in the sacred pagan month of Rajab when killing was forbidden, indignation arose later when they returned to Medina with the caravan's booty and with the traveler's blood on their swords.

The local laws held that killing during the sacred month was a crime committed against humanity. But Muhammad had a new revelation that pardoned the offenders and laid down a precedent followed to this day. According to this revelation, the unbelief of the Quraysh was the greater sin. Killing in Allah's cause was not wrong.[232]

Defining personal unbelief in Allah as a crime, the state of Islam swept aside the customs and laws of the region as well as all future barriers separating civil crimes and religious transgression. Moral absolutes were sacrificed for the financial benefit of the Muslims while the barriers between mosque and state were demolished.[233]

Sins of faith were combined in state matters and measured against civil crimes with the Head of State approving death sentences for some who failed his religious standards while pardoning others by their mere confession in his new religion. Simply put, the raid on Nakhla demonstrated that Allah's justice and mercy preferred Muslim believers. Regarding this principle the Quran states:

> Surely those who believed and those who fled (their home) and strove hard in the way of Allah these hope for the mercy of Allah and Allah is Forgiving, Merciful.[234]

> ... They disbelieved in Allah's communications, therefore Allah destroyed them on account of their faults; surely Allah is strong, severe in requiting (evil).[235]

With such precedents establishing that war making was entwined with religious commitment, the time had come to exact greater revenge on the Quraysh for rejecting Allah and Muhammad. After all, they had committed a crime punishable by death and to avenge that crime by killing them was a matter of religious devotion.

The Al-Abwa and Nakhla raids exercised precedents whereby Islam acted as a state unto itself setting it's own code of laws. For instance, the code established at Al-Abwa permitted attack on unde-fended civilian men, women and children for financial gain. The next new code established was the beheading of unbelievers in public view as a means of establishing authority through fear.

Forward outposts on the trade route reported to Muhammad that a large rich Quraysh caravan laden with money from successful sales in Syria was returning to Mecca. Only this time an army protected it. Promising paradise to slain believers and riches to the victors, Muhammad gave the call to report for battle with instructions to cut off the heads of the unbelieving Quraysh.

> Therefore strike off their heads and strike off every fingertip of them. This is because they acted adversely to Allah and His Messenger; and whoever acts adversely to Allah and His Messenger-- then surely Allah is severe in requiting (evil). [236]

As the band of 300 Muslims came upon the caravan they were met by superior numbers of Quraysh militia. What followed was the battle of Badr. Outnumbered three to one, the Muslims fiercely beheaded their opponents during the battle taking another 70 captives for beheading later.

Paying back his people's rejection was sweet revenge. Standing over the huge stack of dismembered Quraysh body parts heaped together into a pit beneath his feet, Ibn Ishaq records that Muhammad spoke over the mounded gory remains. Deriding them for rejecting Allah he said:

> Have you found what God promised you is true?
> I have found that what my Lord promised me is true.[237]

To this day jihadists wave the battle of Badr as a flag promising devout Muslims victory against superior forces while calling on the faithful to behead non-Muslims in public for all to see.

Such was the case for the American contract worker, Nicholas Berg, who was beheaded by a hooded Muslim sawing a butcher knife back and forth across Berg's throat in front of video cameras in May 2004. When the act was finished the killer held up Berg's severed head by the hair in front of the cameras and shouted, "Allah be praised!"

Al Qaeda leader Abu Musab al-Zarqawi said of the gory act, "The Prophet, *the most merciful*, ordered [his army] to strike the necks of some prisoners in [the battle of] Badr and to kill them... And he set a good example for us."[238]

Following the battle of Badr Muhammad received another timely revelation giving him permission to nullify treaties and make war on anyone he distrusted:

> If thou fearest treachery from any group, throw back (their covenant) to them... Let not the unbelievers *think* that they can get the better (of the godly)... Against them make ready your strength to the utmost of your power, including steeds of war...[239]

This was the next important change that instantly wrote a new kind of law executing punishment for thoughts. No actual deeds were necessary to demonstrate aggression against Islam; mere suspicion that others were *thinking* about doing something wrong against Muhammad was enough evidence to nullify his treaties with them and launch preemptive strikes against them.

At this point Muhammad's only treaty was with the three Jewish tribes in Medina previously permitting the Hijra. That agreement was about to get *thrown back in their faces*. Preemptive sieges and battles were launched based on suspicion, and the new revelation made it the fault of those being attacked.

Consolidating Power

Monotheism had a strong presence in Arabia for nearly 600 years before Islam began. A strong Christian community lived in the city of Najran while three Jewish tribes dominated Medina. These were the three tribes that signed the mutual community protection pact with Muhammad. After his move to Medina tensions quickly arose in Arabia following the caravan raiding as the Muslims attacked civilian travel and caused financial crisis. But further causes were necessary to break the treaty.

Numerous theological debates began to emerge because neither the Christians nor the Jews recognized Muhammad to be God's final prophet with the latest message.

Muhammad told the Christians he was the person to whom Jesus referred when he promised the counselor that was to come after his ascension.[240] Since Muhammad didn't read, he would not have studied the words of Jesus recorded in the New Testament scriptures already used in Arabia. Jesus words clearly described the Holy Spirit as an invisible, indwelling presence that gave Christians power to spread Jesus' message of salvation:

> And I will ask the Father and He will give you another Counselor to be with you forever—the Spirit of truth. The world cannot accept him because it neither sees him nor knows him. But you know him, because he lives with you and will be in you.[241]

> …You will receive power when the Holy Spirit comes on you, and you will be my witnesses in Jerusalem, and in all Judea and Samaria, and to the ends of the earth.[242]

To Christian leadership Muhammad's revelation was a preposterous heresy without scriptural reference. It denied the work of the Holy Spirit revealed through six centuries of church growth, as well as the New Testament scriptures and the Nicean Creed of Orthodoxy. To the converts of Islam, however, it was the bedrock confession of truth. According to the Quran, the spoken revelations from Muhammad's mouth were the absolute will of God, and his conduct was the example for all men to follow.[243]

That meant that the Quran legislated for Muslims, but from the very beginning, there were harsh disagreements with Christianity resulting from Muhammad taking God's place in the person of the Holy Spirit.

For some reason it was also important for Muhammad to deny that Jesus had been crucified, a fact well established by written historical documents and verified by eyewitness testimony. Did he deny this because he wasn't able to read the documents? And why attack the crucifixion of Jesus? What was that to him?

Stranger still, why did Muhammad press this point with the Jewish community? Christians based the forgiveness of sins on the crucifixion of Jesus Christ? The New Testament letter to the Galatians' church clearly stated, "Christ redeemed us from the curse of the law by becoming a curse for us."[244]

The crucifixion was far more important to Christians. Nevertheless, it became a point of heated argument between Muhammad and the Jewish leaders who insisted that Jesus was put to death by crucifixion. After all, they took responsibility for it, but the Quran said otherwise:

> That they said (in boast), "We killed Christ Jesus the
> son of Mary…" but they killed him not, nor crucified
> him…[245]

Curiously enough, the Christian apostle Paul knew people who witnessed the crucifixion of Jesus and wrote (circa 50 AD) in the same Galatians' letter, "before your very eyes Jesus Christ was portrayed as crucified." Calling people to receive the promised Holy Spirit by faith and continue in forgiveness and right standing with God by faith, he connected both Jews and Christians to their founding ancestor, Abraham, calling him the man of faith.

In answer to both these controversies Allah revealed to Muhammad that Jews and Christians knew better but hid the truth from the public in order to promote their own license for wrongdoing. God the Father, God the Messiah, and God the Spirit did not exist. According to Allah there was no Trinity. There was only Allah and Muhammad who was sent to straighten out this confusion of history caused by the deceitful Jews and the Christians who were both cursed according to his progressive revelations recorded in the Quran:[246]

> They say: "Become Jews or Christians if ye would be guided (To salvation)." Say thou: "Nay! (I would rather) the Religion of Abraham the True, and he joined not gods with Allah." [247]
>
> O ye who believe! Take not the Jews and the Christians for your friends and protectors: They are but friends and protectors to each other.[248]

As the religious tensions increased, Muhammad applied his revelation for punishing bad thoughts: "Let not the unbelievers *think* that they can get the better (of the godly)... Against them make ready your strength to the utmost of your power, including steeds of war..."[249]. The Qaynuqa Jews were the first to find out the price of his suspicions about their thinking.

One of the original three Jewish tribes of Medina who signed the pact with the Muslims the year before, the Qaynuqa neighborhood suddenly found itself under a military siege that cut off food and water. When they surrendered only another Muslim pleading to Muhammad on behalf of the Qaynuqa caused him to spare their lives. In exchange the community turned over all their property and accepted banishment from Medina.[250]

One tribe down and two more to go; a year later in the late spring of 625 AD a plot to kill Muhammad was supposedly uncovered involving the Jewish Nadir tribe. By refusing his command to immediately leave Medina, Muhammad claimed the Nadir Jews had declared a war on the Muslims, an innovative reversal of responsibility for his upcoming attack. The subsequent two week long military siege of their neighborhood also forced surrender. As the Qaynuqa before them, the Nadir were banished from Medina and their lands confiscated by the Muslims.[251] That was two down and one more to go.

The last of the Medina Jewish tribes were the Quraiza. Fearing the worst, they made a pact with Muhammad's old enemies, the pagan Quraysh of Mecca. By secret agreement in the spring of 627 AD the Quraysh marched from Mecca and laid siege to Medina from outside the city while the Jewish tribe awaited the attack order to strike the Muslims from inside the city.

After three weeks of siege, the order for attack was given, but the Quraiza inside Medina held off their attack waiting on the Quraysh to attack first from outside. Trust quickly broke down between the two groups and the Quraysh withdrew leaving the Quraiza all alone to face the Muslims. After a month of siege the Quraiza Jews finally surrendered to Muhammad. What followed was one of the most infamous massacres of world history.

Ibn Ishaq tells of one surviving boy's eyewitness account saying that all the Quraiza men were beheaded publicly including many boys. The Muslim army inspected all the Quraiza boys for pubic hair. All those boys who had any pubic hair were beheaded in public view along with the rest of the men while those without pubic hair were left alive. This witness survived to tell the tale because he was a pre-pubescent boy.

In all Ibn Ishaq writes that 600-700 men and boys were beheaded and their dismembered parts heaped together in a trench. The women and children were sold into slavery and all the lands and possessions of the Quraiza Jews were divided among the Muslims.[252]

With the three Jewish communities banished, massacred and sold into slavery Muhammad had complete control of Medina and the trade route between Mecca and Syria. What began five years earlier as immigration revealed itself step by step as a carefully premeditated war strategy for territorial take-over complete with all the trimmings; disrupted trade, military siege, and captured lands. By concealing each step Muhammad maintained the element of surprise against his opponents.

His duping of the Jews of Medina serves as an example for the doctrine of lying and deceit called *taquiyya* or *kithman* that encourages Muslims to lie and deceive non-Muslims to gain an advantage. Author Amir Taheri states, "Muslims have every right to lie and to deceive their adversaries, and a promise made to a non-Muslim can be broken whenever necessary."

Dismembering the truth is a widely used technique of this doctrine. By cutting up the truth into half-truths with other lies attached Muslims can trick their opposition into trusting a false impression. In *Because They Hate* Lebanese author, Brigitte Gabrielle, says that a modern day example of this acknowledges Islam's ambition to spread their religion worldwide but insists that the process is by peaceful persuasion. [253]

The conquest of Medina proved Muhammad's four-step strategy for extending the empire, a war strategy still used today for conquest of non-Muslim nations. Step one; immigrate to the desired nation. Step two; change laws to work in favor of Islam. Step three; attack civilians and disrupt economy. Step four; seize regional control forcing submission by terror.

In his original preaching to the Quraysh in Mecca fourteen years before he presented that Allah wanted him to supervise Arabia. Though he ruled over Medina as the king of a city-state, challenges of Muhammad's complete authority over all Arabia still remained.

One such possible enemy was an ally of the pagan Quraysh of Mecca, the Mustaliq tribe. Taking them completely by surprise, the Muslim army attacked the Mustaliq, "without warning while they were heedless and their cattle were being watered at the places of water. Their fighting men were killed and their women and children and property were taken as booty."[254]

The captured Mustaliq women were so attractive that the aroused Muslim warriors asked permission to have sex with the new captives even before the battle ended and the booty was distributed. Muslims practiced a form of natural birth control known as *azl* (coitus interruptus), which refers to withdrawing the penis before ejaculation.[255] The Muslim soldiers were asking permission for intercourse with the new captives so long as they practiced *azl*. What was the need for that unless some of the women would be passed around?

Muslim law already said that captured women automatically became single permitting them to be owned as slave concubines.[256] So why were the soldiers asking permission for what they already had? After all, what was the concern over getting your concubine pregnant unless that somehow made her damaged goods for someone else to own later? Apparently, the captured women were still available for anybody. Whatever the case, Muhammad told them *azl* wasn't necessary because all conceptions and births came from Allah.[257]

The Muslims already treated captured women as prizes of war. The precedent of the Mustaliq women seemed to reduce that status even further. The jihad warrior had all the rights while the captured woman had none.

Even for Muslim wives there seemed to be a reduced status stated by Muhammad and quoted by Ibn Ishaq:

> You have the right that they (wives) should not defile your bed and that they should not behave with open unseemliness. If they do, God allows you to put them in separate rooms and to beat them but not with severity...lay injunctions on women kindly, for they are prisoners with you having no control of their persons.[258]

Conquering Arabia

With Medina overthrown and his power consolidated Muhammad was ready to conquer the rest of Arabia, particularly Mecca. Leading an army of fifteen hundred he marched against his old hometown in the spring of 628 AD. Representatives of the Quraysh militia met him outside the city at Hudaybiyya where they struck a deal that called for a ten-year truce allowing an annual pilgrimage of the Muslims to Mecca.

Controversy in his army over the agreement arose quickly because the truce meant an end to raiding the Quraysh caravans, an established source of Islam's income for their new empire. According to Professor Efraim Karsh, best-selling author and the Head of Mediterranean Studies at King's College London:

> To deflect this simmering discontent, Muhammad found a handy scapegoat that had served him well in the past: the Arabian Jews. Having eliminated the Jewish presence in Medina he now turned to the affluent Jewish community in the oasis of Khaibar, some ninety miles north of the city.[259]

Muhammad arrived there with his army by night and waited at dawn to hear for the call to prayer among the Jews. When it didn't sound he attacked catching the unarmed citizens as they were walking to their fields to begin the day's work. The Apostle seized the property piece by piece and conquered the forts one by one as he came to them." [260]

A man named Kinana al-Rabi who was in charge of the treasure of the Nadir Jews hidden at Khaibar was captured and tortured with fire to extract information of the treasure's hiding place. He kept the secret until his death at which point his head was cut off, then his father-in-law and many of their relatives were also killed. After Muhammad took Kinana's wife for himself, a guard watched his tent all night fearing she would try to kill him in vengeance. [261]

Following a month of siege the final remnant of the Jews at Khaibar surrendered. Rather than banishing them like the Jews of Medina, Muhammad allowed them to stay as sharecroppers caring for the land and paying an annual tribute to the Muslims of half their produce.

A final condition of subjugation was added: the Muslims could banish the Khaibar Jews at any time in the future if they desired to do so. [262] This became the condition of those conquered in the Muslim empire known as *Dhimmitude* meaning a second-class citizenry subjugated, taxed and existing solely by the good will of the Muslims.

Along with the booty the captured women of Khaibar were distributed among the Muslim soldiers with the instruction to refrain from intercourse with the ones who were either pregnant or menstruating at the time. [263]

There can be no doubt that the conquest of Khaibar set an inspirational precedent used to fan the fires of hatred against Jews even today. For instance, the Islamic website www.alminbar.com encourages Muslims everywhere to irritate Jews with a slogan they supposedly fear: "Khaibar, Khaibar, O Jews, the army of Muhammad will return!"

Using the universal crime of an insult against the worldwide Islamic nation, further text on this website says: "Why do we hate the Jews? We hate them for the sake of our Lord...because they slandered Allah..." [264]

After a few months of enjoying the many satisfactions to be had from their Khaibar conquest the time arrived for the first pilgrimage to Mecca in 629 AD. The victorious army's march into the city made an impression attracting many new converts and leaving Muhammad with the sense it was time to take over Mecca.

In order to do that there had to be a reason to break the truce agreement of Hudaybiyya decided the year before. No problem: a local Meccan killed a Muslim convert in a private quarrel. Of course this violated Islamic sovereignty, and on January 1, 630 AD the Muslim army left Medina to conquer Mecca. Ten days later the city surrendered making Muhammad the de facto emperor of Arabia.[265]

Conquering the World

In eight years the prophet who left in defeat returned as the military conqueror. During those years he had discovered all the successful means that would ever after be employed by Muslims for world conquest. The founding of the state without boundaries made all who offended Islam by word or deed or thought at war with Allah and his prophet. The religion he founded called Muslims to struggle in war during all times in all lands against all men everywhere until they all submitted to Allah. Unbelief was the greatest sin while killing in Allah's cause was not.

Al-Abwa made non-believing women and children fair targets of war. Nakhla made regional laws meaningless compared to Allah's cause. Badr established the cutting off of heads. Treaties meant nothing and were broken when convenient.

The Qaynuqa Jews found they couldn't think against Muhammad without banishment. The Nadir Jews learned that whatever offended the Muslims made a Muslim attack your fault. As for the Quraiza Jews, they became the example of terror for all to see. And the Khaibar Jews helped Islam establish Dhimmitude, the *protection tax* that would help finance the empire.

Muhammad died two years later June 8, 632 AD [266] but in his farewell address he stated the foreign policy Islam echoes today, "I have been ordered (by Allah) to fight against the people until they testify that none has the right to be worshipped but Allah."[267]

Before he died Muhammad invited the Persians to the east and the Byzantine Empire to the north and the west to convert to Islam. They didn't take him up on the offer. Four years later at the head of the Muslim armies Khalid ibn al Rafiq defeated the Byzantines at the Battle of Yarmuk in 636 AD and Lebanon fell under Arab control.[268] By 638 Jerusalem surrendered and Palestine fell to the Arabs as well. From then until today these two countries are considered the *property of Islam* as if to say, "once conquered always owned."

When these countries fell to other governments as history progressed, it became obligatory on all members of Islam to support the reconquest of the territory lost to the infidels.[269] The Islamic scholar, Bernard Lewis, says that today this is mingled with the Islamic doctrine against *apostasy* and: "...Has been developed into a doctrine of insurgency and revolutionary war as a religious obligation and form of jihad."[270]

So starting a civil war in Lebanon was actually an obligation of the Islamic leaders who lived by the code. And reconquering *Israeli occupied Palestine*, well, no question there. Islam was obligated to restore a land fallen into apostasy. So, in that manor the ancient history of Islam influences and motivates today's news headlines.

Outside of actual events, however, in the news business there is a term that refers to the overall philosophy of a reporter or a news organization. That term is, "worldview," and it has a way of appearing in the way producers and reporters tell their news stories to the public. The way they interpret news events is shaped by their idea of who's right and who's wrong. What is justice or injustice? Who are the weak and who are the oppressors, and why? In short, how they view the events they report about shapes the way the facts are presented...or not presented to the public.

At the time I was in the Middle East there was also a fascinating combination of technological limitations that made a narrow worldview the prevailing vision told to the American public about the events unfolding in Lebanon and Israel. That snippet of time helped the American people deceive themselves. What follows next is a glimpse into how that happened.

Part III

What America Misunderstood

Chapter 10
Technical Difficulties

It was 1985 and there was no Internet for research. Personal computers weren't invented yet. No search engines existed, no email, no Microsoft Word Processing software. There were no laptop computers, no ink jet printers, no cell phones and no wireless connections. It was the world of landline telephones and typewriters.

The fastest way to send a written news story from overseas was using a telephone line and a fax machine, but the story would have to be typed first on a typewriter and the finished pages carefully fed into the fax machine after a good connection was established. Yet getting a clear line was another task entirely.

There were more telephones than available phone lines in Israel so on an ordinary day it took a constant half hour of redialing just to get a dial tone to call the next town, never mind an international connection. After finally getting a dial tone all the international lines could be busy. Then, you had to start redialing all over again. If your telephone didn't have an automatic redial function, you were out of luck.

In Beirut, telephone service was even more erratic. Due to the sporadic fighting, service was almost always being repaired. And outside Beirut in South Lebanon, having both phone service and electricity at the same time meant a good day.

Some of the newest electric typewriters had limited word processing and featured a small black screen that permitted viewing written paragraphs in a hard-to-see-orange-lettering. Our chief correspondent in the Jerusalem News Bureau had one of those. But my typewriter would only permit me to write about fifteen words for preview. I scrolled a few words at a time across a one-line-high gray calculator screen; then I'd hit the "enter" button. Still, that was good technology for the time.

Across America evening newspapers had gone out of business because Americans preferred television to newspapers for the news. In broadcasting there were the three networks of ABC, CBS, and NBC. The new kid on the block was CNN who actually had a bureau in Beirut, but their bureau chief got kidnapped.

The only way to send a videotaped report for a news broadcast was by renting a satellite window that cost over $200 / minute. That was an entire process that required a TV broadcasting facility with all the equipment and technicians as well as a working telephone landline with a clear connection permitting network-to-network international coordination. The satellite window was set up by appointment in advance and rented in ½ hour blocks. If the telephone landline was busy or cut off during the ½ hour window…tough luck, money lost, no sending the videotape. Segment producers got fired over that.

But there were even further technical limitations. The receiving station in the U.S.A. used an entirely different broadcasting signal (NTSC) than the Middle East (PAL). The reason for this was that the two systems were based on electrical power differences as well as lines of television picture resolution. For instance, the Middle East PAL signal was based on 50-cycle 220-volt electricity and 650 lines of resolution on the television screen whereas the NTSC signal in America was based on 60-cycle 110-volt electrical power and 525 lines of picture resolution.

The two signals were not compatible. Even if all else went perfectly, the video product sent from Jerusalem through the satellite window arriving in America was unintelligible electrical snow. So, an expensive signal-decoding device had to be linked between the sending recorder and the receiving recorder to translate the signal code from overseas PAL signal code and reassemble it into NTSC in the United States before it was recorded. Otherwise, it couldn't be viewed in the U.S.

With a six to nine hour time difference from the American time zones, in my medium of television I scheduled a camera crew and recorded video for my story. This included scheduling and recording any necessary interviews. Then, I wrote the story and recorded my narration. After that I worked with an editor in the video editing facility to get the final copy that had to be reviewed by the bureau chief before transmitting it by satellite.

The editing suite was a critical time. That's where 15 minutes of raw video pictures and interviews became a neat one minute and thirty second news story. It was a limited session of a couple of hours of cutting and pasting videotape and audio narration. A well-prepared producer would go over his interviews and know exactly where to cut before entering the editing booth.

In Jerusalem our bureau facilities were at the Jerusalem Capital

Studios facility in Benyanei Ha'Uma, "the Nations" building where we rented our editing booth time in advance. Since we didn't know how the news would change from day to day, we couldn't afford to be without an editing suite and an editor when necessary. ABC, CBS, NBC, Canadian TV, Spanish TV, German TV, French TV and others all had their bureaus in that facility. In addition, other production companies would arrive in Jerusalem to make a television special and do their editing at JCS. The competition for equipment and technicians was intense.

In Lebanon we had our own facility at an undisclosed location. The problem there was manpower. To edit a story I had to pull someone in off another daily assignment. So, whether in Jerusalem or in Lebanon, there was no time in the editing booth to be listening to the interview looking for the best two or three sentences. I had to be ready beforehand.

Suppose my interview source had his best fifteen seconds in two different sentences at different parts of a ten-minute interview. That required a cut that appeared imperceptible to the audience. Because my camera was on the interview subject recording the entire time, I'd use a short piece of video of myself taken after the interview called a "turnaround" or some other piece of videotaped subject matter called a "cut-away" to cover up the jump-cut in the words and picture of the person interviewed on camera.

First we put the interview jump cuts together so the audio flowed perfectly. That meant removing all the "uhh's and repetitions" and splicing together the best phrases with the clearest language pronunciation. Then we covered the jump cuts with "video only" in one of the two manners I mentioned above. The effect to the audience was imperceptible because the audio flowed perfectly underneath the smooth video.

Most video editing suites could program a cut in the tape accurate to 1/15 of a second. The blink of an eye takes about 1/3 of a second, so the world of television news cannot only condense reality, it can change reality imperceptibly to the viewing audience. A reporter could record his "stand-up" after an interview or remove the pauses in a sentence. If he didn't like what the interview gave him, he could leave it out or find somebody else to say what his editors wanted to hear.

For reporters the greatest temptation is to change things around to make themselves look perfect while making the interview hold to the editorial viewpoint of their supervisor and network. It's actually the unwritten rule of operation in most companies. What the assignment editor gives you is the story you must report, even if the facts are different. It was deceitful to the public. Long before going to the Middle East I decided it was better to be honest at all times. But, I learned the hard way that some of my stories would get spiked as a result.

That's because the most aggressive way the news is shaped is by what managing editors *choose to tell* the public. It's called "agenda setting". For instance, CBS News anchorman Walter Cronkite had total editorial control over the entire CBS evening newscast.

With so many uncontrollable factors I found it was safest to work my day overseas, get the story edited and send it by a satellite window during newscast prep time in the U.S. That way they had it and knew exactly how long to allot for the piece in their show. We were seven hours ahead of the U.S. East Coast time zone, so after a full workday overseas, you took a break and came back around 9 or 10 p.m. to make the evening news in the states.

If your report went on a morning program, it probably meant 24 hours without sleep, maybe longer depending on the reporting pressures. For me, I had the responsibility of producing and writing reports for a daily 30-minute Middle East broadcast in English. From time to time I also submitted news reports for American audiences. It's a wonder I ever got a full night's sleep.

The Evening News

The American audience traditionally got their world news in ½ hour evening TV broadcasts that condensed major news stories into 1:30 prerecorded video news pieces. A maximum of twenty-four minutes of a 30-minute newscast was actual news content because at least eight to ten minutes were reserved for commercials.

Network anchormen had higher credibility ratings with the American public than the U.S. Presidents. For instance, CBS anchorman Walter Cronkite was the most trusted man in America. Polls said the public put more faith in his words than the President of the United States.[271]

The illusion of truth that television news created convinced the public an anchorman didn't slant a story for political reasons whereas the President might. So six minutes of the precious twenty-four minutes of news-content time was allocated for the anchor's on-air-face-time.

Reading his news copy word for word from the teleprompter that hung over the studio camera's lens, he looked straight into the camera maintaining an illusion of perfect eye contact with the viewing audience. Thus, he appeared truthful and totally sincere as he *told* them the news. But he was actually reading every single word, including his own name.

Whoever had the final editorial control over the news program controlled the content. That person previewed and approved everything and if it didn't pass their scrutiny, it never went on. And that included their political slant and worldview. For instance, before each weeknight broadcast of the CBS Evening News, Walter Cronkite could be seen editing the copy he was to read on-air, crossing out phrases he didn't like.[272]

Even the timing for each section of the broadcast was developed through statistical audience research and these sections were almost identical across the network newscasts. A viewer could switch channels in the middle of the CBS broadcast and find ABC or NBC reporting the same story or subject matter at the same time. After all, hundreds of millions of advertising dollars were riding on how many people watched. That's what the advertisers paid for, audience size, bigger was always better.

The most important factors determining newscast credibility were the factors that determined an anchorman's popularity. Those factors were: likeability, smooth delivery, *appearing believable*, being well-known, and overall professional look. Truthfulness was equal to appearance, yet set decoration and graphic arts were non-determining factors in newscast credibility, except if they were technically bumbled during the broadcast, then they dragged credibility down. So, the audience believed newscasts were truthful because of the anchorman, the professional look and an error free transmission.[273]

Over half the nightly twenty-four broadcast news minutes were designated to national news and politics. There was something about the President from the White House Reporter's viewpoint, something from the Pentagon, the State Department, the Congress on Capitol Hill, the economy, and maybe health or education. Whatever international news actually made it into the program was allocated between three to five minutes at the most including the anchorman's 15 to 30 second read-ins to introduce the video reports. It was generous to allocate one or two

1:30 pieces each broadcast. For the international reporter, then, a highly developed skill for 1:30 "piece-art" was an essential aptitude necessary to succeed.

In that era, whatever the three major networks told the U.S. audience to believe was the gospel truth in America, and their collective content added up over the months was the only means most Americans had to give them perspective. In one minute and thirty seconds, however, an international TV correspondent could rarely go into history or context, and radio reporters seldom had more than sixty seconds to narrate their stories. A maximum of 140-160 words of narration was about the usual in broadcast reports. That's about three paragraphs of print.

Watching faithfully every night, an observer in the television audiences might see two or three minutes during the entire week about Lebanon, Israel and the Middle East on the nightly newscasts. And those two or three minutes had to be packed with the most attention getting scenes in order to keep up with competitors.

The more in-depth reporting was most likely found in the major newspapers like the *New York Times*, and the *Washington Post* who could afford to pay an international correspondent to live in Beirut or Jerusalem. The three wire services had their correspondents and reporters too, and all these print mediums allowed more words.

Let's face it though, realistically; most western reporters had their hands full in keeping up with the latest car bombings and meeting the challenges of formatting their reports to fit the time and space limitations of their information medium. Headlines far outweighed historical reference.

When it came to explaining the Middle East news to Western Civilization, it seems the audience needed a baseball-park-style program to tell the players. Who were the Shiites, the Sunnis, the Druze, the PLO, the PFLP, the Lebanese Forces, the Phalangists and so on? It was confusing to American audiences.

Why were the Christians fighting the Muslims in Lebanon? Why were the Palestinians fighting the Jews in Israel? Where was the Gaza Strip, anyway? Where was Lebanon? Was Beirut in Lebanon or Israel? Who started the fighting? The Palestinians blamed the Jews. The Jews blamed the PLO in Lebanon. And the Arab world blamed America for screwing up the entire Middle East by allowing Israel to exist. How was the average American to unscramble it all? They couldn't, and they never really did. Instead, the agenda setters in the news world told Americans what to think.

Seeing It Their way

Who set the agenda for the American public? Ben Bradlee, the executive editor of the *Washington Post* from 1965-1991 proudly proclaimed, "The power of the *Washington Post* lies mostly in its ability to focus national attention on certain topics." And when asked who set the agenda for the United States besides the *Washington Post* Bradlee said it was collectively controlled by, "*The New York Times* and the television networks and *Time* and *Newsweek*." [274]

To further complicate matters, there was the political viewpoint and values or "worldview" of the writers and editors of the major news media. You might wonder if that could affect the content of the news seen and read in the U.S.A. I think the answer is an obvious "yes."

As a matter of fact, it's so obvious that the public assumes bias as normal operating procedure. Two thirds of the American public says the news media favors one side on political and social issues and that bias favors Democrats. Only one fourth of the public says the media is fair and balanced while only one third of the public says the news organizations get their facts right.

The public's disillusionment centers on the news media claiming that they are truthful and impartial, when the problem identified by the public in polling data is a *liberal and Democrat bias.* Even the most trusted man in America, Walter Cronkite, admitted, "most of us reporters are liberal." Offering a flimsy excuse as his explanation he criticized the medium saying that there wasn't enough time to be balanced.[275]

The credibility problem for newspapers is even worse. Eight out of ten Americans believe newspapers are predisposed and report in a manor supporting their own political and social views while their reporters and editors are seen as dishonest and prone to canceling or changing a story to suit their interests. Nine out of ten Americans believe that newspaper reporters will select and twist the facts of a story to promote their own opinions.[276] How did the public ever get such negative ideas? Read on.

The first major study of this kind in 1981 measured political attitudes and voting patterns of the news decision makers at the *New York Times, Washington Post, The Wall Street Journal, Time, Newsweek, U.S.*

131

News & World Report, ABC, CBS, NBC and PBS. The data demonstrated that journalists and broadcasters held liberal positions on a wide range of social and political issues, liberal attitudes that were opposite from the general publics' views. For instance, nine out of ten voted democrat, favored abortion, wanted strong affirmative action for blacks, and wanted the government prohibited from regulating any sexual behavior.

The very fact that nine out of ten news reporters voted democrat represented a drastic contrast to the voting record of the American public who elected Republican presidents for all but twelve of the forty years between 1952 and 1992.

Other studies showed that eight out of ten reporters and editorial elites wanted decreased defense spending and stricter gun control while 15 out of 16 journalists held a worldview contrary to the general public advocating a liberal prejudice against traditional values.[277] The vast majority of leading journalists embraced a value system that was anti-Christian, anti-military, averse to traditional norms and suspicious of people in governmental authority.[278]

Given the above values and voting records, one can only imagine how suspicious the media elite was of a Republican authority figure with traditional family values. Wouldn't they see that person as an adversary to everything their worldview embraced?

In 1981 conservative Republican Ronald Reagan took office as President of the United States. In a landslide victory winning 44 of the 50 states and 90 percent of the electoral vote, he crushed the democratic incumbent President, Jimmy Carter. But none of the reporters covering the White House voted for Reagan.[279] To them he was the enemy.

He was a member of the National Rifle Association that opposed gun control. He increased defense spending and was passionately respectful of the U.S. military to the point of actually saluting American servicemen in uniform.

This gesture in itself was an extreme sign of respect because the President is Commander and Chief of all U.S. military forces. As such, he's never expected to salute, whereas all U.S. soldiers in uniform are required to salute him. A Christian who believed in God and the Bible, Reagan was pro-Israel and sent the U.S. Marines to supervise the Palestinian army's withdrawal from Beirut. In short, he was everything the media elite despised.

Yet it was the media elite who ran the major newspapers, the news magazines and the television news networks. They had the equipment, the money, the satellite windows, the international correspondents and the overseas news bureaus. The big media chose which information to tell us about Lebanon, Israel and the Palestinians framing it so as to give us the news the way they wanted us to see it. Conspiracy? No. Pack mentality? Yes. Did the truth suffer limitations? You think?

Not only was the technology limiting to international news but also the amount of news available to Americans was constrained to a limited viewpoint that fit a prejudicial vision, a media that saw reality predominantly through an anti-Christian-anti-military lens.

What was the greatest threat to truth for the American audience? Was it the technological limitations of the era or was it the editorial predisposition of the elite media? I believe it was the elite media's viewpoint and that was never so clear to me as on my first trip to Beirut, Lebanon. On that trip I discovered who the real oppressors were.

G. Scott McGregor

Chapter 11
Who's The Real Oppressor?

It was January of 1983. Peering out the airplane window on our landing approach, beneath us I saw the United States Marines stationed close to the Beirut airport. During those fateful days they were part of a multi-national peacekeeping force that also included French and Italian units in other parts of the city. The Israeli Army controlled the territory south of the airport all the way down to the northern border of Israel.

Their forces had invaded Lebanon a few months earlier to put an end to rocket attacks on their northern towns from the Palestinian armies occupying Lebanon. After only two weeks of fighting the Israeli Army had pushed the Palestinian Army (PLO) out of South Lebanon across the Litani River Gorge up past the Awali River Gorge all the way north and cornered them in Beirut. Only a United Nations negotiated cease-fire permitted the withdrawal of the Palestinian forces from Beirut saving them from annihilation at the hands of the Israeli Army.

When I got off the KLM flight that January morning in Beirut, I stepped smack dab into a war zone. It was eerie. Every night I heard automatic weapons fire outside my hotel room and every day I saw the destruction. It was easy to see that the removal of the Palestinian militias did not end the fighting in Lebanon. Something else was brewing.

In the middle of the week our team drove twelve miles south of Beirut and walked the streets of what was once the pristine hillside suburb of Damour. Extending upwards on the hills set back from the coastal highway, its 25,000 Christian residents once had a peaceful unobstructed view of the Mediterranean Sea where they could watch the sun melt into the horizon every evening.

But Damour was a ghost town. Six years earlier in January of 1976 a united Muslim army of 16,000 Syrians, Palestinians, Iranians, Afghanis, Pakistanis and Libyans surrounded the undefended town. Acting as part of the Palestine Liberation Army (PLO) under the command of Zuhair Mohsen, they attacked without notice or negotiation. Describing the unprovoked assault an eyewitness inside Damour said:

> It was an apocalypse. They were coming, thousands
> and thousands, shouting 'Allahu Akbar! God is
> great! Let us attack them for the Arabs, let us offer a
> holocaust to Mohammad 'and they were slaughtering
> everyone in their path, men, women and children…
>
> In the morning I managed to get to one house despite
> the shelling to bring out some of the corpses. And
> I remember something that still frightens me. An
> entire family had been killed, four children all dead,
> and the mother, the father, and the grandfather. The
> mother was still hugging one of the children. And
> she was pregnant. The eyes of the children were
> gone and their limbs were cut off. No legs and no
> arms. It was awful. [280]

Following the carnage they caused, for some reason the Muslim army then desecrated the town cemetery knocking down the crosses and digging up the graves. Skeletons and other remains of the dead were scattered across the ground. One of the churches was turned into a repair facility for their military vehicles.[281] And in the center of town on the wall of what used to be the community center was painted the logo of the Palestine Liberation Army featuring two fists with AK-47 assault rifles X'd over a map of Israel.

Only weeks before arriving in Lebanon I'd seen photos of the Damour massacre on a fact-finding trip to Washington, D.C. Many of the bodies were dismembered and violated, so the only way to get an accurate count of the dead was to literally count the heads. In all, 583 men, women and children were found dead in Damour.

The mutilation of the people was punishment for corrupting a land previously conquered by Islam twelve centuries earlier. Both the Quran and the Hadith commentaries contained references sanctioning such conduct:

> The only reward of those who make war upon Allah
> and His messenger and strive after corruption in the
> land will be that they will be killed or crucified, or

have their hands and feet on alternate sides cut off...[282]

He (Muhammed) ordered to cut off their hands and legs and their eyes to be branded with heated iron pieces...[283]

That sunny morning in Lebanon as I looked at the logo so proudly displayed in the center of the ghost town I wondered, *what did this Christian village in Lebanon have to do with liberating Palestine of the Jews?* Zuheir Mohsen, commander of the PLO army that carried out the Damour massacre, answered that question a year later in an interview with the Dutch newspaper, *Trouw*. In his own words Mohsen said:

The Palestinian people do not exist. The creation of a Palestinian state is only a means for continuing our struggle against the state of Israel for our Arab unity. In reality today there is no difference between Jordanians, Palestinians, Syrians and Lebanese. Only for political and tactical reasons do we speak today about the existence of a Palestinian people, since Arab national interests demand that we posit the existence of a distinct "Palestinian people" to oppose Zionism. For tactical reasons, Jordan, which is a sovereign state with defined borders, cannot raise claims to Haifa and Jaffa; while as a Palestinian, I can undoubtedly demand Haifa, Jaffa, Beer-Sheva and Jerusalem. However, the moment we reclaim our right to all of Palestine, we will not wait even a minute to unite Palestine and Jordan.[284]

Zuheir Mohsen's view of the world was a lawless one that saw sovereign nations and Christian villages as temporary obstacles to *Arab unity*, the slogan designed to sell the west on what was actually *Jihad*, a Muslim war against non-Muslims. Damour was simply part of a brutal process, an obstacle in the way of Islam's control of Lebanon. Under the flag of the PLO their army vented Muslim rage against these Christians as occupiers of Islam's rightful possessions. Just like Muhammad centuries before, they attacked Damour when it was unsuspecting and defenseless.

Evening Revelations

The next day sometime around eight o'clock in the evening I had an appointment for a private briefing with the spokesman of the Lebanese Forces north of Beirut in the port city of Juneih. My driver picked me up at the Alexander Hotel in Ashrafieh at 7:30.

In January the sun went down around six in Lebanon and Beirut had the meanest streets of the world. Traveling those streets by night was next to insanity, but my driver, Halil, had been the personal driver of President Bashir Gemeyal, and he was the best there was. I arrived safely at my destination in Juneih on time at eight o'clock.

Fadi Hayyak was Spokesman for the Lebanese Forces at the time.[285] Giving me the privilege of a private briefing spared me the discomfort of a press corps jammed into his office barking out questions, and gave me the opportunity to ask anything I wanted without interruption.

He was a lawyer, a Lebanese Catholic educated in three languages, English, French and Arabic. Like many leaders in The Lebanese Forces he left his professional life in Beirut to serve in the militia. Personally recruited for the position by President, Bashir Gemeyal, spokesman Hayyak chose to stay on after the newly elected president was assassinated early in his term by a Syrian operative.

Hayyak explained quite accurately that the history of modern Lebanon went back over 3000 years to the ancient Phoenician peoples who were concentrated in the port city-states of Tyre, Sidon, Biblos, and Beirut. An educated sea faring people that traded throughout the Mediterranean, perhaps they were best known for the giant cedar trees they harvested from the mountain forests and sold to the kings of Egypt and Israel in ancient days to adorn their palaces and temples with fine wood.

He explained that in modern times Lebanon had become known as the Switzerland of the Middle East basing their modern economy on banking and recreation.[286] There was skiing in the mountains, casinos, restaurants, resorts and luxurious hotels. All kinds of designer clothes, luxury cars and fine home furnishings could be purchased in the various port cities at greatly reduced prices compared to the rest of the world.

The spokesman explained that after the reestablishment of the state of Israel in 1948, a large community of Palestinians left Israel and moved to other Arab countries. Some of those refugees settled in Lebanon in the southern region of Tyre while a large group moved further north to the outskirts of Beirut.

Within a few years after arriving, however, by the mid 1950's their communities were giving shelter to hit squads of the Pan Arab movement started by Egypt's President Nasser. Their goal was to destabilize the democratic government of Lebanon in hopes of turning it into another Muslim state furthering *Arab Unity.* [287]

Further embittered with the United Nations vote that divided Palestine in 1948, the Palestinian refugees in Lebanon exerted pressure on the Lebanese government to somehow make up for their losses.[288] But the government chose not to build them new homes or make them citizens. In the long run it was a decision that the government probably regretted, but pleasing the Palestinians became a nearly impossible task for diplomats the world over. As author Cynthia Ozick lamented in her article *Where Hatred Trumps Bread*, the Palestinians are not known for their desires to coexist:

> What has been the genius of Palestinian originality, what has been the contribution of the evolving culture of Palestinian sectarianism? On the international scene: airplane hijackings and the murder of American diplomats in the 1970s, Olympic slaughtering and shipboard murders in the 1980s... But the most ingeniously barbarous Palestinian societal invention, surpassing any other in imaginative novelty, is the recruiting of children to blow themselves up with the aim of destroying as many Jews as possible in the most crowded sites accessible.[289]

In short, they were anarchistic and undesirable. Eventually, Lebanon's situation became similar to that of Jordan where the Palestinians tried to overthrow the government of King Hussein. After Black September in the early 1970's the Palestinian militias were thrown out of Jordan and crossed into Lebanon where they set up a state within the state. Soon afterwards Lebanon splintered into civil war.

All this had been explained to me just a few weeks earlier in Washington when I interviewed Lebanese President Camille Chamoun at the Dolly Madison Hotel.[290] Chamoun was in office in 1958 when America's President Eisenhower sent 14,000 United States Marines and Army troops to stabilize the situation in Lebanon.[291] The result was nearly two decades of peaceful coexistence between Muslim and Christian communities.

But after the final expulsion of the Palestinian militias from Jordan in June 1971, 15,000 PLO militiamen flowed into Lebanon. Then, enlistment offices throughout the Arab world swelled their ranks to 40,000 as recruits from numerous Islamic countries joined in the cause. The Palestinian communities inside Lebanon overflowed, so entire Lebanese towns were taken over to serve as new military camps. Such was the fate of Damour.

But with the PLO forced out of Lebanon by the Israeli Army, new pressures were emerging. Fadi Hayyak told me that eventually the Israelis and the multi-national force would leave Lebanon. When that happened the contest for control of the government would resume placing the Christian communities in further peril.[292] *I imagined Damour as he spoke.*

According to the National Pact which created the balance of power in the Lebanese democracy, the President was a Christian, the Prime Minister a Sunni Muslim and the Speaker of the Parliament a Shiite Muslim. It was a *permanent* agreement. But the Shiites felt that since their numbers had increased they deserved the Presidency instead of the Christians and so wanted to change the National Pact to accommodate their desires for more power.[293]

"Is that a workable solution?" I asked Fadi Hayyak.

"Do you want us to become second class citizens?" he answered. "Lebanese Christians have no desire to live in a Muslim state. If they do they can move to Syria where Christians don't have the same rights as Muslims."

"How will you become second class citizens if the Shiites have the presidency?" I asked.

"You mean make both the Prime Minister and the President Muslims?" he replied. "If we agreed to that it will change the constitutional balance of power. Lebanon will no longer be a democracy. It will become another Islamic state!"

"Can you explain that in more detail?" I asked. "How would Lebanon become an Islamic state if the President were a Muslim?"

"Just look at what you're asking!" he shot back. "The Muslims would have both the top positions of power and three large sections of the Parliament because the Druze are Muslims too. That would leave the Christians with just the one section of Parliament. It would be the end of the democracy. The Muslims could change the laws to be whatever they wanted and we would be powerless to stop them." [294]

Hayyak's comments to me were prophetic because within a year the Druze and Shiite militias were teaming up and firing daily artillery barrages into Christian sectors of Beirut as well as around the Presidential Palace at Babda trying to force President Amin Gemeyal to capitulate to the governmental changes they wanted.[295]

But at the time of my interview in that winter of 1983, the Shiite Muslims were simply taking advantage of the unstable situation and pressing for a *constitutional change* that would favor the Muslims and change the legal foundations of the nation.[296]

Sound familiar? It was the same pattern established by Muhammad in the *Hijra* centuries earlier when Islam first expanded out from Medina to conquer the Arabian Peninsula. If America learns anything from the history of Lebanon, this is the lesson. Islam seeks to replace democracy, first by immigration, then by legal changes and finally by violence when necessary to enable political takeover.

Lebanese Christian leaders knew the play was on to supplant Lebanon's democracy with an Islamic state. That's what disconnected them from the western media. There was that unspoken gap that we were supposed to understand. We didn't. Our reporters were supposed to understand the role Islam played historically in attacking the Judeo-Christian heritage of the Middle East throughout fourteen centuries. But the anti-Christian viewpoint of the American news media didn't report it that way. To them the Christians were the bad guys.

Bernard Lewis, the famous Islamic historian, wrote that Christianity had a special place of importance because it was the only serious rival to Islam as a world faith and a world power. In the first century of Islam's existence, this religion of the sword advanced out of Arabia and conquered Syria, Palestine, Lebanon, Egypt and North Africa, all countries that were previously part of Christendom for six hundred years.[297]

So even when the Ayatollah Khomeini declared war on both America and Israel in 1979 in the name of Allah, we couldn't identify it as a religious conflict! That fit into neither the pack mentality of the Commodore Hotel where the American press was nor the political-values-added-package of the media elite news editors setting the agenda for the United States audience. This could only be told to American audiences as a political event in which the Christian religion was an enemy of progress. In short, we weren't allowed to see why terrorism was coming to America.

In fact, the indexes in the books of the time written by the five major media's best selling western correspondents make no mention of the word *jihad*, strangely conspicuous by its absence.[298] Yet, from my research I could see what was all too obvious to the Lebanese Christians; they were struggling to preserve their democracy, not obstruct it. Were we in the American media naïve of Islam's techniques to supplant? Honestly, I think we were.

News content indicated our elite media demonstrated no desire to report with any balance the historic struggles of Christianity to survive against the onslaughts of Islamic jihads through the ages. To our media there was no jihad. So, the Christian leaders in Lebanon weren't acting like Christians.

The news I listened to made the Lebanese Christian militias appear as though they were obstructing the very democracy they were giving their lives to preserve. [300] And that simply wasn't true. Lebanese Christian Leaders knew the dangers to democracy represented by Shiite Muslim aggression because they knew that Islam didn't separate religion and state. Islam was the state. And Lebanese Christians knew the history of the Middle East.

What I mean by that is that the fabric of their country's foundation sought to accomplish what Middle Eastern Christians had hoped to do for centuries, build a state without military competition among religions. That was modern Lebanon: beautiful, vibrant, wealthy, and educated. But one side of the equation simply refused to enter the 20th Century.

I finished my interview with Fadi Hayyak that January night in 1983 and left his office for my room at the Alexander Hotel. I had a lot to process and Halil was polite enough to let me quietly make a few notes on the drive back to Ashrafieh. The spokesman was thinking of the history of the Christians in the Middle East. He even referred to Dhimmitude, the second-class citizenship suffered by so many non-Muslims for so long under the Islamic dominion of their nations.

Perhaps he thought of the five hundred years of Islamic dominion of Spain. Perhaps he thought of the struggles of his ancestors. I'll never know because he didn't say. As Halil drove me through the night, I reflected on my discovery of something both ancient and modern. Ancient because it had been going on since Islam swept out of the Arabian Peninsula in 633 AD, but modern because here we were in the 20th Century unable to avoid the conflict.

I didn't know it on the drive back to the hotel from Juneih that night in Beirut, but soon I would be back in Lebanon just as President Camille Chamoun suggested to me weeks before when I met him in Washington, DC. When I returned, I was the producer for METV Channel 12, the only independent English / Arabic television station broadcasting into seven countries of the Middle East. From then on I compiled the notes and research that made this book possible.

To really understand what's happening today, we have to turn the clock back to a different era. In the Middle East 1000 years is as one day, so events that happened centuries ago are used as precedents for actions today. That's why we have to look back to when the ongoing religious wars of the Middle East actually started. Five hundred years *before* the Christian Crusaders entered the Middle East there were the *Islamic Crusades*.

Chapter 12
The Islamic Crusades

Depending on who is telling the story, a series of religious wars known as *The Crusades* are set into world history with an angry finger pointing at those imperialist Christians from Europe who journeyed to the Middle East and violated the lands of Islam. No, really. If you mention the word *Crusaders* in polite conversation, see if someone doesn't quickly make a condemning remark against Christianity in general. Why is that?

It's because the people of Western Civilization have been taught to feel guilty and apologetic for the Crusades. Yet, very little mention is ever given to the fact that Islam initiated worldwide-armed religious conquest in 622. Their constitution of the *Hijra* made the world outside Islam against them, *dar al-harb,* the world of war. And the religious crusading they began in 622 has continued 1400 years until today. Perhaps you've never heard it put that way. Surprised? That's because it's not politically correct.

According to Muhammad's system of belief, however, only Islam's expansion and subjection of the entire world would bring about true justice for mankind expressing Allah's perfect will on this planet, administered by Muslims of course.[301] He ordered his prophet to fight against all men until all nations were subjugated to Islam.[302] The economic benefits and sheer political power that followed conquests were part of the perks Allah gave to the faithful who slaughtered and conquered as their spiritual service of worship.[303]

After Muhammad died in 632 the Muslim armies crusaded out of the Arabian Peninsula first carrying their *final revelation of Allah* to Iraq. In 633 after the Battle of Olayis that took place between Hira and Basra in Southern Iraq, for two days Islamic soldiers under command of Khalid ibn al-Rafiq rounded up the great multitude of prisoners and fugitives who were then herded onto a dry river bed and butchered until the dirt turned red with their blood. In Islamic lore thereafter, this place proudly bore the title of "The River of Blood." [304]

As if this atrocity wasn't enough, Ibn Rafiq had a sadistic sex ceremony that he carried out after a victory. According to Benjamin Walker in *The Foundations of Islam*:

> A wine-lover and lustful debaucher, Khalid took sickly sadistic delight in beheading a defeated chieftain on the battlefield, selecting his wife (if young) or daughter and celebrating his nuptials with her on the spot soaked with the blood of the victim.[305]

The Christian territories of Palestine, Syria and Lebanon were next. Previously administered by the Eastern Roman Empire whose capital city was Constantinople, these territorial armies of Rome were decisively defeated by the Muslim armies commanded by Khalid ibn al Rafiq at the Battle of Yarmuk in Syria in 636. Two years later Jerusalem surrendered to the Arabs in 638 after an extended siege.

With the seat of their new empire in Damascus, the Muslims continued to raise armies and wealth by conquering more nations and instituting the *protection tax* on all non-Muslims, particularly Christians. By 648 just fourteen years after Muhammad's death, all of Egypt and North Africa had fallen under their control. It was bad news for Christians and Jews.

Dhimmitude, the second-class citizenship for non-Muslims, had laws requiring public gestures by Christians and Jews recognizing Muslims as their superiors. So, not only did Christians pay tax to worship Christ, they had to give deference to Muslims as well. The attitude enforced was that of master to slave. A Christian was to be ordered about and treated with tolerance but never permitted to have any say over a Muslim.[306]

And any Muslim could take a Christian to court over disrespect. Once in the Islamic court, a Dhimmi could not testify against a Muslim, and only Muslim lawyers could argue before the judge. An accused Christian had to pay for a Muslim defense lawyer and other fees to Muslim witnesses to testify on his behalf. [307] It was a racket.

Then, in the summer of 711 the ambitious governor of Tangiers in North Africa raised an army of Islamic crusaders and crossed the Straits of Gibraltar. Tariq ibn Ziyad invaded Spain from the south with an expeditionary force of 12,000 Arabs. The next year he returned to

Morocco and was replaced by Musa ibn Nusair, the Muslim governor of all North Africa. Nusair brought more fresh troops and within two more years by 713 conquered all of Spain except the mountainous regions in the extreme north.[308]

In eighty-one years Islamic armies spread their religious crusade from the Arabian Peninsula to the Atlantic Ocean and were threatening to take France. Only a decisive defeat south of Paris at the Battle of Tours in 732 halted their advance.[309] Described by the 19th Century military historian, Edward Creasy, as one of the fifteen most decisive battles of the world, the Muslims never successfully advanced into France after their defeat at Tours. Historian Edward Gibbon in his *Decline and Fall of the Roman Empire* said that the victory at Tours guaranteed the existence of church spires with crosses in Oxford, England instead of Islamic minarets.[310]

At the farthest corner of the Islamic world, Spain was named Al Andalus and fell under the leadership of the Muslim Caliph of Damascus, so most of the Islamic governors appointed to Spain were Syrian. But nothing in Europe compared at the time to the wealth, power and brilliance of Al Andalus. She was a sparkling jewel adorning the Islamic Empire's crown.

In 976 the Muslim leader Al Mansur came to power in Spain and preached jihad against the Christians on the northern frontier. Under-taking annual summer campaigns against them served to unite Spanish Muslims in a common cause to extend control to the north. Elsewhere, throughout Muslim controlled Spain, the protection tax fell most heavily on the Christian communities who were permitted to exist but prohibited from flourishing.[311]

For five hundred years the Muslims ruled most of Spain, a nation previously evangelized by Christians and flourishing with church worship centuries before their arrival. That should be a sobering thought to Americans because Spain was across the sea from Arabia.

The jihads initiated by Al Mansur only served to unify the move-ment among Christians from the four unconquered states in the north to free Spain from Islamic subjugation. But in North Africa an Islamic revival movement organized a new jihad against Christianity that spilled across into Spain. It was a new invasion in the old Islamic manner, brutal. The Christians of Spain were about to be decimated.

Pope Innocent III called all Christendom to respond and units arrived in mass around the city of Toledo in the northern state of Castile where Alfonso VIII was king. Armies from Germany and Italy arrived to join those of Navarre, Castile, Aragon, Leon and the nation of Portugal. Christian Europe made a stand against Moslem Africa in a war with Spain the prize of victory.

In 1212 Emperor Muhammad An Nassir led the invading Muslim force of 400,000 moving northward in Spain seeking a decisive battle with the Christian armies. The deciding moment approached as King Alfonso led the 100,000 united Christian troops southward to meet the Islamic advance at the battle of Las Navas de Tolosa where these ½ million men fought on the fields of Andalusia.[312] How it shaped up is an amazing story.

Surrounded by mountains about seventy miles east of Cordova on a gently sloping surface lay the grand plateau of the plains of Tolosa, ample space for the vast hosts that met there. But the Muslims arrived first and deployed across the eastern section holding the only mountain pass into the plain from the north. It was the ancient battle of the 300 Spartans against the Persians, only in reverse.

The smaller band of elite forces from ancient Sparta held the pass at Thermopylae in central Greece. Forcing the enormous Persian army to fight through the pass on a limited front, the Greeks held back the Persians advance for three days.

In Spain, however, instead of the smaller force holding the gateway and forcing the larger force into a constrained battlefront, it was the opposite. The larger army of the Muslims held the pass of Losa, nature's only highway to the plains of Tolosa. For the Christian army to enter the field of battle, they would have to fight their way through the pass of Losa exposing themselves to a three-sided attack from the hillsides and the front against the entire Muslim army of 400,000 in reinforcement. Outnumbered four to one, it was an impossible situation for the Christian army. But a military miracle happened.

Martin Halaja, a shepherd that grazed his flocks in that vicinity for years, approached King Alfonso and told him of a pathway through the mountains that was unknown to the enemy. As the Muslim lookouts atop the mountain entrance to the Losa pass saw the Christian camps breaking up, they reported back to Muhammad An Nassir that the Christian army had retreated. Hearing this the Emperor sent off letters to southern cities celebrating their victory.

Then, from dusk on July 14[313] all night until dawn on the 15[313], the shepherd guided Alfonso's army through this little-known mountain by-way. Shaken and furious, an astonished Islamic army gazed on the Christian host the morning of July 15, 1212 watching them flow from the mountains onto the opposite side of the plateau untouched.[313]

That was Sunday. Standing in their battle formation all day the Moslems sent riders across toward the Christian lines to taunt them, but the Christians declined to fight. Then, at midnight the Christians went to worship services and prayed. When dawn came July 16th both armies drew up in battle deployment and the great struggle began.

As the Christian army looked across to the hordes of Islam, one account said that the hosts of Mohammed covered the hillsides and plains like "countless swarms of locusts."[314] From Chapter 24 of *The Latin Chronicle of the Kings of Castile* comes the account of how the battle began:

> They attacked, fighting against one another, hand-to-hand, with lances, swords, and battle-axes; there was no room for archers. The Christians pressed on; the Moors repelled them; the clashing and tumult of arms was heard. The battle was joined, but neither side was overcome, although at times they pushed back the enemy, and at other times they were driven back by the enemy.[315]

At one critical point as the Muslims gained the upper hand, King Alfonso told Archbishop Rodrigo, "Archbishop, you and I must die here."

"No," replied Rodrigo. "Here we must triumph over our enemies."[316] With that the two rode into the thick of the battle. In an effort to protect the King and the Archbishop from death other troops rushed to protect them changing the direction of the thrust and suddenly breaking the Islamic lines:

> The king of Morocco, who was sitting in the midst of his men surrounded by warriors chosen for battle, got up and mounted a horse or a mare, and turned tail and fled. His men were killed and slaughtered in

droves, and the site of the camp and the tents of the
Moors became the tombs of the fallen.[317]

The entire store of Emperor An Nassir's army was captured
including horses, carts, wagons, lances, chests of gold and silver as well
as the food banks of the 400,000. The Emperor's tent was sent to the
Pope in Rome to adorn St. Peter's Cathedral as a symbol of the triumph.
Muhammad An Nassir returned to Morocco in disgrace where he died,
poisoned in Marrakech soon after.[318] The Muslim power over Spain was
broken.

The Christian Crusaders

The victory in Spain took place during the era when the armies
of Europe were united and mobilized to fight against the Muslims in the
Crusades of the Middle East. This era began in 1097 and ended in 1291,
lasting less than 200 years. If we back up and approach the history from
another angle it might become even clearer.

The world of Christendom was Islam's primary target, its
competitor in religion and territorial influence.[319] After all, Christianity
predated Islam by six centuries and won the respect of the Roman
Empire through reason and suffering.[320] Islam on the other hand gained
recognition by hacking and slaughtering their competition on the
battlefield.

So much so that two years after the death of Muhammad in 634
Sophronius, the Patriarch of Jerusalem, said in his Christmas sermon that
the Muslims were savage and barbarous, oppressing Christianity by their
bloody swords.[321] And Michael, the Patriarch of Antioch in Syria, wrote
that Caliph Marwan II's troops, "inflicted many evils on the men: blows,
pillages, and outrages on women in their husbands' presence."[322]

In the early 8th Century Baghdad's Caliph Al-Mutawakkil
designated a yellow badge for Jews, setting a precedent that would be
followed twelve centuries later in Nazi Germany. As a matter of fact,
in comparing Nazi law towards Jews and Dhimmi Law in the Omar
Charter shows how the Nazis copied from the Muslims. [323] Here are a
few examples:

Islam: Jews & Christians must wear identifiable clothing and live in a clearly marked house. For Jews, a yellow banner is to be fixed around the shoulder or arm, as to be recognized as a Jew.

Nazism: A yellow banner is to be fixed around the shoulder or arm, as to be recognized as a Jew. They must live in the Jewish Ghettos.

Islam: He must not ride a horse or bear arms. He must yield the right-of-way to Muslims.

Nazism: Jews are not admitted to serve in the army or navy. They are not allowed to bear arms.

Islam: Dhimmis (Jews & Christians) cannot be a witness in a legal court except in matters relating to other "dhimmis" (Jews & Christians) or be a judge in a Muslim court.

Nazism: Jews cannot hold public offices...be Judges...or serve on juries.

Islam: Jews & Christians must pay "Jizya", a special tax for protection.

Nazism: For their protection Jews must pay double the taxes the Germans pay. [324]

Islamic rule by brutality and violence was common for Christians in conquered territories. For instance, from 1004-1015 Caliph Al-Hakim ordered the destruction of thirty thousand churches and the seizure of all church property throughout Syria and Palestine including the destruction of the Church of the Holy Sepulcher in Jerusalem. When Atiz bin Uwaq and his forces arrived in Jerusalem sixty years later in 1077, they slaughtered three thousand Christians and Jews among the already subjected population; for what? These people had already submitted to Islamic government. The truth...it was an exercise in extermination.

Christians were the subjected peoples, "the guilty" for having distorted Allah's revelation and believing in the Trinity.[325] The non-

Muslim tax was enforced with "belittlement and humiliation" by striking Christians on both cheeks in public as they paid the tax collector.[326]

Display of the cross or Christian education of children was forbidden.[327] They could not raise their voices in prayer and disturb a Muslim. They had to give up their seat to a Muslim. Christians could not own weapons or ride horses and camels. They could not construct a church or a house that was higher than any Muslim structure.[328]

A Muslim was to be sheltered and fed for free in their churches or houses upon request at any hour of the day or night. Christians kept to the side of the street, rode donkeys and could not speak about their faith to a Muslim on sentence of death.[329] All this because they were the second-class citizens, so termed by Islamic law as the *dhimmis*.

Islam oppressed Middle East Christians. The structure of the Byzantine Empire gave protection to the Christians of the Middle East for over three centuries after the Council of Nicea convened by Emperor Constantine. But that structure crumbled under the continuous assault of the Arabs. For nearly five centuries Muslims mounted unholy continuous war against every country in this territory until Alexius I in Constantinople finally called on Pope Urban II in Rome for help in 1095.

At the Council of Claremont Pope Urban II called for the liberation of the oppressed churches. It was the first defensive action taken by European Christendom in answer to five hundred years of Muslim crusades against lands previously dominated by Christian worshipers. Taking the position that military action was long overdue Pope Urban said:

> For your brethren who live in the east are in urgent
> need of your help, and you must hasten to give them
> the aid, which has often been promised them… now
> go against the infidels and end with victory this war
> which should have been begun long ago… [330]

His impassioned speech brought dramatic results motivating kingdoms as the Crusaders came from France, Britain and Italy.[331] In *The Truth About the Islamic Crusades and Imperialism,* historian, James Arlandson said:

> It is a plain and unpleasant historical fact...that the church had to fight back or be swallowed up by an aggressive religion over the centuries.[332]

The Crusader armies assembled at Constantinople and planned for battle. After they crossed the Bosporus into Turkey, their first conquest was the city of Nicea, but it wasn't easy. After suffering heavy casualties trying to break through the city's walls, the Crusaders finally routed the Turkish Muslims in a one-day cavalry battle.[333]

From there they moved on to besiege Antioch in October 1097. But Antioch's walls were nearly impregnable. Supplies and reinforcements arrived five months later in March 1098, but it wasn't until summer that a spy was successfully bought who helped the Crusaders breach the wall in secret and take the city the first week of June.

The Crusaders rushed into the city through the St. George Gate while the Dhimmi Christian citizens joined the fighting through the streets. Two days later, however, the tables turned as the Turkish army arrived in force besieging the Crusaders within the city. On the ropes and nearly starved, the Crusaders exited Antioch in a counter attack that routed the Turks June 28, 1098.[334] From there it was on to Jerusalem.

Taking Jerusalem meant the Crusaders had to build siege ramps and that required wood. Part of the army had to be detached and sent miles away to cut timbers from the forests of Samaria, then transport them outside the walls of Jerusalem to build the ramps. This took weeks. In the meantime Muslim reinforcements were supposedly on the way from Egypt.

Bishop Adhemar, the Pope's representative, ordered a fast for the whole army July 7, 1099. As the Muslim soldiers atop the Jerusalem walls mocked, the Bishop led the Christian army around the city in a prayer and praise march the following day. As evening came preachers addressed the soldiers with sermons on the Mount of Olives.

Moving the siege ramps up, the united Crusader army assaulted Jerusalem and breached the walls on July 15, 1099. That's when the rampage began. For five centuries reports had steadily arrived in Europe of the Muslims atrocities against Christians. For two days the revenge for all those years continued until all the Muslim defenders were dead. Regrettably, they also burned a synagogue with people inside. Order returned on the 17th with only the conquerors left occupying the city. [335]

Nine hundred years ago was a very different era. By their moral standards, the Crusader's sack of Jerusalem was out of bounds. By the military practices of the day, however, it wasn't. Accepted principles of siege warfare allowed for non-resistors to leave a besieged city. Many Jews and Muslims left Jerusalem in safety during the crusader siege in 1099. Nevertheless, those who remained to resist risked being put to death by any conqueror.[336]

The First Crusade was a great success for the Christian armies. Inflicting defeat after defeat on the Muslims and causing heavy casualties, they liberated key cities of the Dhimmi Christians such as Nicea, Antioch and Jerusalem. In addition they gained a controlling sector of territories that enabled them to stay in a governing capacity preventing further Islamic atrocities against Christian settlements. Though enraged by their defeats, the Muslims feared them and two generations of relief came to the Christians living in the Holy Lands.[337]

Ninety years later the Muslim general, Saladin, defeated the Crusader army at the Horns of Hittim above the Sea of Galilee July 1187. The records of Saladin's own secretary, Imad ed-Din, tell us General Saladin was not magnanimous in victory but ordered the mass execution of all his opponents. That was not accepted practice of open field warfare except for Muslims who gleefully exterminated non-Muslims, as in the River of Blood:

> ...A whole band of scholars and Sufis and certain number of devout men and ascetics; each begged to be allowed to kill one of them (the crusader soldiers), and drew his sword and rolled back his sleeve. Saladin, his face filled with joy, was sitting on his dais...[338]

Three months later in October 1187 Saladin recaptured Jerusalem and ordered the execution of every Christian throughout the city. Only the threat made by Balian of Ibelin, the Crusades commander in Jerusalem, stayed Saladin's command. Balian threatened to kill all Jerusalem's Muslims first.[339]

The Third Crusade of 1188 came in response to the defeats and subsequent massacres suffered at the hands of Saladin. And Crusaders remained in the Holy Land another one hundred years until their final defeat at Acre in 1291. There, Islam committed another atrocity.

Sultan al-Ashraf Khalil promised to spare the lives of those Christians who surrendered. He lied. Arab historian, Abu al-Fida, records that the final defenders were all put to death. Al-Ashraf killed everybody allowing his soldiers to tie women, children and even babies between horses to be pulled apart. [340]

In all there were seven Christian Crusades that lasted one hundred and ninety years, not much in comparison to the Muslim jihads that began in 622 and spread into Europe after the Crusaders left the Middle East. Those Jihads lasted for one thousand and sixty years until they were finally halted outside the gates of Vienna, Austria Sept 11, 1683.[341]

Yes, that date is correct. Read it again, September 11th. It is the ignominious date of Islam's defeat, the "high water mark" of Islam's jihads against Christendom, September 11, 1683. For three centuries afterwards Islam was thrown back.

Fast Forward

Not until November 1979 when Iran's Ayatollah Khomeini declared war on "America the Great Satan" did the jihad resurface against Western Civilization.

Then, taking our embassy in Tehran hostage, the Ayatollah grabbed the Great Satan by the tail and kicked him in the butt for the entire world to see as he showed Muslims worldwide on ABC that Allah gives victory over infidels no matter who they are and no matter how powerful they may be. It was his blessing of assurance to every suicide Islamic bomber that Islam would triumph over America.

Twenty years later, listing a long diatribe of America's crimes against Islam, Osama bin Ladin joined with Khomeini and issued his own declaration of war against America on February 23, 1998.[342] Why?

First, Muslims do not see individual nations. Instead, they see the people of Islam as the one nation divided into individual territories that have national names.[343] Second, those outside Islam are in the *dar al-harb*, the world at war with Islam, at war with Allah. Third, any nation conquered by an Islamic army is the property of Islam forever. And I might add that the nations of the Middle East are particularly and most specifically owned under the propaganda phrase of *Arab unity.* Fourth, Islam teaches that it is their divine destiny to rule every nation of the world without exception.

Think about this for a minute. Every reason above is a tenant of the Islamic faith. And all four reasons put them at odds with all peoples and all nations in all times. If you haven't submitted to Islam as a person or as a nation, you must, otherwise the destiny of Islam will not be fulfilled.[344]

In the Islamic view of logic, all crimes committed against Islamic believers anywhere in the world are crimes against Islam, war crimes against Allah and his messenger, Muhammad. They are in a constant state of war with the entire world and there are only two ways to peace, convert or submit to Islamic rule. If you think that's a bit extreme, read it for yourself on page 47 of *The 9/11 Commission Report*:

> Claiming that America had declared war against God and his messenger, they called for the murder of any American, anywhere on earth, as the "individual duty for every Muslim who can do it in any country in which it is possible to do it…"Asked whether he (Osama bin Ladin) approved of terrorism and of attacks on civilians, he replied: "We do not have to differentiate between military or civilian. As far as we are concerned, they are all targets." [345]

In making such a statement Osama bin Ladin was only carrying out the perfect example of his predecessor and Prophet, Muhammad, who gave permission in the Al Abwa raid to kill men, women and children because they were all the same… infidels.[346]

Read it for yourself in the Hadith commentaries of Al-Bukhari on line at the University of Southern California's website sponsored by the Muslim Student Association http://www.usc.edu/dept/MSA/fundamentals/hadithsunnah/bukhari/. Click on Book 52, *Fighting in the cause of Allah (Jihaad),* and scroll down to Number 256.[347]

Then, go on-line to the *Ten Misconceptions about Islam,* http://www.missionislam.com/discover/misconceptions.htm, and read in the second paragraph that religion and state are not separated.[348] Scroll down to *Misconception 2* and read that the best alternative for our represent-ative republic in America is an Islamic state under Sharia Law.[349]

Then, scroll down to *Misconception 7* and read in paragraph eleven that "…jihad is obligatory wherever there is injustice, and Muslims need not acknowledge imaginary lines (national boundaries) around the earth when it comes to upholding this obligation."[350] Since the Muslims have a different set of laws, they are allowed to decide what is unjust towards mankind outside of the laws of nations.

So they are encouraged to make war on any nation not living up to Islam, and that's everywhere Islam doesn't govern. Later on in *Misconception 7* paragraph thirteen says that: "Hence, the Creator obligates us to fight wherever..."[351]

Of course the Crusades were a different time and a different era. The circumstances were not the same. But things were stirred up again in the 20th Century. Khomeini's Islamic Revolution and the Lebanese Shiites united to make Lebanon a base for striking against Israel and America. Within ten years the Harvard University government specialist, Samuel Huntington, addressed the problem saying that Islamic fundamentalism wasn't the issue, instead he wrote:

> "It is Islam, a different civilization whose people are
> convinced of the superiority of their culture and are
> obsessed with the inferiority of their power."[352]

For five hundred years the nations of Europe stayed out of the fight hoping for coexistence, and for five hundred years Europe heard of the ruthlessness of Islam against Christians throughout the Holy Land. Finally, Pope Urban called for the First Crusade in 1096. Today, Western Civilization of the 21st Century is unable to avoid the conflict the same as Europe in the 11th Century.

Why? Because what grew out of the Judeo-Christian religions changed the world and gave birth to new civilizations and new ideas, ideas that don't fit within the aggressive instructions expressed by Muhammad for world conquest and Islamic religious control.[353]

For instance, the archeological findings in Israel are testimony to the accuracy of the Judeo-Christian scriptures. After Jerusalem came under Jewish control following the 1967 Six Day War, archeologists made astounding discoveries that verified the truth of ancient Biblical texts. How could rocks testify you might ask? The stones verified the precision of the words recorded thousands of years before.

Indeed, 230 years ago some of those passages moved a group of colonists in the new world to depend on the character of the Creator they described. Risking all in faith of those words they founded the United States of America.

Today, those ancient stones of Israel still cry out and testify. I saw for myself, and then checked the historical record. It gives a timeline of how America came into being. Starting with the legal foundations of the Ancient Hebrews, that's next.

Chapter 13
When The Rocks Cried Out

The air smelled clean in the strong mid morning Israeli sun. I gazed at the two distinctly different ancient walls in front of me and listened to the lecture of the archeology professor. One wall was directly inside the other, yet each wall was obviously built with different cut stones from a different era of time.

One of the many walking tours of Jerusalem, this one was named, "The City of David Tour" and descended for ten minutes from the streets of modern day Jerusalem outside the wall of the old city at the Jaffa Gate down a path into a gray dusty ravine known as the Kidron Valley. As we walked down the rocky hill, looking back I saw the old city wall and the ancient steps to the entrance of Solomon's temple built over two thousand years ago.

Feeling the rocky path beneath my feet I listened to the beeping of cars and the sounds of trucks shifting gears on the road above that circled outside the old city walls. The contrasts were stunning. I was in one of the oldest cities of the world listening to the sounds of today.

Jerusalem has been continuously inhabited for 5000 years. One of the excavated walls in front of me was 60 feet high and dated back to the Jebusite city that King David of Israel conquered in 1000 BC.[354] Yet another wall was constructed outside a portion of that wall and appeared wider. The guide said this represented a portion of the wall Governor Nehemiah built in 445 BC when he returned to Israel from Persia to rebuild the walls of the city destroyed by the Babylonians.[355]

After the Israeli Army took Jerusalem from the Jordanian Arab Legion in the 1967 Six Day War, archeologists began excavations that dusted off Israel's past. The rocks cried out! Over three thousand years of history written in numerous books of the Bible and other sources were proved true by the physical evidence discovered. As a citizen of the New World I had returned to my roots. These rocks said to the world that the Biblical record of ancient Israel was true.

Yet long before these rocks were uncovered, the founders of the United States staked the success of our new nation on the character of the Creator who revealed Himself to ancient Israel. The centuries in between brought great struggle, however, the new nation was finally born: "conceived in liberty and dedicated to the proposition that all men are created equal." [356]

The concept of a government protecting the rights of free men was not some notion dreamed up by a few colonists avoiding taxes. It was the result of their Creator's revelation to mankind.

Where It Began

According to *The Atlas of Jewish History* Abraham left the city of Ur in Chaldea with his wife Sarah to answer the call of God in 2000 BC. From this region of southern Mesopotamia they journeyed to Canaan where, through his son Isaac's descendants, the Hebrew nation of Israel emerged in the 13th Century BC.[357] But how could something that happened as a religious revelation to one man four thousand years ago have any meaning to our Western Civilization today? Read on.

Abraham's name meant "father of multitudes" yet when he responded to the call of Almighty God, he was childless. When his wife couldn't conceive, out of frustration she gave permission for Abraham to have a child by her handmaid, Hagar. This child born to Hagar was named Ishmael to whom the Arab nations trace their heritage to this day. However, he was not the child God promised Abraham as part of their covenant. Instead, Isaac was later born to Abraham and Sarah as that fulfillment.

Although back in Mesopotamia his ancestors worshipped many gods, Abraham openly declared his faith in the one and only God eternal and almighty who revealed himself by name, Yahweh, creator of heaven and earth, the righteous judge of the nations and all mankind. His character being perfect wisdom, justice, mercy and goodness he dwells beyond the limits of time.

For Abraham the supreme test of his life came when God asked him to sacrifice Isaac, his only son, who was the only means by which the promised nation of Israel would eventually come into being. Nevertheless, Abraham obeyed, believing that God would raise his son from the dead to fulfill the covenant he made to Abraham. The episode concluded when an angel stopped Abraham's hand sparing Isaac, then God provided a ram to sacrifice.

Two thousand years later the author of the New Testament book to the Hebrew churches wrote of the faith shown by past believers naming Abraham as an example of the covenant made to these new Christian believers indicating that from the very beginning of the Hebrew nation God provided the picture to Abraham of what He, himself, would do on their behalf. God would sacrifice His only son to die for the sins of men, and then raise him from the dead.[358] This was part of his agreement with Abraham to create from a childless man a nation of descendents and bring blessing upon the entire world. However, before Israel became a nation that blessed the world, they first became a distinct people.

There was a famine in the land of Canaan that lasted several years and drove Abraham's descendants to move in mass to Egypt. The Prime Minister of Egypt at the time of their immigration was a descendant of Abraham's grandson, Jacob. Spoken of in both the books of Genesis and Exodus in great detail, Joseph, the Prime Minister of Egypt, was betrayed years before by his older brothers and sold as a servant to a caravan heading to Egypt. They expected him to disappear from the face of the earth. He didn't.

Instead, through terrible personal trials that included imprisonment by false accusation, Joseph rose to prominence. By appointment of the King of Egypt Joseph took charge of the agricultural resources of the nation. In this position he prepared the country to withstand a famine.

Fleeing the famine in Canaan seventy descendants of Abraham entered Egypt in 1700 BC. Here they reconciled with Joseph receiving his forgiveness and great favor from the king. Afterwards, they stayed and multiplied for four hundred and thirty years.[359] As their numbers grew over the centuries the Hebrew people prospered and eventually populated an entire section of Egypt known as Goshen. Though they enjoyed great favor with the kings of Egypt in the first centuries of their residence, as the leaders changed after the death of Joseph, so also the attitudes changed towards the Hebrews.

Finally, under Ramses II the entire Hebrew nation of people was under servitude to the Egyptians as slave laborers and 2nd class citizens. It was during the middle of the reign of this king that a brilliant leader arose among the Hebrews. His name was Moses, and through his negotiations with Ramses II, the king was finally persuaded to release the Hebrews after Egypt endured a series of devastating events.

Moses persuaded the king that the events were judgments from God that would cease when the Hebrew nation was released from servitude to Egypt. The king finally released them and thus began the period of the Exodus about 1260 BC. [360]

It was the birth of Israel.[361] The entire nation exited from Egypt and took up residence in the Sinai Peninsula, a section of land between Egypt and modern day Israel that is a strikingly beautiful desert landscape filled with plains and multicolored mountains of red, black, tan and brown stone. These mountains stand directly at the edge of the deep sapphire blue waters of the Red Sea with the Gulf of Aqaba on the east and the Gulf of Suez on the west. The color contrasts are striking like no other place on earth.

It was there beneath Mount Sinai that the entire nation spread their tents and received the Ten Commandments as the basis of law from which to form the conduct of their nation:

1. You shall have no other gods before me
2. You shall not make for yourself a graven image
3. You shall not take the name of God in vain
4. Honor the Sabbath day to keep it holy
5. Honor you father and your mother
6. You shall not murder
7. You shall not commit adultery
8. You shall not steal
9. You shall not bear false testimony against you neighbor
10. You shall not covet anything that is you neighbor's [362]

The first four commandments were about faith and how a person relates to God. The last six commandments made up the basis of the civil law code that constrained all men. Founded on a vision of the personal sacrifice of Christ, Abraham's descendants grew into a nation whose knowledge of God was to cause them to set an example for mankind.

The great Jewish scholar, Paul of Tarsus, wrote about the importance of Israel for the world saying that to them belong the promises, the giving of the law, the worship of the One True God and from their race comes the Christ.[363] So from Abraham and Isaac came the Hebrew race and the nation of Israel and from Israel came the Christ of Christianity.

The Spread of Christianity

Two thousand years ago in the 1st Century AD the civil engineers of the Roman armies had connected the vast territories of the empire with a network of interstate roads. The result was that international travel became possible for the common man. In fact, "the people of the Roman Empire traveled more easily and more extensively than anyone before them did or would again until the 19th Century." [364]

Starting in Jerusalem the new faith immediately took on the uniqueness of a cult spreading rapidly through the twenty-two largest cities of the Roman Empire.[365] This was due to the unique aspect that Christian believers said Jesus of Nazareth rose from the dead on the morning of the third day after his crucifixion and subsequent burial.[366]

At the time Jerusalem's population was around 45,000 but those numbers were swollen to 70,000 as Jews from all nations had traveled to Jerusalem for the Passover Festival.[367] Crowds around the temple witnessed the preaching of the disciples on the Day of Pentecost. And other small groups, together numbering over five hundred people, claimed to be eyewitnesses to the resurrected Jesus.[368]

The account in the Acts of the Apostles says that during these times three thousand converts were added.[369] That is to say that 4 percent of the 70,000 or so people in Jerusalem converted to Christianity in less than two months. And if that were an accurate reporting of events, it would have created quite a stir not only in Jerusalem but also in the other nations where Jews had traveled from…and so it did.

In his study of the rise of Christianity in the ancient world sociology professor Rodney Stark of Baylor University found that the number of Christians grew at around 3.2 percent per year and showed a projected growth of 40 percent per decade through the middle of the 4th Century up to 350 AD. That's an exponential curve.

Professor Stark estimated 7500 converts existed by the year 100; sixty-five years after the new religion began. In the next century converts increased to 217,000 by the year 200, further rising to 6.3 million by the year 300 and topping out at 33 million by 350 AD. That last figure represented 56 percent of the total population of the Roman Empire in the middle of the 4th Century.[370] Emperor Constantine, himself, converted and in 313 issued the *Edict of Milan* that officially recognized Christianity and prohibited persecutions and confiscations of property.

But what caused such a dramatic spread of this new religion across the nations? Why did it grow from an unknown movement at the edge of the Roman Empire to become the dominant faith of their civilization?

Certainly the ease of travel and the distance from Jerusalem were important factors. In addition, a pre-existing network of Jewish communities was already established because the Jews of the Diaspora built synagogues in all these major cities. So, for Christians, it was already possible to travel from city to city presenting the claims of the new faith to interested communities within familiar networks of relatives and friends of Jewish congregations.[371] These new revelations said that Jesus was the prophesied Messiah of the Jewish scriptures who came to die for mankind's redemption.

It quickly became an urban movement and Antioch, the fourth largest city of the Roman Empire, was particularly receptive to the new religion. In fact, many scholars believe that the Gospel of Matthew, the first book of the New Testament, was actually written in Antioch.[372]

However, like many Greco-Roman cities of the epoch, Antioch was founded as a fortress so it was compact and densely populated.[373] Not accounting for public buildings:

> The population density of Antioch was roughly 75,000 inhabitants per square mile or 117 per acre. As a comparison, in Chicago today there are 21 inhabitants per acre; San Francisco has 23, and New York City overall has 37. Even Manhattan Island has only 100 inhabitants per acre…very spread out vertically.[374]

Yet, the crush of humanity was further complicated by the fact that public buildings, monuments, and temples occupied 35 to 40 percent of these cities. Actual resident density was more like 180 to 320 inhabitants per acre,[375] and there were no skyscrapers extending a city's living space vertically.

People lived in tiny cubicles in multistoried tenements without chimneys or running water. Chamber pots were used to remove human waste and daily emptied out windows into open ditches in the streets that served as sewers. The smell of sweat, urine, feces, and decay permeated everything.[376] During times of warm weather the stench of these cities could be picked up miles away.

Modern archeological research in Jerusalem found these societies suffered from "the ingestion of fecally contaminated foods or… unsanitary living arrangements in which people came into contact with human excrement." [377] There were killer epidemics and constant human affliction from the repugnant sanitary conditions. For instance, in the city of Antioch 41 natural and social catastrophes occurred during a period of six centuries, one every fifteen years.[378]

In fact, if it weren't for a constant influx of new inhabitants to cities like Antioch, their populations would have died out. But with the multitude of cultures from across the empire, the waves of traveling newcomers replenished the urban populations; however, they also splintered the cultures of the cities into chaos filling them with traditions and groups from everywhere. Residents were in continual clash with each other with constant tension and an overwhelming sense of isolation.

The amoral structure of the pagan times cheapened life even further. For instance, Romans believed in female infanticide because a male heir was desirable while female children were considered an economic drain. A Roman man serving in Alexandria, Egypt wrote back home to his pregnant wife: "…If you are delivered of a child (before I come home) if it is a boy keep it, if a girl discard it." [379]

The earliest known Roman legal code called *The Twelve Tablets* was written around 450 BC. These statutes permitted a father to expose (naked in the street) any female infant or deformed male infant.[380] And excavations in Ashkelon found the bones of 100 newborn babies apparently murdered and thrown into the sewer.[381]

Small families of one or two children were preferred, so abortion was used as a means of birth control along with mutual masturbation and anal intercourse.[382] Infidelity and prostitution were widely accepted yet no antibiotics existed to treat venereal diseases. And during times of epidemics the sick were put into the streets to die while the healthy would often leave town to escape getting the disease.[383]

In contrast, Christianity taught the sanctity of life, the joy of having children, the absolute need for fidelity in marriage, the power of a loving faithful God, the sacrificial giving of time and money to help needy brethren, the nursing of the sick and the supernatural bonds of the family of believers. This was the new moral order set forth by Jesus of

Nazareth and written in Matthew's Gospel:

> For I was hungry and you gave me food. I was
> thirsty and you gave me drink. I was a stranger and
> you welcomed me. I was naked and you clothed me.
> I was sick and you visited me. I was in prison and
> you came to see me...Truly, I say to you, as you did
> it to one of the least of these my brethren, you did it
> to me. [384]

Because to love God meant to believe in Jesus and to obey his words, Christianity brought a powerful antidote to the cheap life in the filth of the cramped cities. It brought hope to the lonesome and offered a sense of belonging amidst the cultural pagan chaos. In short, it made each person's life valued and important. But it went beyond that and challenged the pagan amoral government.

The Effect of Christian Martyrs

So, although Christianity answered the crying needs of a world in chaos, it personally threatened the belief system of authorities in high places. And since there was no freedom of speech to criticize a divine emperor, many famous Christian leaders were sentenced to death as Roman authority targeted the leaders to terrify the followers.

Eusebius Pamphilus, the Bishop of Cesarea in Palestine, published a two-volume history of the early church around 325 AD called *The Martyrs of Palestine*.[385] It is recognized that the total number of Christians martyred by the Roman authorities was less than a thousand.[386] But each were apparently murdered, tortured and executed publicly in front of numerous witnesses. This being the case, their lives were written about and remembered.

In 62 AD during an interim between two Roman governors James, the brother of Jesus and a leader of the Jerusalem church, was stoned to death by Jewish authorities in the city. Two years later in 64 AD Paul of Tarsus, the preeminent New Testament missionary and scholar was executed in Rome. And one year later in 65 AD the Apostle Peter who delivered the famous Day of Pentecost sermon was publicly executed by crucifixion upside down in Rome. Both Paul and Peter could have escaped their fate, but chose not to. And in the crucifixion account of Peter's death, while dying upside down on the cross, he spoke at length to the crowd of onlookers about faith in Christ.[387]

These most admired and holy figures all died within three years of each other, yet the result was a strengthening of faith by example to believers and a solemn public testimony. Written records from the era state that even pagans found the bravery and steadfastness of the martyrs a proof of Christian virtue.[388] Strong evidence of such an effect comes out in the histories of another two famous martyrs in the church.

Ignatius, the Bishop of Antioch, was condemned to death during the reign of Emperor Trajan (98-117 AD). However, as he journeyed to Rome for his public execution, the attachment of Roman soldiers guarding him allowed Ignatius to preach throughout Asia Minor (modern day Turkey). In addition they also permitted the writing and delivery of seven famous letters of theology to the churches. From this account it's plain to see that instead of abusing Ignatius, the soldiers protected him with respect.

About fifty years passed and Polycarp, the Bishop of Smyrna, was burned alive in a public execution in the year 156. When the fires died down the Christian believers gathered his bones, publicly proclaimed they were more precious than Roman gold, and called all Christian believers to an annual celebration of his death. Though Roman officials witnessed these acts, they did nothing against them.[389]

Such bold devotion flew in the face of the pagan Roman authorities as these beloved and famous non-violent leaders of the faith suffered and died before crowds of onlookers gaining them a well-documented place in history.[390]

Changing an Empire

But Christianity not only gave pagan Roman authority a black eye, it delivered a series of crushing uppercuts, left hooks and incessant jabs to the face. In 300 years fifty percent of the population of the Roman Empire believed in the resurrected rabbi-carpenter from Nazareth.

Instead of mercy being a weakness of character, it became strength of character. Amidst the pagan chaos of the empire people were finding that their lives were of infinite worth to a loving creator who forgave sins and rebuilt broken lives. In short, Christianity brought a new concept of humanity to a world drowning in human cruelty and cheap life.

More than just a popular movement among the poor, belief in Christ captured the minds of scholars, commanding soldiers, political leaders, the rich, the poor, the middle class and even some emperors.

On October 28, 312 AD on the eve of the battle at the Mulvian Bridge, the Roman commander Constantine had a dream in which he saw the initial letters of the name of Christ with the words, "By this sign you will conquer." [391] Although he was not a Christian convert, in obedience to the vision he ordered the sign of the cross with the Chi-Ro (Greek letters) monogram painted on the shields of his soldiers. In the ensuing struggle, Maxentius, the opposing leader, lost the battle and his life, and Constantine won control of the Western Roman Empire.[392]

When he entered Rome in triumph, Constantine remembered to whom he owed his victory. The customary tributes of thanks to the gods of Rome were cancelled. Constantine declared the Christian God as the protector of the empire and the sponsor of his own mission for reform and reconstruction.

It is easily argued that such battlefield conversions disappear after survival or victory. For this reason the leaders of the Christian movement were not satisfied with the mere conversion experience of a pagan leader. According to church historian, Thomas Woods, "…the church had to continue to guide them, both to guarantee that the conversion had truly taken hold and to ensure that the faith would begin to transform their government and way of life." [393]

Constantine's conversion proved authentic. A year after his victory at Mulvian Bridge he issued the Edict of Milan in 313 recognizing Christianity as an acceptable religion, restoring previously confiscated church property and protecting Christian people from persecution. But in the eastern half of the Empire Lucinius, the pagan emperor, scoffed at the Edict of Milan and began persecuting anew the churches, thus dividing the empire over citizens' rights while sticking his finger in the eye of Constantine.

It was a bad move. By this time nearly one of every four Roman citizens was a Christian and Lucinius was soon to find out that the public sport of persecuting Christians was finished. In the first place, Constantine was a highly successful general and commander of the armies of Rome. Secondly, he was also an enthusiastic believer in the Christian religion.

The Emperor in Rome was in a peculiar position that Paul of

Tarsus had specifically taught about in his letter to the Roman churches saying that the purpose of the military authorities was to protect the citizens; reward good conduct and destroy evildoers.[394] The answer was there for Constantine though it would take some time to apply it, a full ten years would pass while diplomatic attempts failed.

As head of the Eastern Empire Lucinius was certainly acting wickedly by confiscating Christian's property, and torturing citizens for belief in Christ. Constantine knew his ultimate responsibility and made the decision to remove him by force. So, in 323 Constantine invaded Lucinius' territories, defeated his armies, and executed Lucinius.[395] The result, citizens across the empire had the protected right to freedom of worship, and that included Christianity.

Some historians have written that Constantine's actions had an "...unfortunate and abiding effect; for the first time Christ became a god of battles." [396] But Constantine acted on correct authority. Roman citizens were being treated unlawfully for their faith, a clear violation of any ruler's true authority. After all, who was Lucinius to kill and torture people because they met in houses and sang songs to God? These people raised no armies and made no plots to overthrow Rome.

But the other part of the equation was that Lucinius was not ruling over another sovereign country, but over another portion of the Roman Empire. And his actions were making void the rights of individual Roman citizens who each by law could appeal to Caesar (the emperor).[397] In political reality regarding the rule of law within the Roman Empire, Constantine acted correctly regardless of whether he was protecting the rights of Christian worshipers.

Then, with the Roman Empire under his sole authority, Constantine responded to the rising popularity of the Arian Heresy that denied Christ's divinity and sponsored the Council of Nicea. [398] Some have argued that he was forcing Christianity on everyone. Realistically, Constantine was responding to the change in society because belief in Christ was accelerating across the civilized world in an explosion of growth that included 27 million new converts in the first half of the 4th Century.[399]

As Emperor of the realm, Constantine's foresight showed political savvy. The Empire was undergoing an enormous social change as half the population was in the process of converting from paganism to Christianity. Such a sweeping and sudden change needed leadership and direction or social chaos might result.

In May 325 AD he summoned all the church bishops throughout the Roman Empire to Asia Minor where they met in the city of Nicea for the sole purpose of establishing a statement of orthodox Christianity. That very creed of orthodoxy hammered out at the Council of Nicea continues to this day. The 220 or so words of the Nicean Creed [400] are regularly recited in all languages wherever Christians worship and its precepts are the foundational concepts written in the statements of faith in countless Christian churches of all denominations.

Christian missions from the Mediterranean World spread into the outer regions of Europe and assisted in establishing new nations and laws in those regions that gave rise to new civilizations. As the old Roman Empire crumbled from inside, one of those new civilizations stopped an ominous conqueror dead in their tracks allowing for the emergence of Western Civilization. Adolf Hitler didn't approve. That story is next.

Part IV

The Facts For Our Survival

Chapter 14
The Christian Church Builds
Western Civilization

A Battle for the Ages

Three centuries after the Council of Nicea the Roman world was falling apart as the Muslim conquests in the east added the territories of Syria, Lebanon, Palestine, Egypt, Persia and Iraq to their growing empire. Mohammed's revelations from an angel in a cave led to this new religion of war, a religion that taught the sure way to heaven was to die in battle.

By 709 the Muslims controlled North Africa and the door was opened to take Western Europe by ferrying an army from the African coast fifteen miles across the Straits of Gibraltar into Spain. That's exactly what happened. Those invasions began in 711 and within two years (713) the Muslims had renamed the Iberian Peninsula in Arabic, *Al Andalus*. In less than 100 years the world was falling at the feet of an Islamic conquest. It was happening exactly as Mohammed foretold before his death in 622.

> I have been ordered (by Allah) to fight against the people until they testify that none has the right to be worshipped but Allah.[401]

According to Islamic world vision the Caliphs (Islamic Emperors) dispatched governor-generals to fight against all men to subject all nations to Islam. So, as the new governor of Al Andalus, Abdul Rahman marched north from Spain across the Pyrenees Mountains into Southern France with an undefeated army reinforced by 80,000 cavalry. As with the back of his hand he captured and sacked the cities of Toulouse and Bordeaux then moved further up to the center of the country where they were met at Tours in 732 by Charles Martel and a Frankish Army of 30,000 foot soldiers.

Having used back pathways instead of Roman roads the Franks

took Rahman's army by surprise. Positioned above them and on a hill walled in by forest on both sides the only attack for the Muslims was a frontal assault up hill into the twenty foot spears of Martel's disciplined phalanx. It was a battle plan they had prepared ten years to execute, and Martel had picked the time and place in such a manner as to negate the advantages of the infamous Muslim cavalry. Rahman tried to get the Franks out into the open with taunts and insults. Martel waited. Seven days he waited enduring the insults as they stood in the way of Abdul Rahman's advance. Finally, Rahman's army charged.

The repeated and ferocious attacks by superior numbers of Muslim cavalry proved unable to break the discipline of the Franks who mauled the Muslims inflicting casualties on a ratio of 10 to 1 that amounted to over 10,000 dead Muslims including their leader. Then with Abdul Rahman dead, his defeated army withdrew from France going back to Spain. The Franks at Tours proved to be the wall and the high water mark of Muslim conquest for some time to come.[402]

But it was the foresight of the church that helped stop the armies of Islam at Tours in the 8th Century. Because in the 6th Century as the protection of Rome faded around the edges of the empire, the church leaders such as Saint Remigius reached out to the barbarian kings. The result was the conversion and spread of Christianity among the Franks in the sixth and seventh centuries.

Their leaders were taught faith, order, and the role of leadership in protecting civilization. The church even guided the peaceful changing of power among the Franks from the Merovingian dynasty to the Carolingian family.[403] By the time the actual battle of Tours took place, Charles Martel had been training his professional army for ten years in anticipation of the Islamic invasion. Knowing the fate of Spain and the fame of the Islamic cavalry, the Franks arrived in stealth, blocked the path of Abdul Rahman's ambitious advance and won.[404]

Historians of our modern era remember the battle of Tours for its importance even though it took place 1300 years ago. According to military historian, Kennedy Hickman: "Charles' victory at the Battle of Tours saved Western Europe from the Muslim invasions and was a turning point in European history."[405] But perhaps even more revealing is the rage expressed against the outcome of the Battle of Tours by Adolf Hitler, himself. In the same breath he praised Islam and attacked Jews and Christianity:

Had Charles Martel not been victorious at Poitiers
(Tours) -already, you see, the world had already
fallen into the hands of the Jews, so gutless a thing
Christianity! -Then we should in all probability have
been converted to Mohammedanism, that cult which
glorifies the heroism and which opens up the seventh
heaven to the bold warrior alone. Then the Germanic
races would have conquered the world. Christianity
alone prevented them from doing so.[406]

Thus, the genocidal dictator of Nazi Germany grudgingly recognized the spread of Christianity for the victory. And from his ramblings
that day in late August of 1942, there is little wonder why Hitler forged
an alliance with Islam during World War II in order to destroy the Jews.
He looked out over the centuries and saw a kindred spirit. And when he
approached the Grand Mufti of Jerusalem he counted on the fact that
thirteen centuries of time had not changed their minds. In fact, he even
said he preferred to be a Muslim by conquest.[407]

Lucky for Western Civilization the Battle of Tours made Hitler
unhappy. While Charles Martel and his army at Tours receive credit for
stopping the advance of Islam and preserving Christian civilization in
Europe, the impact of what that meant came in the next two generations
and has remained with the civilized world ever since.

Charles Martel was leader of the Carolingians and father to the
most famous of all Franks, Charlemagne (768-814) who became known
as "The father of Europe." Under the leadership of Charlemagne and his
son, Louis the Pious, Europe experienced seventy years of scholarship
and development known as the Carolingian Renaissance.[408]

Uncovering God's Treasures

"Charlemagne strongly encouraged education and the arts calling
upon the bishops to organize schools around their cathedrals." [409] He
personally encouraged the Christian scholar, Alcuin, to teach the Latin
language that opened a treasure chest of early church history, ancient
Roman literature and the teaching of the seven liberal arts: astronomy,

music, arithmetic, geometry, logic, grammar, and rhetoric.

Fredegise who developed Carolingian miniscule,[410] a system of upper and lowercase letters that included punctuation and spaces between words, succeeded this great scholar as abbot of Saint Martin's monastery at Tours.[411]

Before Fredegise written language in Europe was regional and extremely confusing because no uniform system of punctuation existed. Words of written documents were strung together without spacing or periods. Philippe Wolff, the award-winning professor of Toulouse University in France said, "It would be no exaggeration to link this development with that of printing itself as the two decisive steps in the growth of a civilization based on the written word." [412]

In short, the church took on the burden of education and the monasteries were the production factories. So much so that Christopher Dawson, the renowned English scholar and author of twenty-six books on cultural history, said that it was the great monasteries that preserved education and scholarship and led to the development of the university system.[413]

No greater example exists than Saint Benedict (480-543) the founder of the monastery of Monte Cassino. By the 14th Century the Benedictine Order he began gave the world 37,000 monasteries.[414] They were the centers of learning that taught agriculture, crop growth, swamp reclamation, land development, cattle rearing, cheese making, bee keeping, wine making, beer brewing and the creation of champagne. Instead of being hidden in the monastery, the monks were out among the people spreading knowledge and creating economy.

In 1098 Saint Robert started the Cistercian Order as a reform within the Benedictines. Meeting annually to share technological progress, they developed industry-harnessing waterpower to crush wheat and tan leather. Extracting phosphates from the slag of their iron forges they created a potent fertilizer and discovered the secret to making a blast furnace two hundred years before the industrial revolution.[415]

Within the monastery walls were cures for sickness and the beds of an infirmary where the poor and destitute received ministry. Ancient manuscripts were carefully copied creating libraries for preserving the brilliance of past eras as well as the accuracy of the scriptures themselves. Add to those achievements metallurgy, glassworks, new crop discovery along with the establishment of schools and it can be truthfully said that the Church laid the foundation of Western Civilization.

Church scholarship connected the knowledge of the ancient past to the Middle Ages and into the present day by a unique phenomenon that didn't exist in ancient Greece and Rome. The church developed the university system, a natural next step since the depositories of scholarship and knowledge were within the monasteries and the cathedrals.

Church teachers in all fields of endeavor founded curriculum of study displaying intense commitment to reason and rational thought such as in the works of Thomas Aquinas that taught theology, law, philosophy and public policy.[416] Far from being a time of ignorance, thanks to Christianity, medieval intellectual life actually delivered Europe from the darkness.

And one of the most important factors of that deliverance was the systematic body of law developed by the church referred to as "Cannon Law." Around 1140 the monk, Gratian, finished the *Decretum,*[417] an enormous work that systematically presented law as a single body interacting as a whole for men and government. Drawing on a thousand years of history and vast in its scope, the Decretum included marriage, property, inheritance, and basics of modern contract law such as mistakes, duress, fraud and free will. Taken from the Decretum, Cannon Law took principles from the old and new testaments such as the Ten Commandments and the Golden Rule as well as traditions from classical eras of the Greeks and Romans.

Other portions covered equity of justice to protect the poor and helpless from the rich and powerful. Extenuating factors, legal liability, wrongful intent, the basis of crime, punishment befitting a violation, remedies equivalent to injury…and finally, rational procedures for hearings and trials; all these concepts were covered. Canon law revealed that law itself was universal protecting and benefiting all mankind regardless of religion. Medieval intellectuals found the work fascinating and flocked to the great law school of Bologna to study it.

The right to due process that is part of the Bill of Rights in the U.S. Constitution today emerged then as part of the universal natural law belonging to all men. So, just as there is a natural right of self-defense against physical assault, so too there exists a right to defend oneself against legal charges through reason and examination of evidence.

Pope Innocent IV actually taught Cannon Law at Bologna. In the middle of the 13th Century he wrote: "God makes his sun to rise on the good and the wicked and he feeds the birds of the air…ownership, possession and jurisdiction can belong to infidels licitly . . . for these things were made not only for the faithful but for every rational creature." [418] The Pope's statement of public policy starkly contrasted Islam's jihad that demanded all nations be conquered and subjected under their leadership.

These rights of man in his natural state, being derived from his creator, surfaced once again with the discovery of the new world. In 1492 King Ferdinand and Queen Isabella conquered Grenada, the final remaining Islamic sector in Spain. With the Muslims expelled and Spain united, Ferdinand and Isabella commissioned Christopher Columbus to find the new world. [419]

However, the rights of man didn't come to the forefront to make a new republic at that time. Instead, a Dominican Friar named Antonio de Montesinos scalded the colonial Spanish authorities for their behavior toward native peoples of the new world. Friar Antonio stirred things up so much with King Ferdinand that he demanded reforms.

Such reforms brought Father Francisco Vitoria's teaching to world attention. His work developed the first body of international law regarding the rights of man and the case for a just war. As the leading authority on the works of St. Thomas Aquinas, he concluded all human being were entitled to proper treatment by their creation as men. Pagan kings could not be deposed simply for their paganism, but all states were held to an international code of conduct in exchange with each other. [420]

A Sum of Achievements

The introduction of Christianity in the 1st Century spread a new moral order across the pagan Roman Empire out of which developed Christian civilization. The foresight of church fathers in the 6th Century led to the evangelizing of the barbarian Franks. Later, their repulsion of the Muslim armies from Western Europe at the Battle of Tours made way for seventy years of scholarship and discovery under Charlemagne, the father of Europe.

The study of Latin uncapped the treasuries of knowledge from the liberal arts and classic civilizations. The church developed a universal punctuation system that enabled the development of libraries and the spread of education. The monastic network founded the university system of higher learning leading to further discoveries in technology, medicine, architecture, civil engineering, and culminating with the law codes of Western Civilization. They included the rights of man originating with God, the responsibility of governments to recognize and protect such rights regardless of religion, and the basic universal law governing the conduct by governments and states towards each other.

In short, by changing the moral absolutes of the ruling governments, winning the peace, uncapping the treasuries of knowledge, and revealing the laws of man and nations, the church built Western Civilization and opened the way for a new world to emerge, a world that gave birth to the most powerful, free and wealthy nation in the history of mankind, The United States of America.

A New Nation Emerges

Less than fifteen years after the death of Jesus Christ in the 1st Century Paul the Apostle spoke in front of the philosophers and lawmakers of Greece in the city center of Athens known as the Areopogus (circa 50AD). In that speech Paul summed up the rights of man, the responsibility of the state, and justice under God. Saying that God created man, the state was responsible to provide order and freedom whereby a person can seek God in worship and live a responsible life knowing God's just character would rule over the final judgment of men. These are the ancient concepts over 2000 years old whose further development led to the birth of Western Civilization, as we know it.[421]

The principles were clearly restated in the one document that founded the United States, The Declaration of Independence. Thomas Jefferson set forth the case that the rights of mankind came from the Creator and not from the state or the church. These rights were to be recognized and protected by the civil government. So, all were gifted with rights merely by being people. With that one stroke of the pen, Jefferson disestablished state religion and guaranteed the liberty of individual worship.[422] In other words the state government couldn't tell a person what church to attend or make them pay money to any denomination. But at the same time the state was obligated to protect everybody's freedom to worship.

179

So bold was this concept, making government the protector of rights and servant of the people, that it rocked the world. And according to the memoirs of the Marquis de Lafayette, "The era of the American Revolution, which one can regard as the beginning of a new social order for the entire world, is...the era of...rights." [423]

Perhaps not for 2000 years were such concepts stated so clearly and briefly as they were affirmed in one paragraph of the United States Declaration of Independence. So overpowering and succinct, it is simply quoted in awe: [424]

> We hold these truths to be self-evident: that all men are created equal; that they are endowed, by their Creator, with certain inalienable rights; that among these are life, liberty, and the pursuit of happiness. That to secure these rights, governments are instituted among men, deriving their just powers from the consent of the governed. [425]

Each of the categorical rights encompasses the one to follow. The right to life is most important permitting personal liberty that opens doors to the pursuit of happiness. Government does not grant the rights to men. Men already have their rights. Government is created to recognize and protect those rights thus serving the people governed.

None of the concepts were new, [426] but had followed first from the Magna Carta of England written in the year 1215 AD. This document announced the power of law over the authority of men in government, stated the rights of man, and established a written contract between the governing authorities and the people. [427]

But the problem remained of enforcement. What if men in the government abused their authority and broke the laws of the Magna Carta? What then? Who would be able to punish them and reverse the unjust laws? The Confirmatio Cartarum of 1297 solved that problem and made the Magna Carta higher law overriding all legislation and court judgments to the contrary. This made the Magna Carta a type of constitution. [428]

So, 500 years before the United States of America, Englishmen established the process. First came a declaration of rights, then a contract of enforcement through a higher law of the land. It also followed the same pattern set by Moses and the Hebrew nation in Sinai 3300 years ago when Moses read the law before the people assembled and they consented to the contract.[429]

Following this pattern in the colonies The Constitution of Virginia was passed June 12, 1776 after the Virginia Bill of Rights was drafted and presented first to their convention a month earlier May 12, 1776.[430] Three weeks later the Declaration of Independence of the United States of America took effect July 4, 1776. Then twelve years afterwards, the Constitution of the United States was adopted September 17, 1787,[431] after the Treaty of Paris was signed by the United States and Great Britain ending the American Revolutionary War on September 3, 1783.[432]

Though The Magna Carta and The Confirmatio Cartarum set the pattern the United States followed for establishing individual rights and enforcing the rule of law, the two documents did not solve the huge problem of the separation of church and state.

Only 80 years after these two documents took effect in England John Wycliffe translated the Bible from Latin to English. "So what?" you might say. Well, he was tried in England three times in five years (1377-1382) for his disagreements with the Church over what he found in the translation process.[433]

Things got worse. Two centuries later William Tyndale's translation of the Bible into English from the original Hebrew and Greek manuscripts revealed corruptions used by the Church of Rome who controlled the Church of England. In 1535 he was brought before the authorities to answer for his "heretical" opinions, then tried, convicted, and burned at the stake in 1536 by Catholic authorities in England.[434] It was a terrible crime against religious freedom of thought and scholarship, as well as freedom of speech.

Both these two famous church scholars were persecuted and prosecuted because their religious teachings disagreed with the political authorities. It was the very same type of suffering that Jesus of Nazareth was put through by the Jewish authorities of his day. In William Tyndale's case, it cost him his life in the same manor as Polycarp, the Bishop of Smyrna who I referred to earlier in the section about church martyrs.

By the time Jefferson was writing the Declaration of Independence in 1776 Christian people had been fleeing to America from

England for 170 years. Jefferson's language was clearly secular citing only the Creator of mankind. Careful not to name God, the designer of the document entrusted a nation's future to the aspects of divine character that applied to civil government. Like a skilled surgeon, Jefferson removed the offense. The rights of mankind were not from any religion. Nobody was to be tried for religious offenses, but for civil rights violations alone. Why? It was because the rights of man are civil rights to be protected by a civil authority.

Twelve years later when The Constitution of the United States of America took effect the concept was extremely clear in the First Amendment that said no law could be made to establish a religion or prohibit the free exercise of worship that included scholarship, speech and artistic expression. [435]

Just imagine, today's nation that survived two invasions, a civil war, two world wars, the cold war and terrorism grew from a few thousand settlers into 300 million citizens with more power, wealth and influence than any nation in the history of man. Powerful testimony to the fact that "ideas have consequences."

The archeology tour was over and I'd walked back up the hill from the Kidron Valley to the old city walls by the Jaffa Gate. Unlocking the door of my Subaru I sat in the driver's seat and revved the engine. Later, as I drove back along the Bethlehem Road to my apartment in Canada Hill out on Mount Gilo, I thought about the storm that was brewing off on time's horizon. Islamic fascism was determined to destroy Israel and take down America as well. It reminded me of when I was in sixth grade.

The middle school I attended had a general science teacher who was a career officer in the United States Marines. A highly decorated veteran of the Korean War, Lieutenant Carter came to school every day dressed in his uniform. One day the school toughs were tormenting a small Jewish boy with glasses, and Lt. Carter found out about it. The next day the boy walked through the door into our class with Lt. Carter at his side. They stood in front of the room and with his hand on the boy's shoulder Lt. Carter said, "This is my friend, Tom Harris. You raise your hand against him, you raise it against me," and suddenly his voice went up to the level of a drill sergeant as he shouted, "Is that very clear!"

The room fell silent and I could hear my own heart beating. I remember the fire in the lieutenant's eyes and the steel warning in his loud voice. It was easy to see the incident disturbed something deep in his soul. He had a purple heart, a bronze star and a silver star for valor in the face of the enemy. Every boy in the room got the message.

As far as the United States and Israel were concerned, on May 14, 1948 eleven minutes after the birth of Israel as a nation, President Harry S. Truman announced that the United States of America officially recognized Israel.[436] A man of history changing decisions and great convictions, Truman effectively put his hand on the shoulder of the tiny Jewish nation as they faced opposition of five Arab countries and pledged the friendship of the United States.

Three years earlier the same man had commanded the dropping of atomic bombs on the Japanese homeland until they surrendered unconditionally. With her hand on Israel's shoulder, The United States was saying, "Is that clear!" to the world.

President Truman knew ancient history and read the *Memoirs of Alexander* in Greek. On behalf of the U.S. he acted on the promise God gave to Abraham centuries before saying, "I will bless those who bless you, and whoever curses you I will curse." [437] No country in the history of the world has experienced greater prosperity than the United States.

How could we do anything else? I thought. The foundations of our freedoms in America come from the Judeo-Christian revelation, and Israel is where it began. I wasn't alone in those thoughts. Peter Marshall, the Chaplain of the United States Senate, referred to America as "The New Israel." [438]

Looking through the eyes of his faith into the future another man saw The United States one hundred and forty years before it was born. John Winthrop stood on the deck of a tiny ship, The Arabella, in 1630 off the Massachusetts coast and said, "We will be as a city upon a hill. The eyes of all people are upon us." [439] And so have his words remained true for nearly 400 years.

In his farewell address from the Oval Office of The White House January 11, 1989, President Ronald Reagan said:

> The past few days when I've been at that window upstairs, I've thought a bit of the "shining city upon

a hill. ... And how stands the city on this winter night? ... After 200 years, two centuries, she still stands strong and true on the granite ridge, and her glow has held steady no matter what storm. And she's still a beacon, still a magnet for all who must have freedom... [440]

To savor the truth of Reagan's words just talk to new immigrants in America. It's refreshing. World history also records that the power of Reagan's legacy freed millions of people only two years later as the Russian Empire fell in 1991 during the Presidency of his successor, George Bush Sr.

Yet, as President Reagan spoke those words that cold January night in 1989, a dark storm was brewing only a few years off on time's horizon. Unknown to America at the time, the cold war continued at a secret training camp in the Caucus Mountains where the Russian KGB trained Al Qaeda terrorist commander, Ayman al Zawahiri.

The first wave of that dark storm broke against our shores September 11, 2001. And today, it 's far from being over. The outcome of that storm is up to Americans. We will choose our own future by the beliefs we hold and the leaders we elect. I'm sorry to say that it is totally possible for Americans to give away their liberty within the next ten years by ignoring our Judeo-Christian foundations. Tyranny waits at the door within our very borders right now. How is that possible? Turn the page and I'll explain.

Chapter 15
Threat Level Orange

"A thief is only there to steal and kill and destroy."

Across from me stood Paul Fynn, 5 feet 6 inches tall and 125 pounds. Born in a grass hut village in Ghana, West Africa that kept no written records, Paul didn't know how old he was. But the missionaries that educated him discovered his brilliance and after mastering English, Paul received scholarships to American universities where he earned his degrees in law and government.

In the hopes of leading his own country to a better life, Paul returned to Ghana and ran for election as President. But he lost to a Communist candidate and had to flee for his life as a political refugee. As I interviewed him, he broke the mold and began quizzing me.

"Do you know what America means to the world?" he asked me.

"Freedom and economic opportunity," I answered confidently.

"That and much more," he said. "America is the great beacon of freedom's light that gives hope throughout the world shining into every corner. Because you exist the darkness of tyranny cannot cover the earth. Do you realize that?"

After a second or two of silence he followed with an ominous warning. "In case you don't realize it, if the light from America ever goes out, darkness will descend across the world very quickly."[441]

Perhaps it took a political refugee from Africa to remind me that outside of the United States in many countries of the world tyranny is crouched at the door just waiting for the right opportunity to get in. We dare not forget that…because what begins "over there" will reach us "over here".

In today's world seventy years have passed since the armies of darkness threatened to defeat America and cover the earth with tyranny in World War II. Now, an entire generation of Americans has no feeling or recollection of the danger of that era save listening to the voice of a grandparent who lived through it or seeing movies like *Saving Private Ryan* and *Schindler's List*. It took the deaths of three thousand Americans on 9/11 for us to realize there even was another war going on that made us the targets.

We weren't listening twenty years earlier in 1989 as thunderous cheers broke out in the Kansas City convention hall where two Muslim organizations held a conference. The speaker at the podium was bragging about killing Americans and Jews on a bus in Israel. He then called for Muslims living in America to take up arms against the U.S.A.[442]

On 9/11/2001 the fascist Islamic jihad to conquer the world succeeded on American soil and won a battle. That war is not over. They want to cause catastrophe and make us live in fear. Even as you read this, further plans are being made by our enemies to create mass destruction and cripple our nation. That's because of the nature of the enemy, their origins and their aspirations. They mean to turn out the light of freedom in America. They mean to chip away at our freedoms through political correctness until they can take over…even if it takes fifty years. Let me explain.

The Pattern for Success

As I wrote in chapter 9, the most important event in the success of Islam is the *Hijra,* or the flight. It took place 1400 years ago in the 6th Century (622 AD) when Muhammad moved the believers in Arabia from the town of Mecca further south to Medina.[443] The pattern of that success has always been the model to repeat worldwide even until today. Here's why.

In order to move his entire community he had to make an immigration agreement with the three Jewish communities that populated the region of Medina. The pact they concluded made a distinction between Muslims and everybody else in the world labeling the Muslims a unique "nation unto themselves" with Muhammad as both the head of their state and their religion as well as the interpreter of Allah's voice.[444] He possessed all the same powers as the Emperor of Rome, but his empire was smaller at least for the time being.

Anybody who offended Muhammad and the Muslims committed a religious offense as well as an international aggression against *the Islamic nation* because the nation and the religion were one and the same…no frontier boundaries, just people. So, from that time onward Islam the religion became Islam the nation, and took on a militant national policy against all offenders.[445] In effect, it established a heritage of rage and a religion of vengeance. Somebody somewhere sometime was offending the believers.

In one clever move Muhammad changed the laws of Medina to favor the Muslims giving them their own country wherever they lived, a state within another state that answered only to itself. [446] Allah and Muhammad were the final say in all matters.[447] So, what appeared to be "legal immigration" on the surface was actually a deceitful prelude to conquest. Within a few years the Jewish communities saw the trickery, but it was too late for their survival.[448]

Western civilization now faces the same crisis. "You have to live like a state within the state until you take over," said the teacher at Green Lane Mosque. "The summit of Islam is jihad," said another. In January of 2007 teacher Abu Usama called for Muslims to begin civil wars to establish an Islamic state wherever they lived.[449]

This follows the "blueprint" of the Hijra in 622 AD. After the immigration and the legal changes in Medina, Muhammad's ongoing revelations justified his militia to attack public transportation, disrupt economy, slaughter the local citizens and confiscate their lands.[450] Islam set their own rules, and those were aggression.[451] Does any of this sound familiar, yet? Public transportation attacked, economy disrupted and innocent citizens slaughtered, 9/11 perhaps? This exact plan of conquest carried out in the Hijra is taking place within America right now, today. Don't believe it? Keep reading.

There is mounting evidence that many Muslim immigrants to the United States seek far more than a better way of life in America. They are actually working to overthrow our nation and change America into a Muslim country. Captured documents presented by the FBI in their indictment of a Muslim charity named The Holy Land Foundation revealed a sinister plan to destroy America and set up a Muslim emperor known as a Caliph. Sounds fantastic, far fetched…but it's happening even now right under our noses.

The Secret Society

Let's start with the Muslim Brotherhood, said to be the largest Islamic movement in the modern era.[452] Today, they openly sponsor other organizations throughout the United States including the Holy

Land Foundation indicted by the FBI. But their dark history should ring the alarm bells for every American who loves liberty.

Looking back eighty years to one ominous evening in 1929 by the banks of the Suez Canal in the town of Ismailiya just seventy miles northwest of Cairo, Egypt, Hassan al-Banna founded the Muslim Brotherhood.[453] Within four years his friendship with Adolf Hitler motivated the Fuehrer to hire the Muslim Brotherhood as a secret arm of Nazi Intelligence. Al-Banna's Arab Nazis extended the German Nazi influence throughout the Middle East by building a spy network. They hated Jews; they hated democracy; and they hated Western culture.[454]

In 1937 Adolf Eichmann (the architect of the German death camps that killed six million European Jews) went to Jerusalem to meet personally with the Grand Mufti, Haj Amin al Husseini, the most powerful Muslim in the world. There, al-Husseini and Eichmann agreed to work together for the mass murder of the Jews. They exchanged cultures. The very next year the Muslim Brotherhood translated Hitler's *Mein Kampf* into Arabic and the Nazis demanded 20th Century Jews in Germany wear the yellow stars required for Jews in 8th Century Islam. The Nazis adopted the Islamic badges for Jews and the Islamic Brotherhood adopted Nazism.[455]

As the scope of their influence expanded during World War II, Haj Amin al-Husseini, the Grand Mufti of Jerusalem (the highest official of Islam in Palestine), headed the Palestinian section of the Muslim Brotherhood and became their personal representative to Adolf Hitler with an office in Berlin.[456]

When the Grand Mufti first met personally with Hitler November 28, 1941, he pledged to help Germany win WW II and exterminate the Jews of Europe and Palestine. Meanwhile, back in Egypt, Hassan al-Banna sent word to Hitler promising that the Muslim Brotherhood would kill the British soldiers when the Nazi armies invaded the Middle East.[457] The plan was set.

To Hitler Islam was the key ally for Nazi world conquest and he said so at his midday table talk session recorded by Martin Bormann, the head of the Nazi Party Chancellery on August 28, 1942.[458] As a result, the Arab Nazis helped the German Nazis with genocide against the Jews of Europe.[459]

Hitler put Adolf Eichmann in command of the German death camps that killed six million European Jews. Then, Grand Mufti Husseini and Eichmann proudly toured the gas chambers and ovens of the death camps together. As Hassan al-Banna's personal representative, Husseini expressed his confidence to both Hitler and Eichmann that the Muslim Brotherhood would carry out the *Jewish final solution* in the Middle East.[460]

Adolf Eichmann's deputy, Dieter Wisliceny said later: "The Mufti … was one of Eichmann's best friends and had constantly incited him to accelerate the extermination measures." [461] Grand Mufti Husseini bragged that he got it straight from the top, "I asked Hitler for an explicit undertaking to allow us to solve the Jewish problem in a manner befitting our national and racial aspirations and according to the scientific methods (gas chambers and ovens) innovated by Germany in the handling of its Jews," said Husseini. "The answer I got was: 'The Jews are yours.'" [462]

Nazism Moves to the Middle East

But the Germans lost the war. American bombers destroyed German industry. Hitler committed suicide. The American Army liberated the death camps and hanged the Nazi leadership team. Testimony at the 1945 Nuremberg trials of Nazi war criminals tied Amin al-Husseini to Hitler, Himmler and Adolf Eichmann in the killing of six million European Jews.[463] Though German Nazism was beaten, in Egypt and the Middle East it lived on. Why? The Mufti returned to the Middle East to continue the movement together with Hassan al-Banna.

Holding dear to him his experience and commission from Hitler, the Mufti escaped Germany and received political asylum in Egypt in 1946. The next year he recruited an intense 5 feet 4 inch street gang leader in Cairo from his own Husseini family clan and put the 17-year-old thug in charge of running guns for the 12,000 Muslim Brotherhood's forces in Palestine during the Israeli War of Independence in 1948.

When Israel defeated the Arab armies, both Amin al-Husseini and Hassan al-Banna promoted their cause blaming failure on the secular Arab governments. And the young gunrunner, Yassir Arafat, launched his own political career with the help of the Muslim Brotherhood.[464]

However, the next year in 1949 Egyptian agents hunted down and shot Hitler's ally, Hassan al-Banna, in return for his part in the assassination of Egypt's Prime Minister.[465] Afterwards, Sayyid Qutb rose to prominence in the Brotherhood and preached worldwide Nazi-Islamic war. Today, he's considered to be the father of modern radical Islam.[466]

Preaching that Islamic peoples brought misery and failure upon themselves by submitting to "manmade governments," Qutb had the answer: Return to religion. Reestablish Allah's favor on Muslims through obedience and world conquest.[467] Sound fascist? Check the Quran. I've provided the references.[468]

Qutb connected the racism and world conquest of the Nazis to the will of Allah. Knowing that Hitler actually praised Islam naming Jews and Christians the obstacles to world conquest, Qutb found no contradictions.[469]

He wrote that all Muslims should resist and overthrow all non-Islamic governments. Quoting from the Quran he said that Allah guaranteed the success of the devout and preached that peace would only come after all peoples of the earth were subjected to Islamic law because only Islam had the right to govern men.[470]

Saying Islam requires unquestioning acceptance of Sharia (strict Islamic law) and rejection of all other laws in any shape or form, Sayyid Qutb wrote in his book, *Milestones*: "This is Islam. There is no other meaning of Islam." [471]

Disguised as a social organization, Qutb's Muslim Brotherhood became accepted at Mosques, schools, universities, and trade associations throughout Egypt. But in 1954 the Brotherhood tried to assassinate President Nasser who banned them from public life in Egypt.

Thousands fled to neighboring Saudi Arabia and were accepted as teachers in the religious schools known as *madrassas*. There, the Muslim Brotherhood mingled their Nazi fascism with fundamentalist Islam. And it was there in a Saudi madrassa where Brotherhood teachers taught a man named, Osama bin Ladin.[472]

Since Egypt is a large country, it was easy for the Brotherhood to migrate back and flourish again. However, like al-Banna his predecessor, Sayyid Qutb was also willing to kill his own country's leaders as punishment for thinking outside the Quran box. In 1966 Qutb was convicted and hanged for trying to overthrow the Egyptian government.[473]

The next year the united Arab armies suffered another crushing defeat as the Israelis won The Six Day War in June 1967. Though both al-Banna and Qutb were gone, Islamic fascism had taken hold in the Arab world. As I explained in the chapter, *Six Days That Changed the*

World, the Arabs met at Khartoum later the same year reaffirming both Nazism and militant Islam with three major premises.[474]

First, all Arab states shared the obligation to destroy Israel together as the universal obligation of Islam. Second, peace could never exist since only cease-fires were permitted between Islam and infidels. And third, cease-fires had to be broken to renew the war for world conquest and fulfill Islam's ultimate destiny to subjugate all non-Muslim peoples of the world.[475]

Since the Arab armies hadn't succeeded in their military conquest, it was determined to wage holy war by indoctrinating and subverting other nations across the world. So for the next twenty years from 1967-1987, Yassir Arafat and the Palestine Liberation Organization waged unconventional war without end. Meanwhile, the Muslim Brotherhood built Mosques, schools, charities, sport clubs and social organizations in non-Muslim as well as Muslim countries all with one goal in mind. According to counter-terrorism specialist, Matthew Levitt, that goal is: "to indoctrinate an entire rebellious generation to explode against Western Civilization." [476]

In the Middle East eleven years after the execution of Sayyid Qutb, Egypt's President Anwar Sadat made a history-changing move by being the first Arab leader to visit Israel on an official visit. He spoke before the Israeli Parliament, was named Time Magazine's *Man of the Year*, and later shared the Nobel Peace Prize with Israeli Prime Minister Menachem Begin for their history breaking Camp David Peace Agreement that made permanent peace between Israel and Egypt.[477]

For this the Muslim Brotherhood labeled President Sadat an Islamic heretic. In sympathy with the Muslim Brotherhood Yassir Arafat publicly called for Sadat's assassination.[478] Then, a blind Brotherhood imam named Omar Abdul-Rahman gave the "death command" from Allah and four Brotherhood soldiers gunned down President Sadat October 6, 1981 at a national military parade in Cairo.[479]

Coming to America

In 1963 the Muslim Brotherhood entered undercover into the United States and founded the Muslim Student Association (MSA) with the purpose of starting a movement to establish Islam in America as "a total way of life". That's code talk for takeover. They actually brag about this on their website. You can easily read it for yourself at http://web.archive.org/web/20021206132514/www.masmn.org/Other/About_Us.htm [480]

According to the chief counter terrorism advisor for both Presidents Clinton and Bush, the Muslim Brotherhood is at the center of a web linked to Islamic terrorist organizations attacking the United States.[481] Following Sayyid Qutb's model, their goal in America became the establishment of Islamic law as the means of controlling the affairs of the state and the society. Of course, that meant replacing the U.S. Constitution with the Quran, and they said as much publicly.[482] For instance, their reading materials distributed to the young in America teach children that all Muslims are duty bound to establish Islamic governments, exterminate Jews and Christians and take up arms in revolt.[483]

In 1992, thirty years after their covert entry into the U.S.A, the Brotherhood founded the Muslim American Society (MAS) as a legitimate non-profit organization saying the time had come for them to fulfill their aspirations in America.[484] Since Hassan al-Banna founded it in Egypt in 1929, the Muslim Brotherhood assassinated or attempted to kill every President of Egypt. One could only imagine what their hopes were for America.

We didn't have to wait long to find out. The next year in 1993 the same blind imam connected to Anwar Sadat's murder came to America on a visa and carried out the first World Trade Center bombing. Since then, the FBI has directly linked the Muslim Brotherhood to fundraising for terrorism.[485]

Today, the Muslim Student Association, the original Muslim Brotherhood organization in the United States, operates 150 chapters nationwide at our top universities intimidating patriotic American and Jewish students with Islamic hate speech according to author, Nonie Darwish in, *Now They Call Me Infidel.*[486]

At one of their meetings in March 2003, 23-year-old Muhammad Faheed went to the podium at Queensborough Community College in New York and said, "We must not recognize any government authority, or any authority at all besides Allah. We are not Americans," he shouted. "We are Muslims... reject America...we don't recognize Congress! The only relationship you should have with America is to topple it!" Faheed finished by calling on the students to join terrorist organizations and prepare for armed confrontation within America.[487]

Who knows what kind of violence will come from students taking the advice of people like Faheed? Will Muslims riot, burn down buildings and kill Christians as they did in Denmark? Perhaps they will start fights to get their own prayer rooms on state properties, or maybe they will give death threats to censor city newspapers and websites who say things they don't like. Why? Because it's never over, there's always an excuse. Somewhere in the world, someone will end up dead for "insulting Islam."[488]

And why is that? It's because the Islamists practice the principles of the Hijra agreement recognizing no laws higher than their own, so they are obligated to subject all mankind to the "Islamic way of life". It's because they believe the indoctrination of the Muslim Brotherhood and Sayyid Qutb who says four times in three pages of his book *Milestones* that the Muslim community has the obligation to take over "leadership of the world" by the conquest of Christendom (those nations where the Christian religion flourishes).[489] In case there's any doubt America, that's us. We have a bull's-eye painted across our backs. Just ask the likes of Osama bin Laden.

"We do not have to differentiate between military or civilian," said bin Laden about Americans. "As far as we are concerned, they are all targets." [490]

When he said this bin Laden summarized an entry from a Muslim commentary of Muhammad's life, *Sahih Bukhari, Book 52, Fighting for the Cause of Allah, (Jihaad).* Saying that pagans were pagans, Muhammad sanctioned killing innocent women and children the same as enemy combatants.[491] In other words, this is a doctrine as old as the first years of the religion.

If the events of 9/11 were a freak accident pulled off by a few kooks, I wouldn't be writing this book. But it wasn't. Investigations revealed a worldwide organization that trained, financed and placed kamikaze operatives on our soil. Raising millions of dollars through racketeering and charitable "Islamic front" organizations in America, they have operated their own crime syndicate.

In his brilliant book *Infiltration* author Paul Sperry lays bare this "Muslim Mafia" and their connections to terror worldwide. We've all heard the names Hamas, Hezbollah, al-Qaeda and so forth. Paul Sperry found that they are all connected to a secret Islamic society known as…

guess who…The Muslim Brotherhood.[492] Imagine that.

Feud or Fact

When I think back to my time in Lebanon, I'm puzzled remembering that it was the leaders of the Christian community in Lebanon who were identified as mafia dons by the American press. Compared to the Muslim Brotherhood, however, they are small time amateurs.

A prize-winning author compared the Middle East conflict to the hillbilly feud Mark Twain wrote about in *The Adventures of Huckleberry Finn* where nobody seemed to know why and where it all started.[493]

But there is a reason. Judaism was preached and practiced throughout the Middle East for 1500 years before Islam came into existence. Born from Judaism, Christianity expanded out of Jerusalem and spread throughout the countries of the Middle East flourishing for six hundred years before Islam started. Fifty-six percent of the total populations of the Middle East countries were Christians by the year 350 AD, two hundred and seventy years before Islam existed. [494] Those countries are Syria, Egypt, Lebanon, Iraq, Jordan, and Israel. And that means six out of ten citizens in those countries were Christians.

For three hundred years before Islam existed Christianity was by far the dominant religion affecting the life of the Middle East. Following the acceleration curve of growth plotted by sociologist, Dr. Rodney Stark, as many as seven in ten citizens of the Middle East region professed Christianity by the year 600 AD.[495] No other multi-state geographical area has been so saturated with the Christian faith until today's 21st Century United States where seventy percent profess Christianity.[496] The Middle East was Christian long before it was forced to become Islamic.

When the armies of Islam spread out of Arabia to conquer the world in the 7th Century, they were attacking a Middle East saturated with churches. They attacked Christendom to force those nations to accept Islam, not the other way around. The conquered peoples were called *dhimmis*, victims who lived as the vanquished under Islamic rule without human rights.[497]

Their lands were confiscated, their young women turned into concubines, their families massacred, their towns pillaged, and entire Christian populations deported.[498] Their art was confiscated while their churches were burned or turned into mosques. All professional and artistic skills of the Dhimmi Jews and Christians were turned to serve the Islamic state.

According to Islamic law it was unlawful to kill children because all children were born Muslim. For this reason the parents could be killed and the children raised Muslim.[499] After four hundred years of subjection under brutal Islamic regimes, Western European nations feared the worst for Middle East Christians. Four and a half centuries passed between the fall of Jerusalem to Islamic armies and the beginning of the first crusade in 1096 AD.[500]

Blaming the Crusaders for attacking innocent and peaceful Islam is a reversal of causality. It's a main plank in the platform of deceit meant to play on guilt in the West and evoke sympathy to Islam. The Middle East was Jewish, then Christian long before it was forced to be Islamic.

In the modern era beginning after World War II the slogan of Islamic fascism became: "Today it is Zionism's turn, tomorrow it will be Christianity's; today is Saturday, tomorrow will be Sunday."[501] That means kill the Jews then kill the Christians.

My time and research in Lebanon and Israel revealed not a feud, but a continuous Islamic war to reconquer the democratic states of Lebanon and Israel and establish Islamic hegemony in those countries. It was fascism vs. liberty. Not seeing that missed the forest through the trees. But even more disturbing, I found the jihad movement planned to come to the United States.

Realistically, to most Americans the Middle East conflicts did seem like nothing more than a big blood feud. As long as they stayed over there, who cared? Then, the Islamists attacked us on United States soil? Was that meant to help the Arab's win the argument over who gets the strip of "Occupied Palestine" called Israel? Certainly they mean to manipulate us with terror on the issue of our support for Israel.

Do they also mean to conquer us as well? Of course they do, otherwise why all the trouble? Why infiltrate our society and our university system? Why set up an elaborate crime syndicate. Why the legal defense and Islamic civil rights organizations run by the Muslim Brotherhood? And why the network of terror cells across our nations cities?[502] Do you suppose it's the pattern of the Hijra, immigration, legal change and takeover?

A 30-Year War

Their strategy goes back 30 years to when Iran's Ayatollah Khomeini held Americans hostage in 1979 for over a year and preached to the Islamic faithful across the world demonstrating that the United States was weak willed and couldn't endure the coming struggle. The time of Islamic world conquest had arrived. America was the great Satan and Israel the little Satan.[503]

Identified as one of the gang leaders who took the U.S. Embassy hostage in 1979, Iranian President Ahmadinejad denied the holocaust saying, "They have invented a myth that Jews were massacred."[504]

"Whoever recognizes Israel," he said, "will burn in the fires of Islam."[505] And quoting Ayatollah Khomeini, Ahmadinejad said, "Our dear Imam ordered that the occupying regime in Israel be wiped off the face of the earth. This was a very wise statement…how can we have *a world without America and Zionism*? But you know well that this slogan can be achieved." [506]

And how will Israel and America disappear from the world? According to John Bolton, U.S. Under Secretary for Arms Control and International Security, "Iran is pursuing two separate paths to nuclear weapons." [507]

What other conclusion can we make? We have the documented words of two generations of Iranian leaders, one the teacher and another the disciple. In pursuit of nuclear weapons and calling for the hellfire destruction of both Israel and America, what are we to think? Not only do they seek nuclear weapons, they brag to the world about what they intend to do with them. Attack America and annihilate Israel.[508] For some reason, the Islamic Revolution believes America lacks the will to fight with nuclear weapons.

Does Iran really want to test our will?

This scenario is not only ridiculous but absolutely tragic for the Iranian nation. The United States has 9,962 nuclear warheads ready to use with a destructive power of 3,405 megatons of TNT.

Both the WW II nuclear bombs dropped on Japan added together were only 34 kilotons with one kiloton equivalent to 1000 tons of TNT. One megaton, however, equals 1 million tons of TNT, or 60 of the bombs from WW II.[509] Right now America has the capability of unleashing the destructive power of 204,300 bombs the size of those dropped in WW II. The question is how to deliver such devastating power successfully against an enemy. For that America can choose stealth bombers, land launched missiles or mobile platforms on Navy ships. Let's just look at the navy.

The U.S. Navy has 280 ships. Ten of those are Nimitz Class nuclear super carriers. With each carrier eleven hundred feet long housing 6000 sailors and pilots, a Nimitz Class aircraft carrier is a city afloat. All ten nuclear-powered Nimitz Class ships might carry nuclear bombs in sealed lockers under 24-hour armed guard. The Navy's F/A 18 jets can deliver the B83, 1.2-megaton thermonuclear bomb to targets 1000 miles away from the carriers.[510] With 600 of these B83 bombs deployed in active service two aircraft carriers could send a wave of 70 birds of death armed with multiple nuclear bombs at Iran.[511] But there is no reason to send a single pilot in harm's way for such a mission.

The United States Navy has 18 Ohio Class Trident nuclear missile submarines (SSBN's) on active duty patrolling the world this very day. They are specifically designed to approach by stealth and shower an enemy with multiple nuclear warheads with absolutely no warning. They submerge and don't surface for their entire cruise making them undetectable by an enemy. They travel submerged at 25 knots (30mph) 800 feet beneath the ocean's surface with refueling necessary once every twenty years.[512]

Each sub has 24 Intercontinental Ballistic Missiles.[513] Launched in stealth from underwater, each of these solid fuel rockets is expected to have a flight time of just 12 to 24 minutes and could hit targets up to 6,000 miles away within an accuracy space of 10 yards. At least one submarine is within range of Iran at this moment.[514]

One sub launched missile packs 8 independent 475-kiloton nuclear warheads. When detonated, the 300,000 degree fireball from each warhead is 3 miles wide sustaining temperatures over 15,000 degrees. Within 3 seconds 165 mph winds blast outward creating 64 square miles of destruction from a single warhead. Since each missile has eight such warheads, using overlapping deployment technique, a total nuclear blast area melts five hundred square miles with one missile.[515] The multiple warheads of one missile from a trident submarine can completely destroy both the Iranian cities of Tehran and Mashhad in less than fifteen minutes. Am I making myself clear?

All 24 missiles on any one trident submarine can be launched within 15 minutes and reach their targets in a half hour. In other words, each trident submarine has the capability of delivering 192 overlapping nuclear explosions within less than an hour anywhere in the world creating a destructive nuclear blast area of 12,000 square miles. The payload from one Trident sub will obliterate Iran in thirty minutes. [516] And since the U.S.A. has 18 SSBN's we could unload more subs if necessary on anybody who might object.

We know that today, Iran seeks nuclear weapons to launch strikes against Israel and the United States. In contrast, twenty four hours a day and seven days a week for over thirty years the United States Navy has possessed the ability to approach with stealth and shower the Iranian civilization and her allies with nuclear destruction the temperature of the sun within any hour of any day. They live because we don't think like they think.

In 1979 when Iran held 52 Americans hostage in the U.S. Embassy in Tehran, the American man-on-the-street wanted to "melt Iran into a parking lot." President Carter's restraint prevented such a tragedy and cost him re-election in 1980.

I can only imagine a post 9/11 America picking up the pieces and burying our dead after a preemptive nuclear strike from Iran. The rage will never be contained. It would mean the destruction of the entire Iranian civilization, a nation rich in history and culture.

I can't imagine the Iranian people want to risk such a tragedy. Perhaps we should find a way to remind President Ahmadinejad of the consequences of a nuclear strike against us. Who knows? Perhaps there is a chance he could stop believing his own foolish posturing.

America is by no means weak; instead we are armed to the teeth and strong willed enough to restrain ourselves. However, given the Islamofascist agenda for world conquest and chaos, the way I see it America has three choices and so does Iran. America's choices are:

1. We can renounce Israel and our freedom.
2. We can wait until Iran launches a nuclear strike that could cost a million dead American and Israeli citizens.
3. We can strike first.

Iran's choices are:

1. They can change their foreign policy.
2. They can attack with nuclear weapons.
3. They can continue to support global terrorism.

But such choices are only my opinion and I am neither a diplomat nor a commander in charge of such destructive power. I am merely a journalist and a writer. But as surely as I discovered 23 years ago on the streets of Bent Jbeil, Lebanon that the jihad was coming to America, a showdown is coming with Iran.

And let's not be naive. To cause maximum damage and chaos such a rogue Arab nuclear attack will seek coordination with the Arab terror cells already established throughout American cities.[517] Since we've already allowed the enemy residency, our foolishness has painted us into a dangerous corner...and our enemies know it. But do we know it?

"Six years after 9/11, we're still asleep," wrote Ron Dreher on September 11, 2007. "Islamic radicals have declared war on us – and some are fighting here in what looks like a fifth column." [518] My fellow Americans, they're taking away our freedoms a little at a time. It's time we wake up!

Husain Haqqani, the Director of the Center for International Relations and Professor at Boston University, agrees with the FBI indictment presented in the Holy Land prosecution. Haqqani confirms that the Muslim Brotherhood runs a network of organizations in the United States as a *jihad process* to destroy the American civilization.[519] Your guess is as good as mine why we permit this nonsense anywhere inside our borders.

In Chapter three I told the story of how my cheap landlord in Kiryat Shemona took the screens off the windows of the apartment I rented from him to keep them for himself. The rats from the streets made a home in my apartment before I moved in. Once the rats were there, they thought my house was theirs and were willing to fight me for it. That's where we are today. Our immigration foolishness took the screens off and let in the rats. Now they mean to fight us for our own living room.

But there is a way you and I can fight back that will be the most effective. We can rediscover who we are as Americans and where our freedoms come from. This one step will thunder doom upon the dreams of a Muslim cultural and legal jihad in America.

Before it's too late my fellow Americans we must reconnect with who we are.

Chapter 16
To Secure These Blessings

President Abraham Lincoln said we are a nation born from liberty and dedicated to living out the proposition that all men are created equal.[520] Those weren't just pretty words when he said them because Lincoln was referring to the system of slavery being abolished through war in the United States and his words were part of the speech he gave dedicating the Gettysburg Battlefield where four days of fighting in 1863 left 50,000 men dead in the American Civil War.

The United States of America was only 87 years old at the time of Lincoln's Gettysburg address yet he asked, "whether that nation, or any nation so conceived, and so dedicated, can long endure." [521] Lincoln asked if America would still exist as originally designed so, "that government of the people by the people for the people *shall not perish from the earth*." [522]

What a powerful statement! It's as if President Lincoln knew there would never be another chance for mankind to build another United States. He was asking the same question that Paul Fynn asked me 116 years later.[523] Do you know what America means?

Who are we? We are the great experiment of liberty in the history of the world that says men have the right to rule themselves under law. What law? Whose law? Answer those two questions wrongly and America will fall into tyranny. Answer them correctly and we will endure as we have for another 230 years; but answer we must.

It's not that difficult. The founding document of the United States of America is The Declaration of Independence. It states that the "Laws of Nature and of Nature's God" entitle a nation of people to separate themselves from tyranny because:

> We hold these truths to be self-evident, that all men are created equal, that they are endowed by their Creator with certain unalienable Rights, that among these are Life, Liberty and the pursuit of Happiness.
> — That to secure these rights, Governments are

instituted among Men, deriving their just powers
from the consent of the governed.[524]

These "Laws of Nature and of Nature's God" were not some
invention of religious men who wanted an excuse to start a nation.
The most respected legal theorist of the time, Sir William Blackstone,
explained their meaning and their use in his *Commentaries on the Laws
and Constitution of England.* [525] The laws of nature referred to the will
of God revealed in creation and the conscience of men while the laws
of nature's God were revealed in the scriptures.[526] These were the laws
that gave every person the right to life, liberty and the ownership of
property.

Samuel Adams, the Father of the American Revolution, said that
the laws of the Creator equally bind all men. And the first Secretary of
the Treasury, Alexander Hamilton, wrote that the laws of nature were
dictated into creation by God and remained binding over all the globe, in
all countries, at all times. Thomas Jefferson who wrote the Declaration
of Independence said, "The God who gave us life gave us liberty at the
same time." [527] So according to these founding fathers, God made the
rules and they don't change over time.

Because the rights of Americans came from God through the laws
of nature and nature's God, what God gives no man can take away.[528]
This is who we are as Americans; people entitled to live free by the
character of the Creator who made us.

But after the United States won its independence in the
Revolutionary War, Americans had to form a government that obeyed
the principles in the Declaration for which they fought and died. That's
the purpose of our Constitution approved twelve years later in 1788,
"...in Order to form a more perfect Union...and secure the Blessings
of Liberty to ourselves and our Posterity."[529] So even the United States
Constitution acknowledges that our liberties are a blessing from God.

Whose God and whose laws? In answering that question plain
speaking President Harry S. Truman left no doubt. He said:

> The fundamental basis of this nation's laws was
> given to Moses on the Mount. The fundamental basis
> of our Bill of Rights comes from the teachings we
> get from Exodus and St. Matthew, from Isaiah and

St. Paul. If we don't have that proper fundamental
moral background, we will finally end up with a
totalitarian government which does not believe in
rights for anybody.[530]

Notice that Truman made no mention of Allah, Muhammad or the
Quran, none at all. Today, it's common to hear someone say, "Oh, that
was what they believed back then and we live in a different era, now."
So, America should throw away its foundation based on unchanging
laws in order to adapt to a different epic of time. How irrational is that?

James Madison, the 4th President of the United States disagreed.
He said, "The belief in a God All Powerful wise and good is... essential
to the moral order of the world and to the happiness of man." And after
serving eight years as the 3rd U.S. President, Thomas Jefferson wrote
in 1809, "We all agree in the obligation of the moral precepts of Jesus
and nowhere will they be found delivered in greater purity than in his
discourses." [531]

We are free today because our forefathers believed, wrote,
thought, lived, died and bet the house on the truth of the Judeo-Christian
scriptures of the Bible, nothing less. In fact, The Supreme Court of The
United States declared, "America was a Christian nation from its earliest
days." [532]

This is who we are, and this is where we must reconnect as
Americans. Put it back upon our lips and defend our rights in every
corner by saying, "We are a Judeo-Christian nation." It's our greatest
defense against Islamic fascism calling upon us to change our legal
structure for their benefit. That's a hoax. We can speak softly and without rancor. And you don't have to be a Christian to say it. Conversion
not required!

It's nothing to be ashamed of because Christianity isn't based
on people being perfect. On the contrary, Christianity is based on the
premise that men are desperately imperfect and in need of a savior's
rescue. That's why the founders wrote a Constitution that created three
branches of government that checked and balanced each other.[533] As
President Truman stated so clearly. The founders combined the three
branches of government spoken of in the book of Isaiah combined with
the writings of St. Paul.[534]

If you enjoy the benefits of living in America, respect who we are, for your liberty has been bought with a price. Americans have always been willing to pay that price. Though at times we are a happy and distracted people, the tyrants who've tested us both inside and outside our borders are gone. We speak softly, but we carry a big stick. Every now and then I like to remind myself of that balance.

Living only a few hours from Norfolk I've visited the U.S. Navy base there throughout the years because it stirs gratitude in my heart and reminds me of those who stand watch on my behalf. From time to time I've taken a special guest there; Brigitte Gabriel was one such guest.

My friend and Middle East colleague married an American from our Jerusalem news bureau and moved to the United States. One day I called her husband and proposed we take a day trip to the Norfolk Naval Base. The two of us didn't tell her our destination. "Where are we going?" she asked. "Come on, tell me."

"No, it's a surprise," we explained. Later, arriving at the base early that beautiful Sunday afternoon we took a private tour.

New to the United States, she'd never seen a U.S. Navy warship. In a few minutes we were as ants standing next to and looking up at a super carrier, the USS Theodore Roosevelt, a full three football fields long. The 4.5-acre flight deck loomed 80 feet above our heads and the control tower rose another 150 feet above the flight deck. I said to Brigitte, "We have ten of these and each has 85 jet fighters. This one is named after the 26th American President, Teddy Roosevelt, who said, 'Speak softly and carry a big stick.' This is the big stick."

Then we walked past a group of destroyers and cruisers and submarines. There was an attack helicopter on display and Brigitte sat in it. As the afternoon ended she turned to me and said, "Are all of these yours?"

"Yes," I replied. "And you're only looking at part of what we've got."

"Nobody can ever beat you!" she exclaimed.

"That's right," her husband and I answered together. There was a brief quiet pause as a big smile appeared on her face. "I want to be an American," she said.

Knowing her story and how her Christian family suffered from Islamic oppression in South Lebanon, I thought to myself about the slogan on the Statue of Liberty. "*Send these, the homeless, tempest-tossed to me.*" Since then, Brigitte has written her story in a moving autobiography, *Because They Hate,* which warns her fellow Americans about radical Islam.

That day Brigitte saw and felt something special. What causes American citizens to voluntarily train to run those ships and to fly those planes lives deep within the fabric of this nation. To feel that I suggest you watch one of my favorite movies, *The Patriot,* staring Mel Gibson as Benjamin Martin.[535]

A legendary war hero long retired from military service, he raises his seven children on a picturesque farm in the hills of South Carolina overlooking the harbor city of Charleston. The movie begins in the period immediately before the signing of the Declaration of Independence in 1776 by the original thirteen colonies that formed the United States of America.

Shortly after the signing of the Declaration, British troops invade Benjamin Martin's farm. A brutal British officer kills one of Martin's sons in front of him and takes another to be hanged as a spy before ordering the house and barns burned. As the buildings fall in flames the legendary warrior known as *The Ghost* comes out of retirement. In the forest he attacks and kills all but one of the British squadron escorting his oldest son to be hanged.

The hand-to-hand combat is particularly gruesome shocking the sensibilities of his sons. Before their eyes the legendary warrior hacks the British soldiers to death with dual tomahawks. The rage of the ghost was loose.

Deep within the soul of the United States sleeps *that Ghost,* a rage that offends onlookers and hacks the soldiers of tyranny to death without apology. Today he walks the decks of aircraft carriers and sits in the cockpit of stealth bombers. He stands beside the missile launch buttons and the targeting computers of our missile subs patrolling 800 feet deep in the oceans. He jumps with paratroopers and proudly sings the Marines Hymn. He sends National Guard units away from home and accompanies navy SEALs into combat.

Americans are a friendly people. The Ghost is not. One of our most popular Presidents left this encouragement to Americans and this warning to foes:

> We dare not forget today that we are the heirs of that
> first revolution... unwilling to witness or permit the

> slow undoing of those human rights to which this
> nation has always been committed... Let every
> nation know, whether it wishes us well or ill, that
> we shall pay any price, bear any burden, meet any
> hardship, support any friend, oppose any foe, to
> assure the survival and the success of liberty. ___
> President John F. Kennedy [536]

Let all of us become vigilant. My fellow Americans, wicked people have come to our own shores and imbedded themselves in our own society. Thinking that from within and from without they will trick us and create a fearful chaos that will eventually make us succumb to Islamic fascism. We won't. Americans will rise up to bear the burdens and meet the hardships necessary.

We prefer that our enemies make peace, but if tyrants and fascists choose otherwise, Americans will introduce them to the ghost.

Chapter 17
Final Thoughts:
Life, Liberty and the Pursuit of Foolishness

For nearly a generation (40 years) our public schools and universities have not been allowed to teach the Judeo-Christian heritage that gave us the language of the Declaration of Independence and the rights of man. As Thomas Jefferson, the writer of the Declaration of Independence wrote of the Creator in 1809, he referred to the discourses of Jesus.[537] Why would we omit that knowledge from our schools? It's part of our heritage and the legal rationale for the existence of The United States of America.

In 1992 twenty-one of the twenty-three people in the office where I worked were college graduates from well known universities, yet not one of them answered correctly when I asked them, "As American citizens, where do our rights come from?" Twelve said, "the Constitution;" six answered, "the government;" and three responded, "the state." One man who was not college educated answered correctly. "Our rights come from God the Creator," he said.

In other words, college graduates in the United States learned that the government is the source of their rights. That makes them all good Marxists. Whenever "the state" wants to take away the rights they endowed, wouldn't that be within their authority? Yet when King George tried to do just that, Thomas Jefferson wrote that he was a tyrant. All thir-teen colonies agreed and signed the Declaration of Independence. Guess why we fought the revolution…excessive taxation and governmental abuse of individual life, liberty and property.

Strange how university graduates are taught just the opposite. In *Indoctrination U.* best selling author, David Horowitz, says that for over thirty years our universities have aggressively taught socialism, "state control." According to the research of the Horowitz Foundation, entire courses of study in our university system are based on Marxist principles.[538]

The United States of America, however, fought the Revolutionary War over the Declaration of Independence. And it was that document Abraham Lincoln referred to in his Gettysburg Address when he spoke of our nation conceived and dedicated to God's proclamation.[539] On that hot August day in 1963 as Martin Luther King stood with a hundred thousand people on the mall in Washington, D.C., he called on our nation to deliver on the promises in The Declaration of Independence.[540]

Apparently, however, that's not what our schools teach. It seems political correctness advocates we go down to the National Archives and tear up the Declaration of Independence and replace it with a new statement, "We hold these truths to be self evident. The government gives you the rights of man because the Creator cannot be mentioned."

The most immediate danger to America is not nuclear war. Who would dare test us would lose their civilization. The greatest danger to us is ourselves. I have gone into considerable detail to demonstrate how the "rights of man endowed by The Creator" came from God to the Ancient Hebrews and subsequently the scholarship of the Christian church through the ages.

Our Judeo-Christian foundation is who we are. The Presidents and even our Supreme Court have recognized this as our heritage. Our identity is our Liberty. Abandon that, and our freedoms have no legal rationale to exist. Abandon the foundations of our liberties and what do we have left but tyranny. The tyranny of a government that proposes to socialize health care and major industries confiscating the wealth of individual Americans to do so.

Legislators have even proposed (S.2433), The Global Poverty Act. This act proposes a new tax on Americans equivalent to 25 percent of the annual budget of the United States to be paid by Americans to the United Nations for redistribution of our wealth to poorer countries.[541] That's 150 percent of the cost of the entire Iraq War.[542] These new taxes fall on every working person in America hidden inside the new carbon emission taxes. So as your government raises your utility bill, they'll give part of that to the United Nations. Do we the people consent to that? If not, it's tyranny.

The only reason this kind of rampant socialism can succeed is because of the near-forty years of socialism taught in American schools that began during the cold war as a means of defeating the United States military power through infiltrating American universities with Marxist ideology.[543]

Apparently, the United States public has become used to the ideas of tyranny. One former Russian communist told me in Moscow, "I never dreamed we'd be as successful as we were in the American university system." [544]

We cannot forget that the Arab nations of the Middle East were first allied with the Nazis during WW II and afterwards allied with the Russian Communists against the free world for more than four decades. It was the Russians who supplied the Arabs with rifles, tanks, airplanes, missiles and military advisors. The Arabs used these weapons to attack the two democratic nations of the Middle East, Lebanon and Israel. That in itself helps explain why today's Islamic Revolution waits for us to act in ignorance of our own history. They know it will mean the end of the United States, as we know it.

Why, because ideas have consequences. If the United States citizens do not wake up and recognize the creeping radical Islamic tyranny within our society, we will lose our liberties. Sooner rather than later we may find America reflecting a socialist state where Islamic citizens have more rights than Christians and Jews. What a tragedy that will be if our great beacon of freedom grows dim through socialist lies and the Worldwide Islamic Revolution against Western Civilization. Think I'm exaggerating?

Shortly after 9/11 in November 2001 Swiss authorities captured documents written by The Muslim Brotherhood. Counter terrorism experts refer to it as "The Project." Islamic expert Patrick Poole outlined twenty-six points of the document translated to English from Arabic and Brigitte Gabriel explains them in her book, *They Must Be Stopped.* The seized documents put forth a detailed one-hundred-year plan to overthrow Western Civilization including the United States, replacing all legal systems with Sharia Law. Realistically, we don't have anywhere near that much time.

Cold war tactics are afoot in the Middle East once more. As proof of Russia's alliance with Islam's jihad, Russian secret agent Alexander Litvinenko told former KGB Col. Preobrazhensky that his colleagues trained al-Qaeda's commander Ayman Al-Zawahiri in the Caucus Mountains of Dagestan.

Elsewhere, Russian military trainers and engineers have returned to Lebanon assisting Hezbollah in building satellite guided missile systems that can hit the heart of Israel. Meanwhile in Iran, the Russians

209

sold their newest air defense missile to the Iranian army. This plan places Israel right in the middle of a two front war. While the United States maneuvers toward financial suicide, Russia, Iran and Islamic fascists steer the world towards an enormously dark storm. The character of Americans is about to be tested. [545]

A Realistic Viewpoint

Are all Muslims bad people? Of course not, that's just common sense. They are similar to all people everywhere. Born and raised in a culture they couldn't choose for themselves, Muslim families want to raise their children in peace and plenty the same as families anywhere. That's why many have immigrated to the United States. But hardening influences within the religion seek to galvanize enough of the masses into replicating the very oppressions they fled from. Once again, Lebanon offers the free world a warning about the current ambitions of the Iranian Islamic Revolution.

Years after my in-country reports and his command of the SLA in the Shiite dominated region of South Lebanon, General Lahad summarized the problem for democracies. Long retired from the South Lebanon Army and living in France, in a very revealing interview in 2006 General Lahad said:

> First of all, the Shiites are no more than 30 percent, at most a third, (of the Lebanese population) and not all of them support Hezbullah...Who is Hezbullah? Hezbullah is a Khomeinist arm of Iran...Hezbullah is just the tail of the snake whose head is Iran and Syria. Did it succeed in conquering one millimeter of Israel? Even in Lebanon people know that it cannot conquer one millimeter, and it certainly can't 'liberate Jerusalem,' but it is using this to increase its strength...[546]

How foolish shall we be? Shall we proceed in America as if everything is equal, sort of "who cares?" Islam is a religion that has undergone no effective reformation in 1400 years. There is no separation of religious law and civil law and so Islam calls for Sharia Law to be instituted in Western Civilization. There is a deep historical alliance with Nazism calling for world conquest, the destruction of Israel and a preemptive nuclear strike against America. Seeing themselves as a state within the state Islam denies the sovereignty of nations [547] calling upon all countries to change their laws to be "more Muslim friendly." What should the modern world do with this?

Oddly, for America, one election cycle could do it. Since Islam does not separate religion from the state a President naïve of Islamic ambitions could allow legislation in favor of Sharia Law forcing a super majority vote in Congress to override his veto power. Thus, Islam could strangle the American Democracy in one election cycle and turn Christians, Jews and all non-Muslims into dhimmis, second-class citizens. However, if we start changing our regional civil laws to favor Muslims, we'll accomplish the same task at a slower pace.

My fellow Americans, you will decide what kind of nation you will live in. You will decide where your rights come from and how the government will spend your money. Our victory and the preservation of the greatest nation God ever gave to mankind await your decision. It's up to you.

G. Scott McGregor

Introduction: Notes

(Endnotes)

1 Art Moore, *Should Muslim Quran Be USA's Top Authority?* WorldNetDaily.com, May 1, 2003. http://www.worldnetdaily.com/news/article.asp?ARTICLE_ID=32341

2 Understanding Islam and the Muslims, *Why Does Islam Often Seem Strange?* IslamiCity.com, http://www.islamicity.com/education/understandingislamandmuslims/default.asp?ContentLocation=/Education/UnderstandingIslamAndMuslims&CurrentPageID=6&Top=&Bottom=&Right=&Left=&SideBarWidth=&RightWidth=&LeftWidth=&SideBarLocation=&Style=&CatID=&Destination=/Education/UnderstandingIslamAndMuslims/6.asp

3 Gregory T. Diaz and Barbara Newman, *Lightning Out of Lebanon, Hezbollah Terrorists on American Soil* (New York: Presidio Press, 2006) p. 44

4 American Memorial Site, *We Will Not Forget,* http://americanmemorialsite.com/beirutembassy.html

5 Elisabeth Smick, "Profile: Imad Mugniyah," http://www.cfr.org/publication/11317/; *Imad Fayez Mugniyah,* Most Wanted Terrorists, *http://www.nctc.gov/site/profiles/capture.html;* "Imad Fayez Mugniyah," *NNDB, http://www.nndb.com/people/445/000092169/;* "Hezbollah No.2 Imad Fayez Moughnieh killed in Syria," *Intelligence and Terrorism Information Center at the Israel Intelligence Heritage & Commemoration Center (IICC),* http://www.terrorism-info.org.il/malam_multimedia/English/eng_n/html/ct_130208e.htm.

6 Richard Marcinko, *Rogue Warrior* (New York: Pocket Books, 1992), p. 265.

7 Ibid., p. 268.

8 Ibid., p. 271.

9 Ibid., p. 266.

10 United State Department of Defense Official Website, *The Battle for Iwo Jima,* http://www.defenselink.mil/home/features/iwo_jima/iwo.html ; IwoJima.com, *The Battle of Iwo Jima,* http://www.iwojima.com/ .

11 Sis Levin, *Beirut Diary* (Downers Grove, Illinois: Intervarsity Press, 1989) p.28-29, 41.

12 Thomas Friedman, *From Beirut to Jerusalem* (New York: Ferrar Straus Giroux, 1989) p.137

13 Lawrence Pintak, *Beirut Outtakes* (Lexington, MA: Lexington Books, 1988) p. xv.

14 Muhammad M. Pickthall, *The Meaning of the Glorious Quran,* (Beltsville, MD: Amana Publications, 1996) p.1-2, Al Fatihah: The Opening. Surah 1:1-7.

15 Maulana Muhammad Ali, *The Muslim Prayer Book,* (Dublin, OH: Ahmadiyyah Anjuman Isha'at Islam, 1992). Al Fatihah: The Opening, explanatory notes p.5.

16 Maulana Muhammad Ali, *The Muslim Prayer Book,* explanatory notes p.2; M.H. Shakir, translator, *The Holy Quran,* (New York: Tahrike Tarsile Qur'an, Inc., 1983) Quran 9:5,29.

17 Sharbel Barakat, *Testimony Before the Senate Foreign Relations Committee, Subcommittee on Near Eastern and Far Eastern Affairs.* Washington, DC: June 7, 1997.

18 *9/11 Commission Report* (Washington, DC: GPO, Dec. 5, 2005) p. xvi, 47; http://www.gpoaccess.gov/911/index.html;
19 American memorial Site, *Americans killed by Terrorism (1980-1989),* http://americanmemorialsite.com/1980.html;
Americans Killed by Terrorists (1990-1999), http://americanmemorialsite.com/1990.html;
Americans Killed by Terrorists (2000 to present), http://americanmemorialsite.com/2000s.html

Chapter 1: Notes

20 Joseph Stalin, *An Interview: Joseph Stalin and H. G. Wells, Marxism VS. Liberalism.* (New York, New Century Publishers, September 1937; reprinted October 1950.) http://www.rationalrevolution.net/special/library/cc835_44.htm
21 "Enrollment, Faculty, staff and alumni at the University of Wisconsin, Madison" http://www.wisc.edu/about/facts/community.php#community.
22 Rachael Bell and Marion Bardsley, *Ed Gein: The Inspiration for Buffalo Bill and Psycho,* http://www.crimelibrary.com/serial_killers/notorious/gein/bill_1.html.
23 Troy Taylor, *Dead Men Do Tell Tales* (Alton, IL: Whitechapel Productions, 2008) "Wisconsin's "Psycho", The Deviant Life and Times of Ed Gein," http://www.prairieghosts.com/ed_gein.html.
24 David Horowitz, Unholy Alliance (Washington, DC: Regnery Publishing, 2004) p.72
25 Peter Kornbluh, National security Archive Electronic Briefing Book No. 5, *The Death of Che Guevara: Declassified,* http://w1.1559.telia.com/~u155900388/death_che.htm; http://www.moreorless.au.com/heroes/guevara.html; Moreorless: "Heroes & killers of the 20th Century, Che Guevara"; Paola Evans et al 1997 "Bolivia on the Day of the Death of Che Guevara: A Chronology" http://www.mindfully.org/Reform/2005/Che-Guevara-Gott11aug05.htm,; http://en.wikipedia.org/wiki/Che_Guevara, "Capture and execution"
26 Donald Selvage, "Che Guevara In Bolivia" April 1, 1985, Abstract, Marine Corps Command and Staff College, http://www.globalsecurity.org/military/library/report/1985/SDR.htm; Ernest (Che) Guevara de la Serna (1928-1967) http://www.kirjasto.sci.fi/guevar.htm; Maurice Zeitlin, Robert Sheer, *Cuba: An American Tragedy* (Mass Market Paperback, Penguin Books Ltd., 1964); http://en.wikipedia.org/wiki/Che_Guevara, The Bolivian Diary
27 David Horowitz, *Unholy Alliance,* p. 73
28 Ibid., p. 74
29 "We Will Bury You," *Time Magazine,* November 26, 1956; "The Cuban Missile Crisis: President Kennedy's Address to the Nation," *The U.S. National Archives and Records Administration,* College Park, Maryland, 1988; John F. Kennedy, "The Soviet Military Buildup in Cuba," speech televised to the world at 7:00 p.m. EST, Monday October 22, 1962, http://www.historyplace.com/speeches/jfk-cuban.htm.
30 Those courses were: The Great Speakers and Speeches of World History, The History of British Public Address, The Rhetoric of Agitation and Control, The Theory and Practice of Persuasion, History of the Roman Republic, Introduction to Computer

Science, Spanish Literature, Intermediate Spanish Conversation, and Introduction to Symphony Music.

31 http://www.brainyquote.com/quotes/quotes/j/josephstal113988.html, Joseph Stalin Quotes

32 David Horowitz, *Indoctrination U.* (New York: Encounter Books, 2006) p.123-127

33 Ibid.,p.113

34 James von Gelden and Lewis Siegelbaum, "Seventeen Minutes in Soviet History, 1991," *End of the Soviet Union,* http://www.soviethistory.org/index.php ; Frank Smith, "The Soviet Union Disintegrates," *Macrohistory and World Report,* http://www. fsmitha.com/h2/ch33.htm .

35 Horowitz, *Indoctrination U.*, p.126-127

36 Ibid.,p.115

37 "Report of the Investigative Committee of the Standing Committee on Research Misconduct at the University of Colorado at Boulder concerning Allegations of Academic Misconduct against Professor Ward Churchill," May 16, 2006, *Summary of Key Points*, pp.1-3. http://www.colorado.edu/news/reports/churchill/download/ ChurchillReportSummary.pdf

38 Ibid., p.3.

39 Horowitz, *Indoctrination U.*, p.127

40 http://www.brainyquote.com/quotes/quotes/j/josephstal113988.html, Joseph Stalin Quotes

41 http://www.answers.com/topic/mary-ann-vecchio, Mary Ann Vecchio

42 Nadine Brozan, "Chronicle," *New York Times*, April 25, 1995, Sec. B, P.4

43 Vicki Goldberg, "In a Rifle's Flash, a Lasting Icon of a Nation's Pain" *New York Times*, April 30, 1995, Sec. 2, Pg. 38; Mat Bai, "25 Years After Kent State, photographer, subject finally meet" *The Boston Globe*, April 24, p.24.; Joseph Mallia, "25 years later, photographer to meet his anguished subject" *Boston Sunday Herald,* April 23, p. 12; Janet Mason, "Caught In Time" *Life Magazine,* May 1995, p.39; Mary Ann Vecchio Gillum Press Conference, Emerson College, Boston, MA, April 23, 1995 transcript.

44 Capital Newspapers http://www.madison.com/library/LEE/sterlinghall.html, Front Page News, *Sterling Hall Bombing*

45 Ibid.

46 Capital Newspapers http://www.madison.com/library/LEE/08261970.pdf, Wisconsin State Journal, *UW Students Arm Selves*, August 26, 1970

47 http://www.madison.com/library/LEE/09051970.pdf *Wisconsin Socialists Condemn Bombing*

48 Col. E. Wright, USAF retired, Winchester, Wisconsin: August 1970.

49 Stanislav Lunev and Ira Winkler, *Through the Eyes of the Enemy*, (Washington, DC: Regnery Publishing, 1998) p. 78; Charles Warner, "Cost-per-Thousand (CPM) and Cost-per-Point (CPP)," *The Museum of Broadcast Communications*, http://www. museum.tv/archives/etv/C/htmlC/cost-per-thou/cost-per-thou.htm; CPI Inflation Calculator, "$1000 in 1970 has the same buying power as $5,562.73 in 2009," http:// data.bls.gov/cgi-bin/cpicalc.pl; William Lerner, *Statistical Abstract of the United States 1971, 92nd Edition* (Washington, D.C.: Bureau of the Census, 1971) p.6; *Super Bowl History* "1970 Super Bowl IV," http://www.super-bowl-history.us/superbowl-

history4.html; Thomas E. Woods, *The Politically Incorrect Guide to American History* (Washington, DC: Regnery Press, 2004) p. 161.

50 John McCain and Mark Salter, *Faith of my Fathers* (New York: Random House, 1999) p.338.

51 Ibid., pp.291-292.

52 Palestinefacts.org, *Why did Jordan expel the PLO in 1970?* http://www.palestinefacts.org/pf_1967to1991_jordan_expel_plo.php,

53 "Fedayeen Leader Arafat," Time Magazine, December 13, 1968.

54 Janet Wallach and John Wallach, *Arafat In the Eyes of the Beholder* (New York: Lyle Stewart, 1990) p. 7

55 Joseph Schechtman, *The Mufti and the Fuehrer* (New York: Thomas Yoseloff, 1965) p.175.

56 Barry M. Rubin and Judith Colp Rubin, *Yassir Arafat, A Political Biography* (New York: Oxford University Press, 2003) p. 11-12; Said Aburish, *Arafat, From Defender to Dictator* (New York: Bloomsbury Publishing, 1998) p. 7-8

57 Brigitte Gabriel, Because They Hate (New York: St. Martin's Press, 2006) p.19.

58 Benjamin Netanyahu, *A Durable Peace* (New York: Warner Books, 2000) p.206.

59 Joseph Schechtman, *The Mufti And The Fuehrer* (New York: Thomas Yoseloff, 1965) "Chapter 4: In Axis Service 1941-1945" pp. 116-166.

60 Christopher Andrew and Vasili Mitrokhin, *The World Was Going Our Way, The KGB and the Battle for the Third World* (New York: Basic Books, 2005) pp. 246-251; Alan Hart, *Arafat: A Political Biography*, revised edn. (London: Sidgwick and Jackson, 1994) p.4; Michel Elbaz, "The Great Secret of the Russian Middle Eastern Policy: Dangerous Liaisons: Covert love affair between Russia and Hezbollah, Part 1," *Axis Information and Analysis*, May 24, 2005, http://www.axisglobe.com/hezbollah1.htm,; Itmar Rabinoivich, *The War for Lebanon 1970-1983* (Ithaca: Cornell University Press, 1984) p.38; Tom Sicking and Shareen Khairallah, "The Shi'a Awakening in Lebanon: A Search for Radical Change in a Traditional Way," *Ceman Report 1974* (Beirut: Center for the Study of the Modern Arab World, 1976) pp.85-126; Frank Smith, "The Soviet Union Disintegrates," *Macrohistory and World Report.* http://www.fsmitha.com/h2/ch33.htm.

61 Multiple sources reference this tradition taught as part of the Islamic religion including: *Taqiya* http://answering-islam.org/Index/index.html; *Kithman* http://answering-islam.org/Index/index.html; Brigitte Gabriel, *Because They Hate, A Survivor of Islamic Terror Warns America* (New York: St. Martin's Press, 2006) p. 149; Robert Spencer, *The Politically Incorrect Guide to Islam* (Washington: Regnery Publishing, 2005) p.80

62 Imam Jafar Sadiq, *Kitab al-Kafi,* (Ft. #1 Usool al Kafi, p.88), (Ft. #2, Ibid, p.522), "k" "kithman," http://answering-islam.org/Index/index.html.

63 "Dispatches - Undercover Mosque (1 of 6)" UK Channel 4, January 15, 2007, YouTube, http://uk.youtube.com/watch?v=peFQWuk4nuo.

Chapter 2: Notes

64 Touraj B., personal interview with the author, Washington, D.C., January, 1999.

65 W.W. Davies, *The Codes of Hammurabi and Moses* (Berkeley: Apocryphal Press,

2006) p. 23.
66 Lawrence Pintak, *Beirut Outtakes* (Lexington, MA: Lexington Books, 1988) p. xv.
67 Camille Chamoun, *The Lebanese President's Interview with the Author*.
The Dolly Madison Hotel, Washington, DC, December, 1982.
68 The Holy Bible, *New International Version* (Grand Rapids: Zondervan, 1984) Old Testament, (Ezekiel 27:9).
69 Cedarland, *The Massacre and Destruction of Damour*, http://www.geocities.com/CapitolHill/Parliament/2587/damour.html
70 Quotation of Father Mansur Labaky, *The Massacre and Destruction of Damour*, http://www.geocities.com/CapitolHill/Parliament/2587/damour.html
71 The Holy Bible, *New International Version* (Grand Rapids: Zondervan, 1984) Old Testament, (Habakkuk 2:17).
72 Ze'ev Schiff and Ehud Ya'ari, *Israel's Lebanon War* (New York: Simon and Schuster, 1984) pp. 41-44, 250, 264, 279.
73 Ibid., p. 250.
74 Ibid., p.305.
75 Ibid., p.300.
76 Camille Chamoun.

Chapter 3: Notes

77 Lt. Col. Jonathan Netanyahu Official Website, Biography section, http://www.yoni.org.il/, p. 2.
78 Ibid., p. 2.
79 BiblePlaces.com, "Megiddo", http://www.bibleplaces.com/megiddo.htm
80 *The Amplified Bible* (Grand Rapids: Zondervan, 1965) New Testament, Revelations 16:16
81 The Holy Bible, *New International Version* (Grand Rapids: Zondervan, 1984) Old Testament, Joel 3:14
82 J. Dwight Pentecost, *Things to Come* (Grand Rapids: Zondervan, 1979) p. 344.
83 Ibid., p. 340.
84 The Holy Bible, *New International Version*, Old Testament, Ezekiel 38:8
85 Mark Twain, *The Innocents Abroad* (New York: Literary Classics of the United States, 1984) p. 485-86.
86 The Holy Bible, *New International Version*, New Testament, Luke 7:22

Chapter 4: Notes

87 Yitzhak Shamir, "171. Interview with Prime Minister Shamir," Israel Ministry of Foreign Affairs, Historical documents 1982-1984, Volume 8: 1982-1984; Israel radio, June 22, 1984.
http://www.mfa.gov.il/MFA/Foreign%20Relations/Israels%20Foreign%20Relations%20since%201947/1982-1984/171%20Interview%20with%20Prime%20Minister%20Shamir%20on%20Israel.
88 Mona El-Nahhas, "Uproar over Israeli smear report," *Al-Ahram Weekly*, Cairo, Issue No. 472, 9 - 15 March 2000; Marwan Bishara, "The Israelisation of America's

war," *Al-Ahram Weekly,* Cairo, Issue No. 583, 25 April – 1 May 2002; "Syria Hails Attack," *Tishreen,* Damascus, April 28, 2000; "Iran warns West on al-Quds day" *Aljazeera,*Qatar, September 26, 2008; Jonny Paul, "London editor prays for nuclear attack on Israel," Jerusalem," *International. Jpost.com,* April 28, 2007, http://www. jpost.com/servlet/Satellite?pagename=JPost%2FJPArticle%2FShowFull&cid=118819 7179708 ; Nadia Abou El-Magd, "Egyptians mark anniversary of Palestinian uprising with calls for Arab solidarity against Israel, U.S." *AP Worldstream,* Cairo, September 28,2002; Hussein Dakroub, "Most Arab papers condemn Tel Aviv bombing, but some say it stems from Palestinian despair," *AP Worldstream,* Beirut, April 18, 2006.

89 Alan Sipress, "Palestinians cheer Arafat visit; Israeli right wing rallies against him," *Knight Ridder/ Tribune News Service, July 2, 1994;* Jamaal Abdul-Alim, "Fireworks and black balloons," *The Milwaukee Journal Sentinel,* May 1, 1998; "Talking with the P.L.O.; The P.L.O.: From Birth Through Terrorism to Dialogue With the U.S." *The New York Times,* December 16, 1988, Section A, page 16.

90 Alfred B. Prados, "Lebanon" (Washington, DC: CRS, Library of Congress, March 16, 2006) Issue Brief 89118, p.2, http://www.fas.org/sgp/crs/mideast/IB89118.pdf.

Chapter 6: Notes

91 Daniel Helmer, "Hezbollah's employment of suicide bombing during the 1980s: the theological, political, and operational development of a new tactic," *Military Review,* July 1, 2006; reference to Heinz Helm, *Shi'a Islam: from Religion to Revolution,* translated from German by Allison Brown (Princeton: Markus Weiner Publishers, 1997) p.136. http://www.encyclopedia.com/doc/1G1-150356900.html

92 Morteza Mutaharri, *Jihad and Shahadat: Struggle and Martyrdom in Islam,* edited and translated by Mehdi Abedi and Gary Legenhausen (Houston: Institute for Research and Islamic Studies, 1986) p.128.

93 Antoine Lahad, *Personal Interview with the author,* SLA Headquarters, Lebanon, March 1985; Roee Nahmias, *Lahad: Syria Behind Gemayel's Murder,* Nov. 26, 2006, Ynetnews.com, http://www.ynetnews.com/articles/0,7340,L-3332868,00.html#n .

94 Steve Inskeep, "Lebanon Struggles to Cope with Conflict's Aftermath," *Morning Edition,* August16, 2006, MidEast Transcripts, http://www.npr.org/templates/transcript/ transcript.php?storyId=5656294.

95"Dispatches - Undercover Mosque (1 of 6)" UK Channel 4, January 15, 2007, YouTube, http://uk.youtube.com/watch?v=peFQWuk4nuo.

96 "Dispatches - Undercover Mosque (1 of 6)" UK Channel 4, January 15, 2007, YouTube, http://uk.youtube.com/watch?v=peFQWuk4nuo.

97 Bernard Lewis, *The Crisis of Islam, Holly War and Unholy Terror* (New York: Random House, 2003) p. 33-37; Muhammad M. Pickthall, *The Meaning of the Glorious Quran,* (Beltsville, MD: Amana Publications, 1996) p.1-2, Al Fatihah: *The Opening.* Surah 1:1-7; Maulana Muhammad Ali, *The Muslim Prayer Book,* (Dublin, OH: Ahmadiyyah Anjuman Isha'at Islam, 1992). Al Fatihah: *The Opening,* explanatory notes p.5; Maulana Muhammad Ali, *The Muslim Prayer Book,* explanatory notes p.2; M.H. Shakir, translator, *The Holy Quran,* (New York: Tahrike Tarsile Qur'an, Inc., 1983)

Quran 9:5,29; Colonel Sharbel Barakat, *Testimony Before the Senate Foreign Relations Committee, Subcommittee on Near Eastern and Far Eastern Affairs.* Washington, DC: June 7, 1997.

98 Lawrence Pintak, p. xiv.

99 Lawrence Pintak, p. xv.

100 Bernard Lewis, *The Crisis of Islam, Holly War and Unholy Terror* (New York: Random House, 2003) p. 33-37

101 Robert Spencer, *The Truth About Mohammed* (Washington, DC.: Regnery Press, 2006) p.7

102 Gregory T. Diaz and Barbara Newman, *Lightning Out of Lebanon, Hezbollah Terrorists on American Soil* (New York: Presidio Press, 2006) p. 15-16

103 Ibid., p.230

Chapter 7 Notes

104 "Why did Jordan expel the PLO in 1970?" Palestinefacts.org, http://www.palestinefacts.org/pf_1967to1991_jordan_expel_plo.php,

105 Michael Oren, *Six Days of War* (New York: Oxford University Press, 2002) p.308; Andrew and Mitrokhin, pp. 139-141.

106 Moshe Dayan, *Moshe Dayan: Story of My Life* (New York: William Morrow and Company, 1976) p.287

107 Peggy Mann, *Golda, The Life of Israel's Prime Minister* (New York: Coward, McCann & Geoghegan, 1971) p.214-215

108 Dayan, p.324

109 Ibid., p.315-316, 335

110 Ibid., p.337

111 Ibid., p.343-344

112 Ibid., p.330

113 Ibid., p.350-353

114 Oren, p.229

115 Ibid., p.305-306

116 Ibid., p.227

117 Ibid., p.230-231

118 Dyan, p.368

119 Oren, p.243

120 Ibid., p.243

121 Kenneth L. Sublett, *Sounding the Shofar* http://www.piney.com/Shofar.html,

122 Dayan, p.364

123 Oren, p.282

124 Chaim Herzog, *The Arab-Israeli Wars*, (NY: Random House, 1982), p. 149

125 Seymour Hersh, *The Samson Option: Israel's Nuclear Arsenal and American Foreign Policy* (New York: Random House, 1991) p.165

126 Oren, p. 303

127 Golda Meir, *A Land of Our Own; An Oral Autobiography of Golda Meir*, ed. Marie Syrkin (New York: G.P.Putnam's Sons, 1973) p. 155

128 *UN Security Resolution 242*, November 22, 1967, MidEast Web Historical

Documents, http://www.mideastweb.org/242.htm

129 *Khartoum Resolutions*, September 1967, MidEast Web Historical Documents, http://www.mideastweb.org/khartoum.htm

130 Oren, p.319-323

131 Chart compiled from multiple sources including: Mitchell Bard, *The 1967 Six-Day War* (Jewish Virtual Library) http://www.jewishvirtuallibrary.org/jsource/History/67_War.html; *1948-1967 Six Day War Result* http://www.palestinefacts.org/pf_1948to1967_sixday_result.php; *Six Day War* http://www.zionism-israel.com/dic/6daywar.htm ; *Six Day War* http://encarta.msn.com/encnet/refpages/RefArticle.aspx?refid=761570433 ; *The Six Day War 1967* http://www.onwar.com/aced/data/9999/6day1967.htm ; Dayan, p.350-354; Oren, p.305-306;

Mann, p. 214-215; Benjamin Netanyahu, *A Durable Peace* (New York: Warner Books, 2000) p. 148

132 Netanyahu, *A Durable Peace* p. 87

133 Bernard Lewis, *The Crisis of Islam, Holy War and Unholy Terror* (New York: Random House, 2003) p. 41-42

134 The Holy Bible, *New International Version* (Grand Rapids: Zondervan, 1984) I Samuel 14:1-23,

135 Ibid., Deuteronomy 20:3,4.

136 Ibid., Deuteronomy 28:7.

137 Ibid., Leviticus 26:7,8.

138 Benjamin Netanyahu, *A Place Among the Nations* (New York: Bantam Books, 1993) p. 81

139 Multiple sources reference this tradition taught as part of the Islamic religion including: *Taqiya* http://answering-islam.org/Index/index.html; *Kithman* http://answering-islam.org/Index/index.html; Brigitte Gabriel, *Because They Hate, A Survivor of Islamic Terror Warns America* (New York: St. Martin's Press, 2006) p. 149; Robert Spencer, *The Politically Incorrect Guide to Islam* (Washington: Regnery Publishing, 2005) p.80; Joel Richardson, *Will Islam be in Our Future, A Study of Biblical and Islamic Eschatology, http://www.answering-islam.de/Main/Authors/JR/Future/index. htm,* Chapter 16, "Understanding Dishonesty and Deceit in Islam" http://www.answering-islam.de/Main/Authors/JR/Future/ch16_understanding_dishonesty.htm

140 *Khartoum Resolutions*, September 1967, MidEast Web Historical Documents, http://www.mideastweb.org/khartoum.htm

141 Bernard Lewis *The Political Language of Islam* (Chicago: University of Chicago Press, 1991) p. 72-73

142 Netanyahu, *A Durable Peace* p. 154-157

143 Energy Information Administration, http://www.eia.doe.gov/emeu/cabs/contents. html, *Table 11.5 World Crude Oil Production, 1960-2005* http://www.eia.doe.gov/emeu/aer/txt/ptb1105.html

144 Energy Information Administration http://www.eia.doe.gov/emeu/cabs/contents. html, Country Analysis Briefs, *Saudi Arabia Country Analysis Brief,* http://www.eia.doe.gov/emeu/cabs/saudi.html

145 Janet Wallach and John Wallach, *Arafat In the Eyes of the Beholder* (New York: Lyle Stewart, 1990) p. 7

146 Time Magazine, December 16, 1968 *Fedayeen Leader Arafat*

147 Barry M. Rubin and Judith Colp Rubin, *Yassir Arafat, A Political Biography* (New York: Oxford University Press, 2003) p. 11-12; Said Aburish, *Arafat, From Defender to Dictator* (New York: Bloomsbury Publishing, 1998) p. 7-8

148 Bernard Lewis, *Semites and Anti-Semites; An Inquiry into Conflict and Prejudice* (New York: W.W. Norton & Co., 1999) p. 152-153

149 Joseph Schechtman, *The Mufti and the Fuhrer: The Rise and Fall of Haj Amin al-Husseini* (New York: Thomas Yoseloff, 1965) p. 156

150 Ibid., p. 160

151 Netanyahu, *A Durable Peace* p. 205-206

152 Ibid., p.202

153 Mitchell Bard, *The Complete Idiot's Guide to Middle East Conflict* (Indianapolis: Alpha Books, 2003) p. 193

154 GlobalSecurity.org, *Jordanian Removal of the PLO,* http://www.globalsecurity.org/military/world/war/jordan-civil.htm,

155 Ibid.

156 Uriya Shavit, "Out of Jordan", *Haaretz Newspaper*, May 28, 2002, EretzYisroel. org, http://www.eretzyisroel.org/~samuel/september.html

157 EretzYisroel.org, *Black September, the PLO's attempt to take over Jordan in 1970* http://www.eretzyisroel.org/~samuel/september.html

158 Bernard Lewis, *The Crisis of Islam, Holy War and Unholy Terror* p.89

159 Dayan, p.238

160 Camille Chamoun, Lebanese President Chamoun's Interview with the Author, 1982

161 Rubin and Rubin, p.11-12

162 Camille Chamoun, 1982

163 Michel Elbaz, http://www.axisglobe.com/hezbollah1.htm, *Dangerous Liaisons: covert love affair between Russia and Hezbollah*, part 1

164 Ibrahim Nawar, http://weekly.ahram.org.eg/2006/788/op32.htm, *Unexpected Gifts*, Al-Ahram Weekly, 30 March - 5 April 2006, Issue No. 788

165 Jewish Virtual Library, *Sabra and Shatila,* http://www.jewishvirtuallibrary.org/jsource/History/Sabra_&_Shatila.html

166 Palestine Facts, *What Happened at the LOD Airport in 1972?* http://www.palestinefacts.org/pf_1967to1991_lod_1972.php

167 Netanyahu, *A Durable Peace*, Appendix E, "The PLO Charter, Articles 19-22," p.426-427.

168 "The 1973 Yom Kippur War," *Israel Record,"* http://www.adl.org/ISRAEL/Record/yomkippur.asp; Hersh, pp. 211, 215.

169 P.J. Vatikiotis, *The History of Modern Egypt*, Fourth Edition (Baltimore: Johns Hopkins University, 1992) p. 443.

170 Hersh, p. 319.

171 Ibid., p.318.

172 Mahmoud Ahmadinejad, *Transcript of speech at "World Without Zionism" conference in Tehran*, Iran Focus, October 28, 2005.

173 The Holy Bible, *New International Version,* Genesis 17:1-8.

174 Pentecost, p. 392-393.

175 Sayyid Qutb, *Milestones* (Salimiah, Kuwait: I.I.F.S.O., 1978) p.12-15.

Chapter 8: Notes

176 Robert Spencer, *The Truth About Muhammad* (Washington, DC: Regnery Publishing, 2006) pp. 33-35

177 Mitchell Bard, *The Complete Idiot's Guide to Middle East Conflict* (Indianapolis: Alpha Books, 2003) p.49

178 Quran Formation, http://www.angelfire.com/ny/dawahpage/quran.html

179 Philip Hitti, *The Arabs: A Short History* (Washington: Regnery, 1996) p. 36,37

180 Bernard Lewis, *The Political Language of Islam* (Chicago: The University of Chicago Press, 1988) p.73

181 Ibid.

182 George F. Moore, *Judaism in the First Centuries of the Christian Era*, Vol. 1 (Cambridge: Harvard University Press, 1927) p. 324

183 *The Holy Bible*, New International Version, The Old Testament, Isaiah 49:6 (Grand Rapids, Michigan: Zondervan Bible Publishers, 1984)

184 Rodney Stark, *Cities of God* (New York: HarperCollins, 2006) p. 6

185 Martin Gilbert, *The Atlas of Jewish History,* revised edition (New York: William Morrow and Company, 1993) p. 2

186 Ibid., p.6

187 "King Solomon's Reign: Israel's Golden Years, Enter the Queen of Sheba," *The Good News,* http://www.gnmagazine.org/issues/gn15/archaeologysolomon.htm

188 Jewish Virtual Library, *Aliyah from Ethiopia,* http://www.jewishvirtuallibrary.org/jsource/Judaism/ejim.html

189 Library-Religion, *Judaism, Origins, History and Spread* http://www.abc.net.au/religion/stories/s796551.htm;
Judaism, *The Bare Essentials of Judaism,* http://www.tqnyc.org/NYC052116/Judaism.htm

190 *The Holy Bible*, New International Version, The Old Testament, Psalms 110:2,3

191 Ibid., I Samuel 10:10; I Samuel 16:13; Judges 6:34; Judges 16:13

192 *The Holy Bible*, New International Version, The New Testament, John 18:36.

193 *The Holy Bible*, New International Version, The Old Testament, Isaiah 53: 5,10,11.

194 *The Holy Bible*, New International Version, The New Testament, Acts 1:1-9.

195 Timeline of Bible History, *English Bible History: Timeline on how we got the English Bible,* http://www.greatsite.com/timeline-english-bible-history/

196 Stark, p. 7

197 *The Holy Bible*, New International Version, The New Testament, John 14:15,16

198 *First Council of Nicea: 325 AD*, http://www.piar.hu/councils/ecum01.htm

199 Adolf von Harnack, *The Mission and Expansion of Christianity in the First Three Centuries* Vol. 1 (New York: Putnam, 1904) p.1-10

200 All About The Truth, *How many people wrote the Bible*, http://www.allabouttruth.org/how-many-people-wrote-the-bible-faq.htm

201 Timeline of Bible History

202 Spencer, *The Truth About Muhammad*, p. 37

203 The council of Nicea, *The Role of Constantine*, http://www.columbia.edu/cu/

augustine/arch/sbrandt/nicea.htm

Chapter 9: Notes

204 Ibn Ishaq, *The Life of Muhammad: A Translation of Ibn Ishaq's Sirat Rasul Allah,* A. Guillaume, translator, (Oxford: Oxford University Press, 1955) p.82

205 Spencer, *The Truth About Muhammad,* p. 38

206 Prophet of Doom, *With Whom am I Speaking,* http://prophetofdoom.net/Prophet_of_Doom_07_With_Whom_Am_I_Speaking.Islam

207 Bearman, PJ, (ed.), *Encyclopedia of Islam, 2nd edition.* Brill (Leiden), 98b-99a, "Tahanuth"; Francis Peters, *Muhammad and the Origins of Islam* (New York: State U of New York Press, 1994) p.130.

208 Ibn Ishaq, p. 105

209 Al-Bukhari, vol. 9, book 87, Number 111, USC-MSC Compendium of Muslim texts, http://www.usc.edu/dept/MSA/fundamentals/hadithsunnah/bukhari/087.sbt.html#009.087.111; Marmaduke Pickthall, *The Glorious Qur'an* (Beltsville, MD: Amana Publications, 2006) p. 660, (Sura 96:1-5)

210 Al-Bukhari, vol. 9, book 87, Number 111

211 Ibn Ishaq, p.107

212 *The Holy Bible,* New International Version, The Old Testament, Exodus 33:11; Numbers 12:6; Deuteronomy 5:5; 34:10

213 Ibid., Numbers 12:6

214 *The Holy Bible,* New International Version, The New Testament, Galatians 1:8

215 Ibn Ishaq, p.107

216 Ibn Ishaq, p.106

217 Al-Bukhari, vol. 9, book 87, Number 111

218 Efraim Karsh, *Islamic Imperialism, A History* (New Haven: Yale University Press, 2006) p.10

219 Ibid., p.10,11

220 Ibn Ishaq, p.115

221 Ibid., p.118

222 *The Holy Qur'an,* translated by M.H. Shakir, (Elmhurst, NY: Tahrike Tarsile Qur'an, Inc., 1983) 111:1-5 on line at the Andover-Harvard Theological Library, http://www.hds.harvard.edu/library/research/resource_detail.cfm?resource_id=73&pagetype=ebook

223 A few Examples: 1) The Muslim Brotherhood assassinated Egyptian President Anwar Sadat October 6, 1981 for apostasy to Islam after he made a peace treaty with Israel. 2)Ayatollah Khomeini called on all zealous Muslims to execute the author Salman Rushdie and the publishers of *The Satanic Verses.* Rushdie was forced into hiding when an aide to Khomeini offered a million-dollar reward for his death. 3) In 1993 Rushdie's Norwegian publisher William Nygaard was wounded in an attack outside his house. 4) After Britain's Queen Elizabeth II made Rushdie a knight in 2007, a Muslim government official in Pakistan declared that Rushdie's knighthood justified suicide bombings in England. 5) In November 2004 Dutch filmmaker Theo Van Gough was murdered on the streets of Amsterdam for making the movie *Submission* about a woman who left Islam. 6) The Somali woman in his film, Ayaan Hirsi Ali, is the author of two books, *The Caged Virgin* and *Infidel.* Her life has a death contract on it by the

same Muslim group that killed Van Gough.

224 Ayaan Hirsi Ali, *The Caged Virgin* (New York: Free Press, 2006) p.x-xii

225 Ibn Ishaq, p.130

226 Ibid., p.213

227 Karsh, p. 12

228 Ibid.

229 Ibid.

230 Al-Bukhari, Volume 4, Book 52, Number 256

231 Spencer, *The Truth About Muhammad,* p. 98

232 Ibn Ishaq, p. 288

233 Spencer, *The Truth About Muhammad,* p. 99

234 *The Holy Qur'an*, translated by M.H. Shakir, 2:218

235 Ibid., 8:52

236 Ibid., 8:12,13

237 Ibn Ishaq, p.306

238 Steven Stalinsky, "Dealing in Death" *National Review Online*, May 24, 2004, http://article.nationalreview.com/?q=MjdjMTcyMDQ1YmI3M2E2ZDdiYzY5ZTgxN DYzMWRjM2Q=

239 *The Holy Qur'an*, Abdullah Yusuf Ali, Translator 14th edition, (Elmhurst, NY: Tahrike Tarsile Qur'an, Inc., 1999) 8:58-60; Marmaduke Pickthall, Translator Revised edition, *The Glorious Qur'an* (Beltsville, MD: Amana Publications, 2006) p.159

240 Ibid., 61:6

241 *The Holy Bible*, New International Version, The New Testament, John 14: 15,16.

242 Ibid,. Acts 1:5,8.

243 Answering Islam, Index to Islam, "M" *Muhammad: Model to Mankind,* http:// answering-islam.org/Index/index.html; *The Holy Qur'an*, Abdullah Yusuf Ali (Translator), 33:21; 68:4

244 *The Holy Bible*, New International Version, New Testament, Galatians 2:13, with reference to legal code written 1200 years before by Moses in the Old Testament Torah, Deuteronomy 21:22,23

245 *The Holy Qur'an*, Abdullah Yusuf Ali (Translator) 4:157

246 Ibid., 3;110 ; 5:13,14.

247 Ibid., 2:135

248 Ibid., 5:51

249 Pickthall, p.159, Quran 3;110;5:13,14.

250 Spencer, p.113

251 Karsh, p.13

252 Ibn Ishaq, p.464-469

253 Amir Tahiri, *Holy Terror: The Inside Story of Islamic Terrorism* (Bethesda, MD: Sphere Books, 1987); Brigitte Gabrielle, *Because They Hate: A Survivor of Islamic Terror Warns America* (New York: St. Martin's Press, 2006) p.149,150

254 Al-Bukhari, Volume 3, Book 46, Number 117; Ibn Ishaq, p.490

255 Sam Shamoun. *Islam and Birth Control, Should Muslims Observe It or Not?* Answering Islam, Index to Islam "A" azl, http://answering-islam.org/Muhammad/ Inconsistent/azl.html

256 Answering Islam, Index to Islam, "M" *Marriage,* http://answering-islam.org/Index/

index.html; *The Holy Qur'an*, Muhammad M. Pickthall (Translator), 04:24

257 Al-Bukhari, Volume 9, Book 93, Number 506

258 Ibn Ishaq, p.651

259 Karsh, p.15

260 Ibn Ishaq, p. 511

261 Ibid.,p.517

262 Ibid.,p.515

263 Ibid, p.512

264 Muhammad Al-Munajjid, "The true nature of the enmity between the Muslims and the Jews," http://www.alminbar.com/khutbaheng/9022.htm

265 Karsh, p.16

266 Al-Bukhari, Volume 5, Book 59, Number 742

267 Al-Bukhari, Volume 1, Book 2, Number 24

268 Ted Thorton, History of the Middle East DataBase, *Islamic Conquests 623-661*, http://www.nmhschool.org/tthornton/mehistorydatabase/islamic_conquests_632.php; Lebanon's History, *Medievil Lebanon*, http://www.ghazi.de/medieval.html

269 Bernard Lewis, *The Political Language of Islam*, p. 90

270 Ibid.

Chapter 10: Notes

271 Laura Tuma, *Walter Cronkite, The Most Trusted Man in America*, Texas Tribute (Spring 1997), The University of Texas at Austin, http://txtell.lib.utexas.edu/stories/c0003-full.html; Paul Westman, *Walter Cronkite: The most trusted man in America*, (New York: Dillon Press, 1980) p. 39; Joseph Farah, *The Most Trusted Man in America?*, WorldNetDaily, July 10, 2000, http://www.worldnetdaily.com/news/article.asp?ARTICLE_ID=15007

272 Paul Westman, p. 34.

273 Journalism.org, Project for Excellence in Journalism: Understanding news in the Information Age, *Network TV Audience Trends*, 2006 Annual Report Nightly Newscasts, March 13, 2006, http://www.journalism.org/node/1190; Chart in millions of viewers: *Evening News Viewership, All Networks, November 1980 to November 2005*. http://www.journalism.org/node/1190; Robert Schihl, *Some components of television station image projected and perceived through local news programs* (Thesis (Ph. D.)--State University of New York at Buffalo, 1982)

274 "Ben Bradlee," *NNDB, Tracking The Entire World*, http://www.nndb.com/people/875/000022809/; Michael Gartner, "The First Rough Draft of History," an interview with Benjamin C. Bradlee, *American Heritage* (Oct.-Nov. 1982) pp.37, 38.

275 Evan Coyne Maloney, *Cronkite Admits: Media Liberal*, Brain terminal, August 27, 2003. http://brain-terminal.com/posts/2003/08/27/cronkite-admits-media-liberal

276 The Center for Media and Public Affairs and Harris Pole study in 1997, *What the People want from the Press*; American Society of Newspaper Editors Journalism Credibility Project, 1998, *Examining Our Credibility: Perspectives of the Public and the Press*; Pew Research Center for The People and the Press, October 15, 2000 Report, *The People and the Press, 2000*; The Gallop Organization, Polls 2001-2005: *More See*

225

Media As "Too Liberal" The Missouri School of Journalism's Center for Advanced Social Research, *Results 2005, Key Findings*; Gannett's First Amendment Center in Nashville, *2005 poll of Americans about their attitudes towards the media*, published in the American Journalism Review, August/ September, 2005

277 Robert Lichter and Stanley Rothman, "Media and Business Elites" Public Opinion, October/November 1981, The American Enterprise Institute; Lichter, Rothman and Lichter, *The Media Elite* (New York: Hastings House, 1986) p. 29; The Los Angeles Times, The Los Angeles Times Survey of Journalists and the Public, 1985

278 Michael J. McManus, *Anti-Christian Bias In Media*, VirtueOnline, The Voice for Global Orthodox Anglicanism, http://www.virtueonline.org/portal/modules/news/article.php?storyid=3623; Lichter, Rothman, Lichter, *The Media Elite*, p. 294-295

279 Media Research Center, *Media Bias Basics, How the Media Vote*, White House Reporters, Key Findings, http://www.mediaresearch.org/biasbasics/biasbasics3.asp

Chapter 11: Notes

280 Cedarland, "The Massacre and Destruction of Damour" http://www.geocities.com/CapitolHill/Parliament/2587/damour.html

281 Abu Afak, *The Massacre at Damour, Jan. 9, 1976,* Free Republic.com, http://www.freerepublic.com/focus/f-news/1555079/posts

282 *The Holy Qur'an*, translated by M.H. Shakir, (Elmhurst, NY: Tahrike Tarsile Qur'an, Inc., 1983) 5:33
On line at the Andover-Harvard Theological Library, http://www.hds.harvard.edu/library/research/resource_detail.cfm?resource_id=73&pagetype=ebook

283 Al- Bukhari, vol.8, book 82, num.794-797 Anas bin Malik narrating included, "The Prophet cut off the hands and feet of the men belonging to the tribe of 'Uraina and did not cauterize (their bleeding limbs) till they died."; Also narrated by Abu Qilaba in Al-Bukhari, Volume 1, Book 4, Number 234; also repeated by Anas bin Malik narrating in Al-Bukhari, Volume 2, Book 24, Number 577; Another variation of this is to say that no unbeliever is killed unjustly because of Adam's son who invented murder: as narrated by Abdullah bin 'Umar in Al-Bukhari, Volume 9, Book 83, Number 6 .

284 Zuheir Mohsen, head of Syrian branch of PLO 1971-1979, as quoted in an interview in the Dutch newspaper "Trouw", March 1977, cited on: http://forum.svt.se/jive//svt/report.jspa?messageID=82410 March 6, 2006; *The New York Times accidentally points out the elephant in the Living Room*, Thursday, May 25, 2006, Israel Matzav, http://israelmatzav.blogspot.com/2006/05/new-york-times-accidentally-points-out.html; *Jordan is Palestine: Palestine is Jordan,* by Mati Alon, IsraelForum.com, http://www.israelforum.com/board/showthread.php?t=6693 ; Robert Spencer, *Saddam, Just Before Execution, Shouts, "God is great. The nation will be victorious and Palestine is Arab!"* December 30, 2006, Jihad Watch, http://www.jihadwatch.org/archives/014615.php

285 Fadi Hayyak, *Personal interview with the Author*, Beirut: January 1983.

286 Ibid.

287 Ibid.

288 Ibid.

289 Cynthia Ozick, *Where Hatred Trumps Bread, What does the Palestinian nation offer the world?* http://www.opinionjournal.com/editorial/feature.html?id=110003690

290 Camille Chamoun, *Personal interview with the author*, Washington, DC: December 1982.

291 Globalsecurity.org, Military: Agencies: Marines; *Marine Forces Atlantic [MarForLant] U.S. Marine Corps Forces, Europe (MARFOREOUR)*; http://www. globalsecurity.org/military/agency/usmc/marforlant.htm;
Jack Schulimson, *Marines In Lebanon, 1958.* (Washington, DC: Historical Branch, G-3 Division, Headquarters, U. S. Marine Corps, 1966) p. 4-7
http://www.au.af.mil/au/awc/awcgate/usmchist/lebanon.txt

292 Hayyak.

293 Levin, p. 28-29.

294 Hayyak.

295 John Cooley, *Payback: America's Long War in the Middle East* (New York: Macmillan, 1991) p. 100

296 All democracies are not designed in the same manor. The Lebanese democracy shared power through representation in the Parliament according to religious communities; the manor designed for the three majority sects to share the top three offices balanced out the power. What the spokesman referred to were the legal consequences resulting from transferring both of the top offices of President and Prime Minister to the Muslims. Since they already occupied enough seats of Parliament and two of the top three offices, the only remaining check and balance mechanism for Christian representation was the Presidency.

297 Bernard Lewis, *What Went Wrong? The Clash Between Islam and Modernity in the Middle East* (New York: Harper Collins, 2002) p.3-4

298 Those books and correspondents are: New York Times Correspondent, Thomas Friedman, *From Beirut to Jerusalem* (New York: Farrar Straus Giroux, 1989); CBS News Correspondent, Larry Pintak, *Beirut Outtakes, A TV Correspondent's Portrait of America's Encounter with Terror* (Lexington, MA: Lexington Books, 1988); ABC News Correspondent, John Cooley, *Payback, America's Long War in the Middle East* (New York: Macmillan, 1991); Ze'ev Schiff, Military Correspondent of Israel's largest daily newspaper, Ha'aretz and Ehud Ya'ari, Middle East Affairs Correspondent of Israeli Television, *Israel's Lebanon War* (New York: Simon and Schuster, 1984)

299 Though farfetched, an equivalent change in the United States would be to pass a constitutional amendment removing the veto power from the President and placing it in the hands of a new Islamic Congressional Committee. Such a move would give power to Muslims in America to leverage all laws in their favor. Only super majority votes in the House and Senate could override their veto of any legislation. However, the election of a Muslim as President of the United States might also have the same effect. Since the religion of Islam does not recognize a separation between religion and the state, a Muslim President could veto any legislation he wanted in favor of Islam forcing a super majority vote in the Congress to override his veto power. Thus, Islam could strangle American Democracy, as we know it.

300 John Cooley, *Payback: America's Long War in the Middle East*, (New York, Brassey's U.S., Inc., 1991) pp 69-71, 76, 95-97; *New York Times*, 2/9/83; "Final Report of the Israeli Commission of Inquiry," *Journal of Palestine Studies*, Spring 1983, pp. 89-116; Ze'ev Schiff and Ehud Ya'ari, *Israel's Lebanon War* (New York, Simon and Schuster, 1984) P.225; Victor Ostrovsky and Claire Hoy, *By Way of Deception*, (New

York, St. Martin's Press, 1990) P. 321; *New York Times*, 9/14/83; *New York Times*, 9/13/83; *New York Times*, 9/29/83; *New York Times* 04/14/83; "NBC Nightly News" 03/17/86; *Washington Post*, 6/16/82.; *New York Times*, 1/4/84; *New York Times*, 9/29/83; Friedman, *From Beirut to Jerusalem*, pp. 200-01; *New York Times*, 9/25/83; Tamar Sternthal, "Lebanon's Civil War and Jennings' Historical Revisionism," *Committee For Accuracy in Middle East Reporting*, November 14, 2003; "Is Your TV News Lying?" admin at americancoalition.org, http://www.bio.net/bionet/mm/ageing/2001-August/004449.html ; John Corry, "TV: View Of NBC Coverage of Lebanon Invasion," *New York Times*, Feb 18, 1984; *NBC in Lebanon: A Study of Media Misrepresentation (1983)*, 57 minute documentary directed by Peter Goldman.; *Dishonest Reporting "Award" for 2001-2008*, http://www.honestreporting.com/articles ; *Al-Dura, What Really Happened?* Youtube, http://uk.youtube.com/watch?v=E3Z4_11wLjw&feature=related.

Chapter 12: Notes

301 Fred M. Donner, *The Early Islamic Conquests*, (Princeton: Princeton University Press, 1981) p. 270

302 Al Bukhari, narrated by Ibn Umar, Volume 1, Book 2, Number 24

303 Donner, p.271

304 M.A. Khan, "Islamic Terrorism, Is It A New Threat," Armenian Diaspora News Forum, May 17, 2007, http://www.armeniandiaspora.com/forum/showthread.php?t=93320

305 Benjamin Walker, *The Foundations of Islam* (London: Peter Owen Publishers, 1998) p. 316

306 Rafiq Shoebat, "Israel and the World's Mock Trial, The Shame" Monthly Pearl, March 2004, Edition 55, http://www.pushhamburger.com/mar04.htm

307 Mitchell Bard, *The Complete Idiot's Guide to Middle East Conflict* (Indianapolis: Alpha Books, 2003) p.56

308 Byzantium: The Byzantine Studies Page, Introduction http://www.fordham.edu/halsall/byzantium/; Ancient Worlds, The Egyptian World, *Chronology of Islamic Spain-Al Andalus*, http://www.ancientworlds.net/aw/HomesiteRoom/603942

309 Edward Creasy, *Fifteen Decisive Battles of the World: From Marathon to Waterloo* (London: R. Bentley, 1851) 168-169

310 Battle of Poitiers, 17 October, 732; http://sinclair.quarterman.org/history/med/battleofpoitiers.html; Medieval Sourcebook: Anonymous Arab Chronicler: *The Battle of Pointiers, 732* http://www.fordham.edu/halsall/source/arab-poitiers732.html; Paul Akers, *Why Islam Didn't Conquer the World. From the Plains of Medievil France to the Modern MidEast, Muslims test Christians and Jews*, October 30, 2005, http://fredericksburg.com/News/FLS/2005/102005/10302005/141401/printer_friendly

311 About.com, *Religion in Spain*, *Al Andalus, Islam in Spain*, http://atheism.about.com/library/world/KZ/bl_SpainAlAndalus.htm

312 Ibid.

313 El Asomado, *La Batalla de Las Navas de Tolosa, The Battle of Las Novas de Tolosa, The Pastorcillo*, article written May 4, 2007, http://pobrespain.blogspot.com/2007/05/

la-batalla-de-las-navas-de-tolosa.html

314 Charles Morris, Las Navas de Talosa, The Baldwin Project, http://www.mainlesson. com/display.php?author=morris&book=spanish&story=tolosa

315 The Battle of Las Navas de Tolosa, *The Latin Chronicle of the Kings of Castile*, Chapter 24-26, translated by Joseph F. O'Callaghan, Medieval & Renaissance Texts & Studies vol. 236 (Tempe, AZ, MRTS, 2002), pp. 49-56.

316 Charles Morris, Las Navas de Tolosa, The Baldwin Project, http://www.mainlesson. com/display.php?author=morris&book=spanish&story=tolosa

317 The Battle of Las Navas de Tolosa, *The Latin Chronicle of the Kings of Castile*, Chapter 24-26

318 Charles Morris, Las Navas de Tolosa, The Baldwin Project, http://www.mainlesson. com/display.php?author=morris&book=spanish&story=tolosa

319 Lewis, *What Went Wrong?* p. 3

320 Adolf von Harnack, *The Mission and Expansion of Christianity in the First Three Centuries* Vol. 1 (New York: Putnam, 1904) p.1-10; *First Council of Nicea: 325 AD*, http://www.piar.hu/councils/ecum01.htm

321 Robert Spencer, "Speaking of Playing Fast and Lose with History," Dhimmi Watch, May 8, 2005, http://www.jihadwatch.org/dhimmiwatch/archives/006071.php

322 Bat Ye'or, *The Decline of Eastern Christianity Under Islam* (Madison, NJ,: Fairleigh Dickenson Press, 1996) p.78

323 Bard, p. 56; Rafiq Shoebat, "Israel and the World's Mock Trial, The Shame" under subtitle, "The Nazi Islam Connection" Monthly Pearl, March 2004, Edition 55, http://www.pushhamburger.com/mar04.htm; Ilana Mercer, "Did Muhammad Invent Profiling?" WorldNetDaily, January 9, 2002, http://www.worldnetdaily.com/news/ article.asp?ARTICLE_ID=25982

324 Shoebat, "The Nazi Islam Connection," Regarding Islam quoting from: Omar Charter, Faqeeh Al-Muluk, volume 2, pages 124-136; Regarding Nazi law quoting from: Lucy Dawidowicz, *The War Against The Jews 1933-1945* (New York: Bantam, 1986) pp.48-70

325 "Ten Misconceptions About Islam" *Misconception 5* http://www.usc.edu/dept/ MSA/notislam/misconceptions.html#HEADING5

326 Bat Ye'or, *Islam and Dhimmitude: Where Civilizations Collide* (Madison, NJ: Fairleigh Dickenson Press, 2002) p.70

327 Robert Spencer, *The Politically Incorrect Guide to Islam and The Crusades* (Washington: Regnery Press, 2005) pp. 120-125

328 Bard, p. 56

329 Spencer, *The Politically Incorrect Guide to Islam and The Crusades* pp. 29-51

330 Bongars, Gesta Dei per Francos, 1, p 382 f., translated to English in Oliver J. Thatcher and Edgar Holmes McNeal, eds., *A Sourcebook of Medieval History* (New York: Scribners, 1905) pp. 513-517;

A History and Mythos of the Knights Templar, "Pope Urban II – 1042-1099" http:// www.templarhistory.com/urbanii.html

331 E.L. Knox, A History of the Crusades, Boise State University online course, http:// crusades.boisestate.edu/1st/index.shtml

332 James Arlandson, *The Truth About Islamic Crusades and Imperialism*, American Thinker, November 27, 2005, http://www.americanthinker.com/2005/11/the_truth

about_islamic_crusad.html

333 Thomas Madden, editor, *Crusades, The Illustrated History* (Ann Arbor: University of Michigan Press, 2005) p.41; Paul Williams, *The Complete Idiot's Guide to the Crusades* (New York: Alpha Books, 2001) pp. 62-64.

334 E.L. Knox, A History of the Crusades

335 Ibid

336 Spencer, *The Politically Incorrect Guide to Islam and The Crusades,* p. 137

337 Ibid., p. 147

338 Thomas Madden, *The New Concise History of the Crusades* (Lanham, MD: Rowman .& Littlefield, 2005) p. 76

339 Ibid., p. 78

340 Paul Crawford ed., *The Templar of Tyre: Part III of the 'Deeds of the Cypriots'* (Hampshire: Ashgate Publishing, 2003) p.114; David Nicolle et al., *Acre 1291, Bloody Sunset of the Crusader States* (Oxford: Osprey Publishing, 2005) p. 76; Madden, *Crusades, The Illustrated History,* p.171.

341 Lewis, *What Went Wrong?* P. 16.

342 Osama bin Ladin, "World Islamic Front's Statement Urging Jihad Against Jews and Crusaders" London, *Al-Quds al-'Arabi*, February 23, 1998, Page 3

343 Zuheir Mohsen

344 Qutb, p.13.

345 *The 9/11 Commission Report* (Washington: USGPO, 2004) p.47.

346 Al-Bukhari, Volume 4, Book 52, Number 256; Qutb, p. 12-13.

347 Al-Bukhari, Volume 4, Book 52, Number 256, http://www.usc.edu/schools/college/crcc/engagement/resources/texts/muslim/hadith/bukhari/052.sbt.html.

348 "Ten Misconceptions About Islam" http://www.missionislam.com/discover/misconceptions.htm

349 "Ten Misconceptions About Islam" *Misconception 2* http://www.missionislam.com/discover/misconceptions.htm

350 "Ten Misconceptions About Islam" *Misconception 7* http://www.missionislam.com/discover/misconceptions.htm.

351 Ibid.

352 Samuel Huntington, *The Clash of Civilizations and the Remarking of World Order* (New York: Simon and Schuster, 1996) p. 217-218.

353 Al-Bukhari, Volume 1, Book 2, Number 24.

Chapter 13: Notes

354 *The Illustrated Bible Dictionary* (Wheaton: Tyndale House Publishers, 1980) Vol. I, "Chronology of the Old Testament", p.273; *The Holy Bible*, Revised Standard Version, (Philadelphia: A.J. Holman Company, 1962) Old Testament, II Samuel 5:4-7

355 Etgar Lefkovits, "Nehemiah's Wall Uncovered" Jerusalem Post, November 28, 2007, JerusalemPost.com, http://www.jpost.com/servlet/Satellite?cid=11955467534 93&pagename=JPost%2FJPArticle%2FShowFull; *The Holy Bible*, Revised Standard Version, Old Testament, Nehemiah 1:1-3 and 2:1-6

356 Abraham Lincoln, "The Gettysburg Address" November 19, 1863; The Library of Congress, http://www.loc.gov/exhibits/gadd/gadrft.html

357 Martin Gilbert, *The Atlas of Jewish History* (New York: William Morrow and Company, 1993) p.1

358 Yigal Lossin, *Pillar Of Fire* (Jerusalem: Shikmona Publishing, 1983) p.5-7; *The Illustrated Bible Dictionary*, Vol. I, "Abraham" pp.5-8, 257, 271; *The Holy Bible*, Revised Standard Version, (Philadelphia: A.J. Holman Company, 1962) Old Testament, Genesis 11:26-32 and 12:1-7, New Testament, Acts of the Apostles 7:2-8, Ephesians 1:21 and Hebrews 11:17-22

359 *The Illustrated Bible Dictionary*, Vol. I, "Exodus", p.489; *The Holy Bible*, Revised Standard Version, Old Testament, Exodus 12:40, 41

360 *The Illustrated Bible Dictionary*, Vol. I, "Chronology of the Old Testament", p.270

361 Ibid., p.489

362 *The Holy Bible*, Revised Standard Version, Old Testament, Exodus 20:2-17

363 Ibid., New Testament, Romans 9:4-5

364 Wayne Meeks, *The First Urban Christians* (New Haven, Yale University Press, 1983) p. 17

365 Rodney Stark, *The Rise of Christianity* (San Francisco, Harper Collins, 1997) p. 135

366 Ibid., p.44

367 William Smith, *Smith's Bible Dictionary*, "Jerusalem" 1901; http://www.bible-history.com/jerusalem/firstcenturyjerusalem_smith_s_bible_dictionary.html

368 Stark, p. 44

369 *The Holy Bible*, New King James Version, (New York, Thomas Nelson, 1982) New Testament, Acts of the Apostles 2:41.

370 Stark, pp. 6-7

371 Ibid., p.137

372 Ibid., p.147

373 Barbara Levick, *Roman Colonies in Southern Asia Minor* (Oxford: Clarendon, 1967)

374 Stark, pp.150-151

375 Ibid., p.150

376 Jerome Carcopino, *Daily Life in Ancient Rome* (New Haven: Yale University Press, 1940) p.44

377 Jane Cahill et al, "Scientists Examine Remains of Ancient Bathroom" *Biblical Archeological Review* 17 (May-June, 1991) pp.64-69

378 Stark, p.160

379 Naphtali Lewis, *Life in Egypt under Roman Rule* (Oxford: Clarendon, 1985) p.54

380 Michael Gorman, *Abortion and the Early Church* (Downers Grove: InterVarsity Press, 1982) p.25

381 Patricia Smith and Gila Kahila, "Bones of a Hundred Infants Found in Ashkelon Sewer," *Biblical Archeology Review* 17 (July-August, 1991) p.47; Lawrence Stager, "Eroticism and Infanticide at Ashkelon", *Biblical Archeology Review* 17 (July-August, 1991) pp. 34-53

382 Stark, pp. 117-122

383 Ibid., pp.82-87

384 *The Holy Bible*, Revised Standard Version, (Philadelphia: A.J. Holman Company,

1962) New Testament, Matthew 25:35-40

385 Eusebius, (Ca.325) *The Ecclesiastical History and The Martyrs of Palestine.* 2 vols. Vol.1 translated by Kirsopp Lake. Vol.2 translated by Hugh Jackson Lawlor and John Ernest Leonard Oulton. (Cambridge: Harvard University Press, 1949)

386 W.H.C. Frend, *Martyrdom and Persecution in the Early Church* (Oxford: Basil Blackwell, 1965) p.413

387 Ibid., pp.186,187

388 Stark, p.164

389 Ibid., pp.180-182

390 Peter Brown, *The Cult of the Saints* (Chicago: University of Chicago Press, 1981) p.79

391 Lactantius, *On the Deaths of the Persecutors*, Cited in *A History of the Christian Church*, 4th ed. by Williston Walker, Richard A. Norris, David W. Lotz, and Robert T. Handy (New York, Charles Scribner's Sons, 1985), p. 125.

392 "The Battle at Mulvian Bridge" Unique Historical Events in the Christian religion, http://www.christianitysite.com/MilvianBridge.htm; "The Battle of Mulvian Bridge" https://richardsonworldhistory.wikispaces.com/News+Story+-+The+Battle+of+Mulvian+Bridge; The Christian Empire: 313- 476, http://gbgm-umc.org/UMW/Bible/ce.stm

393 Thomas Woods, Jr., *How the Catholic Church Built Western Civilization* (Washington, DC: Regnery Press, 2005) p.13

394 *The Holy Bible*, Revised Standard Version, (Philadelphia: A.J. Holman Company, 1962) New Testament, Romans 13:4

395 Walker, et. al., p.125

396 A. S. Peake and R.G. Parsons editors, *An Outline Of Christianity; The Story Of Our Civilization.* 5 Vols. (London: Waverly Book Company, 1926) Vol. II, *The Birth of Christianity*, p. 80

397 *The Holy Bible*, Revised Standard Version, (Philadelphia: A.J. Holman Company, 1962) New Testament, Acts of the Apostles 25:12, 21

398 H. Leclercq, "The First Council Of Nicea," *The Catholic Encyclopedia*, Volume XI. (New York: Robert Appleton Company, 1911) New Advent, http://www.newadvent.org/cathen/11044a.htm

399 Stark, pp.6-7

400 William Jurgens, *The Faith of the Early Fathers,* Volume 3 (Collegeville, MN: Liturgical Press, 1980) p. 338; James Kiefer, "The Nicene Creed" http://www.spurgeon.org/~phil/creeds/nicene.htm; "The Nicene Creed" http://www.christianitysite.com/NiceneCreed.htm

Chapter 14: Notes

401 Al Bukhari, narrated by Ibn Umar, Volume 1, Book 2, Number 24

402 Paul Davis, *100 Decisive Battles From Ancient Times to the Present* (New York: Oxford University Press, 1999) p.106; Victor Hanson, *Carnage and Culture, Landmark Battles in the Rise of Western Power* (New York: Anchor Books, 2002) pp.137-143; "The Battle of Tours" Jewish Virtual Library, http://www.jewishvirtuallibrary.org/jsource/History/Tours.html

403 Woods, p.15

404 Davis, pp. 105-106

405 Kennedy Hickman, "Muslim Invasions: Charles Martel" Kennedy Hickman's Military History Blog, About.com; http://militaryhistory.about.com/b/2007/08/23/muslim-invasions-charles-martel-born.htm; http://militaryhistory.about.com/od/army/p/martel.htm

406 H.R. Trevor-Roper, *Hitler's Table Talk 1941-1944*, Translators: Norman Cameron and R.H. Stephens (New York: Enigma Books, 2008) p.504; Entry # 303, 28 August 1942, midday.

407 Ibid.

408 Woods, pp. 12- 17

409 Ibid.,p.16

410 "The Carolingian Empire, Carolingian Handwriting" http://history.boisestate.edu/WESTCIV/charles/16.shtml

411 Classics: Their History and Present Status in Education, A Symposium of Essays, edited by Felix M. Kirsch, 1977, p.62

412 Philippe Wolff, *The Awakening of Europe* (New York: Penguin Books, 1968) p.57

413 Christopher Dawson, *Religion and the Rise of Western Culture* (New York: Image Books, 1991) p.66

414 "Saint Benedict of Nursia" New Advent, Catholic Encyclopedia, http://www.newadvent.org/cathen/02467b.htm

415 "Cistercians" New Advent, Catholic Encyclopedia, http://www.newadvent.org/cathen/03780c.htm; Woods, p.37

416 Thomas Aquinas, *Summa Theologica* (Benziger Brothers edition, 1947) Translated by Fathers of the English Dominican Province, Christian Classics Ethereal Library, http://www.ccel.org/ccel/aquinas/summa.titlepage.html

417 *Decretum Gratiani*, Bayerische StaatsBibliotek, http://mdz.bib-bvb.de/digbib/gratian; "Domus Gratiani" http://pantheon.yale.edu/~haw6/gratian.html;

418 Brian Tierney, "The Idea of Natural Rights-Origins and Persistence" *Northwestern University Journal of International Human Rights,* Volume 2 (April 2004) paragraphs 15-16; http://www.law.northwestern.edu/journals/jihr/v2/2/

419 "King Ferdinand V King of Castile and Aragon (1452-1516)" http://goofy313g.free.fr/calisota_online/exist/ferdinandV.html

420 Woods, pp. 137-141

421 *The Holy Bible,* The New International Version, (Grand Rapids, Michigan: Zondervan, 1984) New Testament, Acts 17:29-31

422 Dumas Malone, *Jefferson The Virginian* (Boston: Little, Brown and Company, 1948) p. 237

423 Ibid., pp. 236, 237

424 Richard Perry ed., *Sources of our Liberties* (Chicago: American Bar Foundation, 1978) pp. xx

425 Ibid., p.319

426 Ibid., p.318

427 Ibid., p.1

428 [70] Ibid., p. 432

429 *The Holy Bible,* The New International Version, Old Testament, Exodus 19:7-9

430 Ibid., p.303

431 Ibid., p.399

432 The History Place, *American Revolution, An Unlikely Victory 1777-1783*, http://www.historyplace.com/unitedstates/revolution/revwar-77.htm

433 Rit Nosotro, *John Wycliffe, Morning Star of the Reformation*, hyperhistory.net, http://www.hyperhistory.net/apwh/bios/b2wycliffejohn.htm,

434 David W. Cloud ed, *William Tyndale: The Father of Our English Bible* (Port Huron: Way of Life Literature, 2001) http://www.wayoflife.org/articles/williamtyndale.htm,

435 Perry, p. 432

436 Michael T. Benson, *Harry S. Truman and the Founding of Israel* (Westport: Preager, 1997) reviewed by Daniel Pipes, *Middle East Quarterly*, September 1998, http://www.danielpipes.org/article/783 ; Palestinefacts.org, "Why did the United States immediately recognize the State of Israel?" http://www.palestinefacts.org/pf_independence_recognition_us.php

437 The Holy Bible, New International Version, Genesis 12:3.

438 Peter Marshall and David Manuel, *The Light and the Glory* (Grand Rapids: Fleming H. Revell, 1977) p.67

439 Ronald Reagan, "We Will Be As A City Upon A Hill", Conservative Political Action Conference, Washington, DC, January 25, 1974, The American Conservative Union, http://www.conservative.org/pressroom/reagan/reagan1974.asp

440 Ronald Reagan, "Farewell Address to the Nation" Broadcast from the Oval Office of The White House, Washington, DC, January 11, 1989, http://www.reaganlibrary.com/reagan/speeches/farewell.asp

Chapter 15: Notes

441 Paul Fynn, *Interview on the progress of communism in Africa*, Chicago, January, 1980.

442 Steven Emerson, *American Jihad, The Terrorists Living Amongst Us* (New York: Free Press, 2002) p.2.

443 Philip Hitti, *The Arabs: A Short History* (Washington: Regnery, 1996) p. 35-37

444 Karsh, p.12; Ibn Ishaq, pp.231-233

445 Hitti, p.36

446 Ibn Ishaq, *The Covenant Between The Muslims And The Medinans And The Jews*, pp.231-233.

447 Ibn Ishaq, *The Covenant Between The Muslims And The Medinans And The Jews*, pp.231-233; Lewis, *The Political Language of Islam*, pp.69,70; Bard, *The Complete Idiots Guide to Middle East Conflict*, p.49

448 Pickthall, (2:217,218) pp.31,32; Lewis, *The Political Language of Islam*, pp.66, 71; Hitti, p. 36; Ibn Ishaq, p.464

449 "Dispatches - Undercover Mosque (1 of 6)" UK Channel 4, January 15, 2007, YouTube, http://uk.youtube.com/watch?v=peFQWuk4nuo

450 Ibn Ishaq, p.464; Karsh, p.13; Gabriel, p.149; Lewis, *The Political Language of Islam*, p.73

451 Lewis, *The Crisis of Islam, Holy War and Unholy Terror*, pp.6,10,20; Pickthall, (2:191) p.28, (8:57-60) p.159, (9:29) p.166, (9:111) p.176; Al-Bukhari, Narrated by Ibn

Umar, Volume 1, Book 2, Number 24; Al-Bukhari, Narrated by Abu Huraira, Volume 1, Book 2, Number 25, http://www.usc.edu/dept/MSA/fundamentals/hadithsunnah/bukhari/002.sbt.html.

452 Boaz Ganor, *Hamas-The Islamic Resistance Movement in the Territories*, Jerusalem Center for Public Affairs, Survey of Arab Affairs, No. 27, February 2, 1992, http://www.jcpa.org/jl/saa27.htm

453 Matthew Levitt, *Hamas, Politics, Charity and Terrorism in the Service of Jihad* (New Haven: Yale University Press, 2006) p.20.

454 Matthias Kuntzel, *Hitler's Legacy; Anti-Semitism in the Middle East,* Paper presented at the international seminar series "Anti-Semitism in Comparative Perspective" Yale University, New Haven, November 30, 2006; John Loftus, *The Muslim Brotherhood, The Nazis and Al-Qa'ida,* Nexus Magazine, Volume 12, Number 6 (October - November 2005) http://www.nexusmagazine.com/articles/Fascist%20Roots%20of%20Al-Qaeda.html; Marc Erikson, *Islamism, fascism and terrorism (Part 2),* Asia Times Online, November 8, 2002, http://www.atimes.com/atimes/Middle_East/DK08Ak03.html; Joseph Zyble, *Al Queda Terrorists Nazi Connection,* September 12, 2007, Warriors For Truth, http://www.warriorsfortruth.com/al-queda-terrorists-nazi-connection.html; Herbert Eiteneier, *The Nazi-Islamist Connection,* Jerusalem Center for Public Affairs, Jewish Political Studies Review 18:1-2 (Spring 2006), http://www.jcpa.org/phas/phas-eiteneier-s06.htm

455 David Pryce-Jones, "Their Kampf, Hitler's Book in Arab Hands," *National Review On-Line,* July 18,2002, http://www.nationalreview.com/nr_comment/nr_comment071802a.asp; "Who was the Grand Mufti, Haj Muhammed Amin al-Husseini?" *Palestine Facts,* 2009, http://www.palestinefacts.org/pf_mandate_grand_mufti.php .

456 Bernard Lewis, *Semites and Anti-Semites; An Inquiry into Conflict and Prejudice* (New York: W.W. Norton & Co., 1999) p. 152-155; Daryl Hunter, *Militant Islam 101: A History*, Citizens For A Free America, http://www.free-press.biz/usa/Islamism-101.htm.

457 Bernard Lewis, *Semites and Anti-Semites,* p. 152-153; Daryl Hunter, *Militant Islam 101: A History*, Citizens For A Free America, http://www.free-press.biz/usa/Islamism-101.htm; Matthias Kuntzel, *Hitler's Legacy; Anti-Semitism in the Middle East,* Paper presented at the international seminar series "Anti-Semitism in Comparative Perspective" Yale University, New Haven, November 30, 2006.

458 Hugh Redwald Trevor-Roper ed., *Hitler's Table Talk 1941-1944*, translators: Norman Cameron and R.H. Stephens (New York: Enigma Books, 2008) #302 Midday, August 28, 1941, p.504; *From the Fuhrer to Florida*, Militant Islam Monitor, August 8, 2005.

459 J.B. Schechtman, *The Mufti and the Fuhrer: The Rise and Fall of Haj Amin al-Husseini* (New York: Thomas Yoseloff, 1965) pp. 159, 160.

460 Ibid.

461 Ibid.

462 J.B. Schechtman, p.156-160; Hugh Redwald Trevor-Roper ed., *Hitler's Table Talk 1941-1944*, translators: Norman Cameron and R.H. Stephens (New York: Enigma Books, 2008) #302 Midday, August 28, 1941, p.504; *From the Fuhrer to Florida*, Militant Islam Monitor, August 8, 2005, http://www.militantislammonitor.org/article/id/926; Daryl Hunter, *Militant Islam 101: A History*, Citizens For A Free America,

http://www.free-press.biz/usa/Islamism-101.htm

463 Schechtman, p. 160

464 Barry M. Rubin and Judith Colp Rubin, *Yassir Arafat, A Political Biography* (New York: Oxford University Press, 2003) p. 11-12; Said Aburish, *Arafat, From Defender to Dictator* (New York: Bloomsbury Publishing, 1998) pp.14-18, 20-23.

465 Daryl Hunter, *Militant Islam 101: A History*, Citizens For A Free America, http://www.free-press.biz/usa/Islamism-101.htm; UXL Newsmakers 2005, *Hassan al-Banna*, BNET Business Network, http://findarticles.com/p/articles/mi_gx5221/is_2005/ai_n19134442/pg_1

466 Judith Palmer Harik, *Hezbollah, The Changing Face of Terrorism* (London: J.B. Tauris & Company, 2004) p.10.

467 Bernard Lewis, *What Went Wrong, The Clash Between Islam and Modernity in the Middle East* (New York: Oxford University Press, 2002) p.158; Ayaan Hirsi Ali, *The Caged Virgin* (New York: Free Press, 2006) p.19

468 Pickthall, (Surah 5:33-35, 59-60) pp. 97-101, (Surah 5:78-80) p. 103; Al Bukhari, narrated by Ibn Umar, Volume 1, Book 2, Number 24; Maulana Muhammad Ali, *The Muslim Prayer-Book*, Notes on "The Opening" p.5.

469 Hugh Redwald Trevor-Roper ed., *Hitler's Table Talk 1941-1944*, translators: Norman Cameron and R.H. Stephens (New York: Enigma Books, 2008) #302 Midday, August 28, 1941, p.504

470 Sayyid Qutb, *Milestones* (Salimiah, Kuwait: International Islamic Federation of Student Organizations, 1978) pp.10, 11,63; Sayyid Qutb, *The Right To Judge*, http://www.islamworld.net/justice.html; Pickthall, (Surah 5:35) p.98, (Surah 12:40) p.208; Omar Nasiri, *Inside The Jihad* (New York: Basic Books, 2006) pp.150, 329; Judith Palmer Harik, *Hezbollah, The Changing Face of Terrorism* (London: J.B. Tauris & Company, 2004) p.10.

471 Qutb, *Milestones,* p. 63.

472 Daryl Hunter, *Militant Islam 101: A History*, Citizens For A Free America, http://www.free-press.biz/usa/Islamism-101.htm

473 Meir Hatina, *Islam and Salvation in Palestine* (Tel Aviv: Moshe Dayan Center Papers, 127, 2001) p.19; Boaz Ganor, Survey of Arab Affairs, No. 27; *Biography: Sayyid Qutb,* Answers.com,http://www.answers.com/topic/sayyid-qutb-1; Omar Nasiri, *Inside The Jihad* (New York: Basic Books, 2006) p.150.

474 *Khartoum Resolutions*, September 1967, MidEast Web Historical Documents, http://www.mideastweb.org/khartoum.htm

475 Bernard Lewis *The Political Language of Islam* (Chicago: University of Chicago Press, 1991) p. 72-73; *Khartoum Resolutions*, September 1967, MidEast Web Historical Documents, http://www.mideastweb.org/khartoum.htm

476 Levitt, pp. 21-23

477 P.J. Vatikiotis, *The History of Modern Egypt*, Fourth Edition (Baltimore: Johns Hopkins University, 1992) p. 443.

478 Michael Oren, *Power, Faith and Fantasy* (New York: W. W. Norton & Company, 2007) p. 541.

479 Lawrence Wright, *The Looming Tower: Al-Queda and the Road to 9/11* (New York: Knopf, 2006) pp. 49-50.

480 Muslim American Society, *What Is MAS*, http://web.archive.org/

web/20021206132514/www.masmn.org/Other/About_Us.htm; Noreen S. Ahmed-Ullah, Sam Roe, and Laurie Cohen, "A Rare Look at Secretive Brotherhood in America," *Chicago Tribune*, September 19, 2004; Guilain Denoelcx, *Hassan al-Banna*, "Biographies of 20th Century Leaders" Muslim American Society, http://web.archive.org/web/20031118091359/www.masmn.org/Biographies/20th_Century/Hasan_Al_Banna.htm; Ahmed El-Kadi, *Sayyid Qutb*, "Biographies of 20th Century Leaders" Muslim American Society, http://web.archive.org/web/20040816041832/www.masmn.org/Biographies/20th_Century/Sayyid_Qutb.htm.

481 Richard Clark, Senate Committee on Banking, Housing, and Urban Affairs, October 22, 2003.

482 "The Principles of the Muslim Brotherhood," The Muslim Brotherhood (Ikhwan) Official English Website, June 8, 2006, http://www.muslimbrotherhood.co.uk/Home.asp?zPage=Systems&System=PressR&Press=Show&Lang=E&ID=4584 ; Art Moore, *Should Muslim Quran be USA's top authority?*, WorldNetDaily, May 1, 2003, http://www.worldnetdaily.com/index.php?fa=PAGE.view&pageId=18561;

483 Noreen S. Ahmed-Ullah, Sam Roe, and Laurie Cohen, "A Rare Look at Secretive Brotherhood in America," *Chicago Tribune*, September 19, 2004; Steven Emerson, *American Jihad*, p.6.

484 *About MAS, When And Where It All Started,* The Muslim American society, masnet.org, http://www.masnet.org/aboutmas.asp.

485 *US v Holy Land Foundation,* 04-CR-240, "Indictment" (NDTX, July 27, 2004); Paul Sperry, *Infiltration* (Nashville: Nelson Current, 2005) pp. 88-90; Art Moore, *CAIR leader convicted on terror charges,* WorldNetDaily, April 14, 2005, http://www.worldnetdaily.com/index.php?fa=PAGE.view&pageId=29850; *About MAS, Where it all began,* Muslim American Society, http://www.masnet.org/aboutmas.asp; Noreen S. Ahmed-Ullah, Sam Roe, and Laurie Cohen, "A Rare Look at Secretive Brotherhood in America," *Chicago Tribune*, September 19, 2004.

486 Nonie Darwish, *Now They Call Men Infidel* (New York: Sentinel, 2006) pp. 246, 247.

487 Aaron Klein, "Soda, pizza and the destruction of America," *WorldNetDaily*, Mar. 18, 2003, http://www.worldnetdaily.com/news/article.asp?ARTICLE_ID=31571.

488 Michelle Malkin, "Religion of Perpetual Outrage alert: Another Mohammed cartoon riot", February 11, 2008 10:02 AM http://michellemalkin.com/2008/02/11/religion-of-perpetual-outrage-alert-another-mohammed-cartoon-riot/; Sarah Dallof, "Is it illegal to pray on public property?" KSL TV Channel 5, January 31st, 2008 @ 6:04p.m., KSL.com, http://www.ksl.com/?nid=148&sid=2583566; Susan Duclos, "Muslim Students Kill 3 Over Muhammad Caricature", Wake Up America. February 11, 2008. http://wwwwakeupamericans-spree.blogspot.com/2008/02/muslim-students-kill-3-over-muhammed.html.

489 Sayyid Qutb, *Milestones*, pp. 12-14, 303.

490 *9/11 Commission Report* (Washington, DC: GPO, Dec. 5, 2005) Sec. 2.1, "A Declaration of War", p.47, http://www.gpoaccess.gov/911/pdf/sec2.pdf ; "Hunting Ben Ladin," PBS *Frontline* broadcast, May 1998.

491 Sahih Bukhari, translator: M. Mushin Kahn, Vol. 4, Book 52, *Fighting for the Cause of Allah (Jihad)* Number 256, USC-MSA, Compendium of Muslim Texts, http://www.usc.edu/dept/MSA/fundamentals/hadithsunnah/bukhari/.

492 Paul Sperry, *Infiltration* (Nashville: Nelson Current, 2005) pp. 89-91.

493 Friedman, page after copyright, p. 137.

494 Stark, pp. 6-10.

495 Stark, p.10.

496 "Largest Religious Groups in The United States of America" National and World Religious Statistics, Adherants.com, http://www.adherents.com/rel_USA.html#gallup

497 Bat Ye'or, *The Dhimmi, Jews and Christians Under Islam* (Rutherford, NJ: Farleigh Dickinson, 1985) pp. 30-35.

498 Bat Ye'or, *Islam and Dhimmitude, Where Civilizations Collide* (Rutherford, NJ: Farleigh Dickinson, 2002) p. 201; Bat Ye'or, *The Dhimmi, Jews and Christians Under Islam* p. 347.

499 Al Bukhari, narrated by Abu Huraira, Vol. 2, Book 23, Number 467, http://www.usc.edu/dept/MSA/fundamentals/hadithsunnah/bukhari/023.sbt.html#002.023.463; Bat Ye'or, *The Dhimmi, Jews and Christians Under Islam*, "Document 45: Massacre of Christians in Damascus" (1860), p. 268.

500 Robert Spencer, *The Politically Incorrect Guide to Islam and the Crusades* (Washington, DC: Regnery, 2005) p. 126.

501 Bat Ye'or, *Islam and Dhimmitude, Where Civilizations Collide*, p. 179.

502 Steven Emerson, *American Jihad, The Terrorists Living Amongst Us* (New York: Free Press, 2002) Appendices A & B, pp.198-201.

503 Ian Black, "Great Satan' warned of a burning hell" *World Dispatch*, February 16 2005, http://www.guardian.co.uk/world/2005/feb/16/worlddispatch.usa

504 Nazila Fathi, "Wipe Israel off the map, Iranian says" *International Herald Tribune*, October 17, 2005, http://www.iht.com/articles/2005/10/26/news/iran.php; Azadeh Moaveni, "Mahmoud Ahmadinejad" *Time Magazine*, April 30, 2006, http://www.time.com/time/magazine/article/0,9171,1186909,00.html; "Profile: Mahmoud Ahmadinejad" BBC News, April 28, 2006, http://news.bbc.co.uk/1/hi/world/middle_east/4107270.stm; "Iranian Leader: Holocaust a myth" CNN.com, December 14, 2005, http://www.cnn.com/2005/WORLD/meast/12/14/iran.israel/

505 Mahmoud Ahmadinejad, *Transcript of speech at "World Without Zionism" conference in Tehran*, Iran Focus, October 28, 2005.

506 Ibid.

507 John R. Bolton, "Preventing Iran from Acquiring Nuclear Weapons" Remarks to the Hudson Institute, Washington, DC, August 17, 2004, U.S. Department of State Website, http://www.state.gov/t/us/rm/35281.htm;

508 Norman Podhoretz, "The Case For Bombing Iran" *Commentary Magazine*, June 2007, Commentarymagazine.com, http://www.commentarymagazine.com/viewarticle.cfm/The-Case-for-Bombing-Iran-10882.

509 "U.S. Nuclear Weapon Enduring Stockpile" NuclearWeaponArchives.Org, August 31, 2007, http://nuclearweaponarchive.org/Usa/Weapons/Wpngall.html.

510 "The B83 (Mk-83) Bomb" http://nuclearweaponarchive.org/Usa/Weapons/B83.html; "F-16 and F-18 Everywhere and Forever" http://www.strategypage.com/htmw/htairfo/articles/20051109.aspx

511 "Nimitz Class Nuclear-Powered Aircraft Carriers, USA," Navaltechnology.com, http://www.naval-technology.com/projects/nimitz/ ; "The B83 (Mk-83) Bomb" http://

nuclearweaponarchive.org/Usa/Weapons/B83.html.

512 "U.S. Submarine Classes," The Pentagon, Millnet.com, http://www.milnet.com/pentagon/subclass.htm; "SSBN-726 Ohio-Class FBM Submarines," Federation of American Scientists, http://www.fas.org/nuke/guide/usa/slbm/ssbn-726.htm.

513 "Fleet Ballistic Missile Submarines - SSBN" The United States Navy Fact File, http://www.navy.mil/navydata/fact_display.asp?cid=4100&tid=200&ct=4

514 Andreas Parsch, "Lockheed Martin UGM-133 Trident II," *Directory of U.S. Military Rockets and Missiles* http://www.designation-systems.net/dusrm/m-133.html ; Elaine Grossman, "DoD Defends New Sub-Launched Missiles" *Today In The Military*, March 10, 2006, Military.com, http://www.military.com/features/0,15240,90477,00.html .

515 "Ohio Class Submarines" http://en.wikipedia.org/wiki/Ohio_class_submarine "Nuclear Weapon Effects" http://www.nukefix.org/weapon.html

516 Elaine Grossman, "DoD Defends New Sub-Launched Missiles" *Today In The Military*, March 10, 2006, Military.com, http://www.military.com/features/0,15240,90477,00.html

517 Steven Emerson, *American Jihad, The Terrorists Living Amongst Us* (New York: Free Press, 2002) Appendices A & B, pp.198-201.

518 Rod Dreher, "What the Muslim Brotherhood means for the U.S., Memo lays bare group's plans to destroy U.S. from within," *The Dallas Morning News*, Tuesday, September 11, 2007, Dallasnews.com, http://www.dallasnews.com/sharedcontent/dws/dn/opinion/points/stories/DN-dreher_09edi.ART.State.Edition1.4235f88.html

519 Ibid.

Chapter 16: Notes

520 Abraham Lincoln, "The Gettysburg Address" November 19, 1863; The Library of Congress, http://www.loc.gov/exhibits/gadd/gadrft.html

521 Ibid.

522 Ibid.

523 Paul Fynn, *Interview on the progress of communism in Africa*, Chicago, January 1980.

524 *The Unanimous Declaration of the Thirteen United States of America, In Congress July 4, 1776*, The Declaration of Independence, ushistory.org, http://www.ushistory.org/declaration/document/index.htm .

525 William Blackstone, *The Commentaries of Sir William Blackstone, Knt. on the Laws and Constitution of England*, Elibron Classics Unabridged Facsimile Replica (Boston: Adamant Media Corporation, 2005) pp. 13-14.

526 Stephen McDowell, *America, a Christian Nation? Examining the Evidence of a Christian Foundation of America* (Charlottesville: Providence Foundation, 2005) p.8.

527 Ibid., pp.8-10.

528 Mark Beliles and Douglas Anderson, *Contending for the Constitution* (Charlottesville: Providence Foundation, 2005) p. 100.

529 *The United States Constitution,* The United States Constitution Online, "Preamble" http://www.usconstitution.net/const.html#Preamble

530 Harry S. Truman, *Harry S. Truman: Public Papers of the Presidents of the United States Containing the Public Messages, Speeches and Statements of the President---*

January 1 to December 31, 1950 (Washington, D.C.: USGPO, 1965) p.197. Quoted in Beliles and Anderson, p. 70.

531 McDowell, pp.34, 35.

532 *Church of the Holy Trinity v. U.S.*; 143 U.S. 457, 458 (1892).

533 Beliles and Anderson, pp. 127-129.

534 Ibid., pp. 127,128.

535 *The Patriot,* Written by Robert Rodat and directed by Roland Emmerich, (Mutual Film Company and Centropolis Entertainment, 2000) DVD Columbia Pictures.

536 John F. Kennedy, *Inaugural Address*, Washington, D.C., January 20, 1961, John F. Kennedy Presidential Library and Museum, http://www. jfklibrary.org/Historical+Resources/Archives/Reference+Desk/Speeches/ JFK/003POF03Inaugural01201961.htm

Conclusion: Notes

537 McDowell, pp.34, 35.

538 Horowitz, *Indoctrination U.,* pp. 123-127.

539 Abraham Lincoln, "The Gettysburg Address" November 19, 1863; The Library of Congress, http://www.loc.gov/exhibits/gadd/gadrft.html

540 Martin Luther King, "I Have a Dream" Washington, D.C.: August 28, 1963, *U.S. Constitution Online*, http://www.usconstitution.net/dream.html.

541 *The Global Poverty Act,* (S. 2433); "Obama, Hagel, Cantwell, Smith Hail Committee Passage of the Global Poverty Act" Barak Obama, http://obama.senate. gov/press/080213-obama_hagel_can_1/ ; "Obama Bill: $845 Billion More for World Poverty" *WorldNet Daily*, February 14, 2008; Cliff Kinkaid, "AIM Says Media Cover-Up Obama's Socialist-Oriented Global Tax Bill," Accuracy in Media, Washington, D.C., February 13, 2008.

542 "The War in Iraq costs, 535 billion" The National Priorities Project, July 8, 2008, http://www.nationalpriorities.org/costofwar_home.

543 Horowitz, *Indoctrination U.,* p.126-127; Lunev and Winkler, p. 78; Col. E. Wright, USAF retired, Winchester, Wisconsin: August 1970.

544 Vinyamin Poloubiarava, "Communism's effects in America", *Interview with author,* Moscow, April, 1995.

545 Brigitte Gabriel, *They Must Be Stopped* (New York: St. Martins Press, 2008) p.73-76; Konstantin Preobrazhensky, "Russia and Islam are not Separate: Why Russia backs Al-Qaeda," (Alexandria: The Center for Counterintelligence and Security Studies, 2009), http://www.cicentre.com/articles/kpk_russia_islam.html;AxisInformationandAnalysis, "Alexander Litvinenko: Complete Profile," November 24, 2006, http://www.axisglobe. com/article.asp?article=1137 ; Peter Bergin, "Aymin al-Zawahiri," *Time Magazine*, Sunday April 30, 2006, http://www.time.com/time/magazine/article/0,9171,1187180,00. html; Michel Elbaz, "Russian Secrets of Al-Qaeda's Number Two," *Axis Information and Analysis*, July 19, 2005, http://www.axisglobe.com/article.asp?article=256.

546 Roee Nahmias, *Lahad: Syria Behind Gemayel's Murder,* Nov. 26, 2006, Ynetnews. com, http://www.ynetnews.com/articles/0,7340,L-3332868,00.html#n .

547 "Dispatches - Undercover Mosque (1 of 6)" UK Channel 4, January 15, 2007, YouTube, http://uk.youtube.com/watch?v=peFQWuk4nuo

Listings of References

ABC.com. *Judaism, Origins, History and Spread.* Library-Religion,
http://www.abc.net.au/religion/stories/s796551.htm.

About.com, *Al Andalus, Islam in Spain.*
http://atheism.about.com/library/world/KZ/bl_SpainAlAndalus.htm

Aburish, Said. *Arafat, From Defender to Dictator.* New York: Bloomsburg
Publishing,1998.

ADL. *The 1973 Yom Kippur War.* Israel Record.
http://www.adl.org/ISRAEL/Record/yomkippur.asp

Afak, Abu. *The Massacre at Damour, Jan. 9, 1976,* Free Republic.com.
http://www.freerepublic.com/focus/f-news/1555079/posts

A History and Mythos of the Knights Templar. *Pope Urban II – 1042-1099.*
http://www.templarhistory.com/urbanii.html

Ahmadinejad, Mahmoud. *Transcript of speech at "World Without Zionism" conference
in Tehran.* Iran Focus, October 28, 2005.

Akers, Paul . *Why Islam Didn't Conquer the World. From the Plains of Medieval France
to the Modern MidEast, Muslims test Christians and Jews.*
October 30, 2005, Fredricksburg.com.
http://fredericksburg.com/News/FLS/2005/102005/10302005/141401/
printer_friendly

Al Bukhari, Muhammad ibn Ismail. *Sahih Bukhari, Vol. 1-9.* Commentaries translated
to English by M. Mushin Kahn. USC-MSA Compendium of Muslim Texts:
University of Southern California. http://www.usc.edu/dept/MSA/
fundamentals/hadithsunnah/bukhari/.

AllAboutArcheology.org. *Biblical Archeology-Cities of Scripture;
Biblical Archaeology: Ancient Civilization.* http://www.allaboutarchaeology.
org/biblical-archaeology.htm,

_____ *Black Obelisk of Shalmaneser.*
http://www.allaboutarchaeology.org/black obelisk-of-shalmaneser-faq.htm.

_____ *Merneptah Stele.*
http://www.allaboutarchaeology.org/merneptah-stele-faq.htm.

_____ *Moabite Stone.*
http://www.allaboutarchaeology.org/moabite-stone-faq.htm.

_____ *Shishak Relief .*
http://www.allaboutarchaeology.org/shishak-relief-faq.htm.

_____ *Sumerian King List .*
http://www.allaboutarchaeology.org/sumerian-king-list-faq.htm.

_____ *House of Yahweh Ostracon.*
http://www.allaboutarchaeology.org/house-of-yahweh-ostracon-faq.htm.

_____ *The House of David Inscription.*
http://www.allaboutarchaeology.org/the-house-of-david-inscription-faq.htm.

_____ *Why was the Hammurabi Code of Law such an important archaeological discovery?* http://www.allaboutarchaeology.org/hammurabi-code-of-law-faq. htm.

All About The Truth. *Origin of the Bible - The Reliability of Ancient Manuscripts.* http://www.allabouttruth.org/Origin-Of-The-Bible.htm.
_____ *How many people wrote the Bible.* http://www.allabouttruth.org/how-many-people-wrote-the-bible-faq.htm.
_____ *When was the Bible Written?* http://www.allabouttruth.org/when-was-the-bible-written-faq.htm.

Alon, Mati. *Jordan is Palestine: Palestine is Jordan.* IsraelForum.com: http://www.israelforum.com/board/showthread.php?t=6693.

Al-Munajjid, Muhammad. *The true nature of the enmity between the Muslims and the Jews.* Islam Q A. http://www.alminbar.com/ khutbaheng/9022.htm.

American Memorial Site, *We Will Not Forget,* http://americanmemorialsite.com/beirutembassy.html.
_____ *Americans killed by Terrorism (1980-1989).* http://americanmemorialsite.com/1980.html.
_____ *Americans Killed by Terrorists (1990-1999),* http://americanmemorialsite.com/1990.html
_____ *Americans Killed by Terrorists (2000 to present).* http://americanmemorialsite.com/2000s.html.

American Society of Newspaper Editors Journalism Credibility Project, 1998. *Examining Our Credibility: Perspectives of the Public and the Press*

Amos, Gary T., *Defending The Declaration.* Brentwood, Tennessee: Wolgemuth & Hyatt, 1989.

Ancient Worlds. *Chronology of Islamic Spain-Al Andalus.* AncientWorlds.net. http://www.ancientworlds.net/aw/HomesiteRoom/603942.

Angelfire.com. *Quran Formation.* http://www.angelfire.com/ny/dawahpage/quran. html.

Ansari, Ali. *Confronting Iran.* New York: Basic Books, 2006.

Answering Islam. *Taqiya, Marriage, Kithman, Fatwa, Hadith, Kharijites, Shi'a, Sunni, Mut'a, and Muhammad: Model to Mankind.* http://answering-islam.org/Index/index.html.

Answers.com, *Mary Ann Vecchio* http://www.answers.com/topic/mary-ann-vecchio.

Aquinas, Thomas. *Summa Theologica.* Benziger Bros. edition, 1947. Translated by Fathers of the English Dominican Province, Christian Classics Ethereal Library. http://www.ccel.org/a/aquinas/summa/home.html.

Arlandson, James. *The Truth About Islamic Crusades and Imperialism*, American Thinker, November 27, 2005. http://www.americanthinker.com/2005/11/the_truth_about_islamic_crusad. html.

Avigad, Nahman, *Discovering Jerusalem.* Jerusalem: Shikmona Press, 1983.

Awwad, Tawfiq Yusuf. *Death In Beirut.* Translated by Leslie McLoughlin. London: Lynne Reinner Publishers, 1976.

Bacon, Josephine. ed. *All Israel.* London: Quintet Publishing Limited, 1988.

Bai, Mat. *"25 Years After Kent State, photographer, subject finally meet.*
The Boston Globe, April 24, 1995.

Barakat, Sharbel. *Testimony Before the Senate Foreign Relations Committee,*
Subcommittee on Near Eastern and Far Eastern Affairs.
Washington, DC: June 7, 1997.

Bard, Mitchell. *The Complete Idiot's Guide to Middle East Conflict.* Indianapolis:
Alpha Books, 2003.

_____ *The 1967 Six-Day War.* Jewish Virtual Library:
http://www.jewishvirtuallibrary.org/jsource/History/67_War.html.

_____ *Myths and Facts Online, Israel and Lebanon.* Jewish Virtual Library:
http://www.jewishvirtuallibrary.org/jsource/myths2/IsraelLebanon.html

Bayerische StaatsBibliotek. *Decretum Gratiani.* http://mdz.bib-bvb.de/digbib/gratian.

BBC News. *Profile: Mahmoud Ahmadinejad.* April 28, 2006,
http://news.bbc.co.uk/1/hi/world/middle_east/4107270.stm;

Bell, Rachael and Bardsley, Marion. *Ed Gein: The Inspiration for Buffalo Bill and*
Psycho, http://www.crimelibrary.com/serial_killers/notorious/gein/bill_1.
html.

Beliles, Mark and Anderson, Douglas. *Contending for the Constitution.*
Charlottesville: Providence Foundation, 2005.

Benson, Michael T. *Harry S. Truman and the Founding of Israel.*
Westport: Preager, 1997.

Bin Ladin, Osama *World Islamic Front's Statement Urging Jihad Against Jews and*
Crusaders. Al-Quds al-'Arabi, London: February 23, 1998.

Black, Ian. *Great Satan warned of a burning hell.* World Dispatch. February 16,
2005. http://www.guardian.co.uk/world/2005/feb/16/worlddispatch.usa

Black, Ian and Benny Morris. *Israel's Secret Wars, A History of Israel's Intelligence*
Services. New York: Grove Weidenfeld, 1991.

Blackstone, Sir William. *The Commentaries on the Laws and Constitution of England.*
Oxford: Clarendon Press, 1765. Reprinted by Adamant Media Corporation,
2005.

_____ *Sir William Blackstone's Commentaries on the Laws of England.*
Vol. 1, 1735. http://www.agh-attorneys.com/4_william_blackstone.htm.

BNET Business Network. *Hassan al-Banna.* UXL Newsmakers 2005.
http://findarticles.com/p/articles/mi_gx5221/is_2005/ai_n19134442/pg_1.

Bolton, John R. *Preventing Iran from Acquiring Nuclear Weapons.* Remarks to the
Hudson Institute. Washington, DC: U.S. Department of State Website, August
17, 2004. http://www.state.gov/t/us/rm/35281.htm.

Bongars, Gesta Dei per Francos. translated to English by Oliver J. Thatcher and Edgar
Holmes McNeal, eds., *A Sourcebook of Medieval History.*
New York: Scribners, 1905.

Brainy Ouote. *Joseph Stalin Quotations.*
http://www.brainyquote.com/quotes/quotes/j/josephstal113988.html.

Brandt, Steve ed. *The Council of Nicea, The Role of Constantine.*
http://www.columbia.edu/cu/augustine/arch/sbrandt/nicea.htm

Brown, Peter. *The Cult of the Saints.* Chicago: University of Chicago Press, 1981.

Brozan, Nadine. *Chronicle: A Historic Photo and Now a Meeting.*
   The New York Times. April 25, 1995.
Cameron, Norman. *Hitler's Table Talk 1941-1944.* Translators: R.H. Stephens and
   Hugh Redwald Trevor-Roper, New York: Enigma Books, 2000.
Cahill, Jane et al. *Scientists Examine Remains of Ancient Bathroom.* Biblical
   Archeological Review 17 (May-June, 1991) pp.64-69.
Capitol Newspapers. *Sterling Hall Bombing.* Front Page News.
   http://www.madison.com/library/LEE/08261970.pdf.
_____ *UW Students Arm Selves.* Wisconsin State Journal, August 26, 1970.
   http://www.madison.com/library/LEE/08261970.pdf.
_____ *Wisconsin Socialists Condemn Bombing.*
   http://www.madison.com/library/LEE/09051970.pdf.
Carcopino, Jerome. *Daily Life in Ancient Rome.* New Haven:
   Yale University Press, 1940.
Cedarland. *The Massacre and Destruction of Damour.*
   http://www.geocities.com/CapitolHill/Parliament/2587/damour.html.
Chamoun, Camille. *The Lebanese President's Interview with the Author.*
   The Dolly Madison Hotel, Washington, DC, December, 1982.
ChristianitySite.com. *Unique Historical Events in the Christian religion,*
   The Battle at Mulvian Bridge. http://www.christianitysite.com/MilvianBridge.
   htm.
_____ *The Nicene Creed.* http://www.christianitysite.com/NiceneCreed.htm .
Clan Sinclair. *Battle of Poitiers, 17 October, 732.*
   http://sinclair.quarterman.org/history/med/battleofpoitiers.html
Clark, Richard. *Statement of Richard A. Clark to the Senate Committee on Banking,*
   Housing, and Urban Affairs. October 22, 2003.
   http://en.wikisource.org/wiki/Statement_of_Richard_A._Clarke_to_the_
   Senate_Committee_on_Banking,_Housing,_and_Urban_Affairs.
Cloud, David W. ed, *William Tyndale: The Father of Our English Bible.*
   Port Huron: Way of Life Literature, 2001. http://www.wayoflife.org/articles/
   williamtyndale.htm.
CNN.com. *Iranian Leader: Holocaust a myth.* December 14, 2005.
   http://www.cnn.com/2005/WORLD/meast/12/14/iran.israel/.
Collelo, Thomas. ed. Federal Research Division - Library of Congress. December,
   1987. Lebanon's History. *"Medievil Lebanon"* http://www.ghazi.de/
   medieval.html.
Collins, Larry and Dominique Lapierre. *O Jerusalem.* New York:
   Simon and Schuster, 1972.
Cooley, John, *Payback, America's Long War in the Middle East.* New York:
   Bracey's US, 1991.
Coulter, Ann. *Godless, The Church of Liberalislm.* New York: Crown Forum, 2006.
Creasy, Edward. *Fifteen Decisive Battles of the World: From Marathon to Waterloo*
   London: R. Bentley, 1851.
Crystalinks, *Gods and Goddesses of Fertility; Baal, Ishtar, Inanna,*
   http://www.crystalinks.com/fertilitygods.html.
Darwish, Nonie. *Now They Call Me Infidel, Why I Renounced Jihad for America,*

Israel, and The War On Terror. New York: Sentinel, 2006.

Dawson, Christopher. *Religion and the Rise of Western Culture.*
New York: Image Books, 1991.

Davies, W.W. *The Codes of Hammurabi and Moses.* Berkeley: Apocryphile Press,
2006.

Davis, John. *Davis Dictionary of the Bible.* Old Tappan, New Jersey:
Flemming H. Revell, 1972.

Davis, Paul. *100 Decisive Battles From Ancient Times to the Present.* New York:
Oxford University Press, 1999.

Dawidoowicz, Lucy, *The War Against the Jews: 1933-1945.* New York:
Bantam Books, 1986.

Denoelcx, Guilain. *Hassan al-Banna.* Biographies of 20th Century Leaders.
Muslim American Society.
http://web.archive.org/web/20031118091359/www.masmn.org/
Biographies/20th_Century/Hasan_Al_Banna.htm.

Diaz, Tom and Barbara Newman. *Lightning Out of Lebanon.* New York:
Ballantine Books, 2005.

Diker, Daniel, ed. *Iran, Hezbullah, Hamas and the Global Jihad.*
Jerusalem: Jerusalem Center for Public Affairs, 2007.

Dolan, David. *Holy War for the Promised Land.* Nashville: Thomas Nelson
Publishers, 1991.

Dallof, Sarah. *Is it illegal to pray on public property?* KSL TV Channel 5.
January 31, 2008 @ 6:04p.m.
KSL.com. http://www.ksl.com/?nid=148&sid=2583566.

Donner, Fred M. *The Early Islamic Conquests.* Princeton: Princeton University Press,
1981.

Douglas, J.D. et al ed., *The Illustrated Bible Dictionary,* Vol. 1-3
Wheaton: Tyndale House, 1980.

Dreher, Rod. *What the Muslim Brotherhood means for the U.S., Memo lays bare
group's plans to destroy U.S. from within.* The Dallas Morning News.
Tuesday, September 11, 2007. Dallasnews.com.
http://www.dallasnews.com/sharedcontent/dws/dn/opinion/points/stories/
DN-dreher_09edi.ART.State.Edition1.4235f88.html

D'Souza, Dinesh, *What's So Great About Christianity.* Washington, DC:
Regnery Publishing, 2007.

Duclos, Susan. *Muslim Students Kill 3 Over Muhammad Caricature.*
Wake Up America. February 11, 2008. http://wwwwakeupamericans-spree.
blogspot.com/2008/02/muslim-students-kill-3-over-muhammed.html.

Dyan, Moshe. *Living With The Bible.* New York: William Morrow and Company,
1978.

_____ *Moshe Dyan: Story of My Life.* New York: William Morrow and Company,
1976.

Eiteneier, Herbert. *The Nazi-Islamist Connection,* Jerusalem Center for Public Affairs,
Jewish Political Studies Review 18:1-2, Spring 2006. http://www.jcpa.org/
phas/phas-eiteneier-s06.htm.

El Asomado. *La Batalla de Las Navas de Tolosa, The Battle of Las Novas de Tolosa,*

The Pastorcillo. May 4, 2007. http://pobrespain.blogspot.com/2007/05/la-batalla-delas-navas-de-tolosa.html.

El-Kadi, Ahmed. *Sayyid Qutb*, Biographies of 20th Century Leaders. Muslim American Society. http://web.archive.org/web/20040816041832/www.masmn.org/Biographies/20th_Century/Sayyid_Qutb.htm.

Emerson, Steven. *Jihad Incorporated, A Guide to Militant Islam In The US.* New York: Prometheus Books, 2006.

_____ *American Jihad, The Terrorist Living Among Us.* New York: Free Press, 2002

Energy Information Administration. *Table 11.5 World Crude Oil Production, 1960-2005.* http://www.eia.doe.gov/emeu/aer/txt/ptb1105.html.

_____ *Saudi Arabia Country Analysis Brief.* http://www.eia.doe.gov/emeu/cabs/saudi.html.

EretzYisroel.org, *Black September, the PLO's attempt to take over Jordan in 1970.* http://www.eretzyisroel.org/~samuel/september.html.

Erikson, Marc. *Islamism, fascism and terrorism (Part 2),* Asia Times Online, November 8, 2002. http://www.atimes.com/atimes/Middle_East/DK08Ak03.html.

Eusebius. *The Ecclesiastical History and The Martyrs of Palestine.* 2 vols. Vol.1 translated by Kirsopp Lake. Vol.2 translated by Hugh Jackson Lawlor and John Ernest Leonard Oulton. Cambridge: Harvard University Press, 1949. http://www.tertullian.org/fathers/.

Evans, Paola et al. *Bolivia on the Day of the Death of Che Guevara.* Mindfully.org, 1997. http://www.mindfully.org/Reform/2005/Che-Guevara-Gott11aug05.htm.

Elbaz, Michael. *Dangerous Liaisons: covert love affair between Russia and Hezbollah, part 1.* Axis Information and Analysis,http://www.axisglobe.com/hezbollah1.htm.

Farah, Douglas. *The Muslim Brotherhood in America Defined as "Threat Organization"in DOD Memo,* http://www.douglasfarah.com/article/245/the-muslim-brotherhood-in-america-defined-as-threat-organization-in-dod-memo.com

Farah, Joseph. *The Most Trusted Man in America?* , WorldNetDaily, July 10, 2000, http://www.worldnetdaily.com/news/article.asp?ARTICLE_ID=15007.

Fathi, Nazila . *Wipe Israel off the map, Iranian says.* International Herald Tribune. October 17, 2005. http://www.iht.com/articles/2005/10/26/news/iran.php.

Feder, Don. *A Jewish Conservative Looks At Pagan America.* Lafayette, Louisiana: Huntington House Publishers, 1993.

Federation of American Scientists. *SSBN-726 Ohio-Class FBM Submarines.* http://www.fas.org/nuke/guide/usa/slbm/ssbn-726.htm.

First Council of Nicea 325 AD. *Professions of Faith of the 318 Fathers, Canons, Letter of the Synod in Nicea to the Egyptians.* http://www.piar.hu/councils/ecum01.htm.

Flapan, Simha. *The Birth of Israel, Myths and Realities.* New York: Pantheon Books, 1987.

Frend, W.H.C. *Martyrdom and Persecution in the Early Church.*

Oxford: Basil Blackwell, 1965.

Friedman, Thomas. *From Beirut to Jerusalem*. New York: Ferrar Straus Giroux, 1989.

Fynn, Paul. *Interview on the progress of Communism in Africa*. Chicago: January, 1980.

Gabriel, Brigitte. *Because They Hate*. New York: St. Martin's Press, 2006.

Gannett's First Amendment Center in Nashville. *2005 poll of Americans about their attitudes towards the media.* The American Journalism Review. August/September, 2005.

Ganor, Boaz. *Hamas-The Islamic Resistance Movement in the Territories*. Survey of Arab Affairs, No. 27. Jerusalem Center for Public Affairs: February 2, 1992. http://www.jcpa.org/jl/saa27.htm.

Gartner, Michael. *The First Rough Draft of History, an interview with Benjamin C. Bradlee*. American Heritage. Oct.-Nov. 1982.

Gheith, Abu. *Why We Fight. Al-Qu'ida Sokesman Explains September 11 and Declares Intentions to Kill 4 Million Americans With Weapons of Mass Destruction*. Middle East Media Research Institute, Special Dispatch 388, June 12, 2002. http://www.memri.org/bin/articles.cgi?Page=archives&Area=sd&ID=SP38802.

Gilbert, Martin, *The Atlas of Jewish History*. New York: William Morrow and Company, 1993.

Global Ministries. *The Christian Empire: 313- 476.*
http://gbgm-umc.org/UMW/Bible/ce.stm

Global Policy Forum. *Two Views: Can the Koran Condone Terror?*
http://www.globalpolicy.org/wtc/fundamentalism/1013koran2.htm.

GlobalSecurity.org. *Jordanian Removal of the PLO.*
http://www.globalsecurity.org/military/world/war/jordan-civil.htm.

_____*Marine Forces Atlantic [MarForLant] U.S. Marine Corps Forces, Europe (MARFOREOUR).*
http://www.globalsecurity.org/military/agency/usmc/marforlant.htm.

Gold, Dore. *The Iraq Study Group: Implications for Israel*. Issues Brief, Vol. 6, No. 15.Jerusalem: Jerusalem Center For Public Affairs, December 8, 2006.

_____*The Opening Round of Iran's War Against the West.*
Jerusalem Issue Brief Vol. 6, No. 1. Jerusalem: Jerusalem Center for Public Affairs, July 17, 2006. http://www.jcpa.org/brief/brief006-1.htm.

Goldberg, Bernard. *Bias*. Washington, DC: Regnery Press, 2002.

Goldberg, Vicki. *In a Rifle's Flash, a Lasting Icon of a Nation's Pain.*
The New York Times. April 30, 1995.

Gorman, Michael. *Abortion and the Early Church*. Downers Grove:
InterVarsity Press, 1982.

Greatsite.com. *English Bible History.*
http://www.greatsite.com/timeline-english-bible-history/pre-reformation.html.

Grossman, Elaine . *DoD Defends New Sub-Launched Missiles.*
Today In The Military. March 10, 2006. Military.com. http://www.military.com/features/0,15240,90477,00.html .

Hanson, Victor. *Carnage and Culture, Landmark Battles in the Rise of Western Power*

New York: Anchor Books, 2002.

Harik, Judith Palmer. *Hezbollah The Changing Face of Terrorism.* London: I.B. Tauris, 2004.

Harris, Bill. *Israel The Promised Land.* Jerusalem: Steimatzky Publishers, 1985.

Helm, Heinz. *Shi'a Islam: from Religion to Revolution,* translated from German by Allison Brown. Princeton: Markus Weiner Publishers, 1997. http://www.encyclopedia.com/doc/1G1-150356900.html.

Hatina, Meir. *Islam and Salvation in Palestine.* Tel Aviv: Moshe Dayan Center Papers, #127, 2001.

Helmer, Daniel. *Hezbollah's employment of suicide bombing during the 1980s: the theological, political, and operational development of a new tactic.* Military Review. July 1, 2006.

Hersh, Seymour. *The Sampson Option.* New York: Random House, 1991.

Hersi Ali, Ayaan. *Infidel.* New York: Free Press, 2007.

_____ *The Caged Virgin, An Emancipation Proclamation for Women and Islam.* New York: Free Press, 2006.

Herzog, Chaim. *The Arab-Israeli Wars.* New York: Random House, 1982.

Hickman, Kennedy . *Muslim Invasions: Charles Martel.* http://militaryhistory.about.com/od/army/p/martel.htm .

Hirsh, Michael and Maziar Bahari. *A Collision Course With Iran.* Newsweek Magazine. February 13, 2007.

History of Jihad. *The History of Jihad against the Austrians (1500 - 1683).* http://www.historyofjihad.org/austria.html.

Hitchcock, Mark. *Iran: The Coming Crisis.* Sisters, Oregon: Multnomah Publishers, 2006.

Hitti, Philip. *The Arabs: A Short History.* Washington, DC: Regnery, 1996.

Horowitz, David. *Unholy Alliance, Radical Islam and the American Left.* Washington, DC: Regnery Press, 2004.

_____ *Indoctrination U. The Left's War Against Academic Freedom.* New York: Encounter Books, 2007.

Hughes, Thomas Patrick. *A Dictionary of Islam.* London: W.H. Allen and Company, 1895. http://answering-islam.org/Books/Hughes/f.htm.

Hunter, Daryl. *Militant Islam 101: A History.* Citizens For A Free America. http://www.free-press.biz/usa/Islamism-101.htm.

Huntington, Samuel. *The Clash of Civilizations and the Remarking of World Order.* New York: Simon and Schuster, 1996.

Hutchinson, Robert J. *The Politically Incorrect Guide To The Bible.* Washington, DC: Regnery Publishing, 2007.

Ibn al-Hajjaj, Muslim. *Sahih Muslim.* Abdul Hamid Siddiqui translator. Book 041, Number 6985. http://www.iiu.edu.my/deed/hadith/muslim/index.html.

Imad Fayez Mugniyah, *Most Wanted Terrorists,* http://www.fbi.gov/wanted/terrorists/termugniyah.htm.

Inskeep, Steve. *Lebanon Struggles to Cope with Conflict's Aftermath.* NPR Morning Edition. August16, 2006. MidEast Transcripts. http://www.npr.org/templates/transcript/transcript.php?storyId=5656294.

International World History Project, *Sumeria, The City of Ur,*
http://history-world.org/ur.htm.

_____ *The Genesis narrative in the light of recent scholarship,*
http://history-world.org/genesis_narrative_in_the_light_o.htm.

Ishaq, Ibn. *The Life of Muhammed.* Translation by A. Guillaume. Oxford:
Oxford University Press, 1955.

Islamic Affairs Department at the Royal Embassy of Saudi Arabia. *The Religion of
Islam, Introduction to Islam, Understanding Islam and the Muslims .*http://
www.iad.org/.

_____ *The Five Pillars of Islam, Why Do We Pray?* http://www.iad.org/.

IslamiCity.com. *Understanding Islam and the Muslims, Why Does Islam Often Seem
Strange?*
http://www.islamicity.com/education/understandingislamandmuslims/
default.asp?ContentLocation=/Education/UnderstandingIslamAndMuslims&
CurrentPageID=6&Top=&Bottom=&Right=&Left=&SideBarWidth=&Righ
tWidth=&LeftWidth=&SideBarLocation=&Style=&CatID=&Destination=/
Education/UnderstandingIslamAndMuslims/6.asp

Israel Matzav. *The New York Times accidentally points out the elephant in the Living
Room.* Thursday, May 25, 2006. http://israelmatzav.blogspot.com/2006/05/
new-york-times-accidentally-points-out.html.

Israel Information Center. *Facts About Israel.* Jerusalem: Hamakor Press, 1992.

Israeli Defense Forces, *Captured PLO Documents,* Philadelphia: Pavilion Press, 2004.

IwoJima.com, *The Battle of Iwo Jima.* http://www.iwojima.com/.

Jewish Virtual Library. *The 1967 Six-Day War.*
http://www.jewishvirtuallibrary.org/jsource/History/67_War.html.

_____ *Sabra and Shatila.*
http://www.jewishvirtuallibrary.org/jsource/History/Sabra_&_Shatila.html.

_____ *Aliyah from Ethiopia.*
http://www.jewishvirtuallibrary.org/jsource/Judaism/ejim.html.

_____ *The Battle of Tours.*
http://www.jewishvirtuallibrary.org/jsource/History/Tours.html.

Jeans, Ike. *Nuclear Weapon Effects.* Nukefix.com. http://www.nukefix.org/weapon.
html.

Jorisch, Avi. *Beacon of Hatred.* Washington, DC: Washington Institute for
Near East Policy, 2004.

Jurgens, William. *The Faith of the Early Fathers, Volume 3.*
Collegeville, MN: Liturgical Press, 1980.

Kabbani, Muhammad Hisham. *The Approach of Armageddon? An Islamic
perspective.* Washington, DC: Islamic Supreme Council of America, 2003.

Khan, M.A. *Islamic Terrorism, Is It A New Threat.* Armenian Diaspora News Forum,
May 17, 2007. http://www.armeniandiaspora.com/forum/showthread.
php?t=93320.

Karsh, Efraim. *Islamic Imperialism, A History.* New Haven: Yale University Press,
2006.

Katz, Joseph E. *Battleground, Fact and Fantasy in Palestine.* New York:
Bantam Books,1972.

_____ *Black September, the PLO's attempt to take over Jordan in 1970.*
http://www.eretzyisroel.org/~samuel/september.html.

Kennedy, John. *Inaugural Address*, Washington, D.C., January 20, 1961, John F.
Kennedy Presidential Library and Museum. http://www.jfklibrary.
org/Historical+Resources/Archives/Reference+Desk/Speeches/
JFK/003POF03Inaugural01201961.htm.

Kiefer, James. *The Nicene Creed.* http://www.spurgeon.org/~phil/creeds/nicene.htm.

King, Martin Luther. *I Have a Dream.* Washington, D.C.: August 28, 1963,
U.S. Constitution Online, http://www.usconstitution.net/dream.html.

Kirk, Russell. *Rights and Duties, Reflections on Our Conservative Constitution.*
Dallas: Spence Publishing Company, 1997.

Kirsch, Felix M. ed. *Classics: Their History and Present Status in Education,
A Symposium of Essays.* Freeport, NY: Books for Libraries Press.1977.

Klein, Aaron. *Soda, pizza and the destruction of America.*
WorldNetDaily. March 18, 2003. http://www.worldnetdaily.com/news/article.
asp?ARTICLE_ID=31571.

Knox, E.L. *A History of the Crusades.* Boise State University online course,
http://crusades.boisestate.edu/1st/index.shtml.

_____ *The Carolingian Empire, Carolingian Handwriting.*
http://history.boisestate.edu/WESTCIV/charles/16.shtml.

Kornbluh, Peter. *The Death of Che Guevara: Declassified.* National security Archive
Electronic Briefing Book No. 5. http://w1.1559.telia.com/~u155900388/
death_che.htm.

Kuntzel, Matthias. *Hitler's Legacy; Anti-Semitism in the Middle East.*
Paper presented at the international seminar series "Anti-Semitism in
Comparative Perspective" Yale University, New Haven, November 30, 2006

Kushner, Harvey. *Holy War on the Home Front, The Secret Islamic Terror Network in
The United States.* New York: Sentinel Press, 2004.

Lahad, Antoine. *Personal Interview with the author,* SLA Headquarters, Marjayoun,
Lebanon, March 1985.

Leclercq, H. *The First Council Of Nicea.* The Catholic Encyclopedia, Volume XI.
New York: Robert Appleton Company, 1911. http://www.newadvent.org/
cathen/11044a.htm .

Lefkovits, Etgar. *Nehemiah's Wall Uncovered.* Jerusalem Post, November 28, 2007,
JerusalemPost.com, http://www.jpost.com/servlet/Satellite?cid=1195546753
493&pagename=JPost%2FJPArticle%2FShowFull .

Levick, Barbara. *Roman Colonies in Southern Asia Minor.* Oxford: Clarendon, 1967.

Levin, Mark. *Men in Black.* New York: Regnery Publishing, 2005.

Levin, Sis. *Beirut Diary.* Downer's Grove, Illinois: Intervarsity Press, 1989.

Levitt, Mathew. *Hamas; Politics, Charity and Terrorism in the Service of Jihad.*
New Haven: Yale University Press, 2006.

Lewis, Bernard. *Cultures In Conflict, Christians, Muslims and Jews In The Age of
Discovery.* New York: Oxford University Press, 1995.

_____ *Semites and Anti-Semites, An Inquiry Into Conflict and Prejudice.*
New York: W.W. Norton & Co., 1986.

_____ *The Crisis of Islam: Holy War and Unholy Terror.* New York: Random House,

2003.

_____ *The Political Language of Islam.* Chicago: University Of Chicago Press, 1988.

_____ *What Went Wrong? The Clash Between Islam and Modernity in the Middle East.* New York: Oxford University Press, 2002.

_____ *What Went Wrong: Western Impact and Middle Eastern Response.* New York: Oxford University Press, 2002.

Lewis, Naphtali. *Life in Egypt under Roman Rule.* Oxford: Clarendon, 1985.

Library-Religion, *Judaism, Origins, History and Spread.*
http://www.abc.net.au/religion/stories/s796551.htm.

Lichter, Robert and Stanley Rothman. *Media and Business Elites.* Public Opinion, October/November 1981.

Lichter, Robert, Stanley Rothman and Linda Lichter. *The Media Elite.* Bethesda, Maryland: Adler and Adler, 1986.

Lincoln, Abraham . *The Gettysburg Address.* November 19, 1863; The Library of Congress. http://www.loc.gov/exhibits/gadd/gadrft.html

Locke, John. *The Second Treatise of Civil Government.* Chapter 2, Sec.4 & 6. London: 1690. Reprinted by The Constitution Society.
http://www.constitution.org/jl/2ndtreat.htm.

Loftus, John. *The Muslim Brotherhood, The Nazis and Al-Qa'ida.* Nexus Magazine, Volume 12, Number 6. October - November 2005. http://www.nexusmagazine.com/articles/Fascist%20Roots%20of%20Al-Qaeda.html

Lossin, Yigal, *Pillar of Fire The Rebirth of Israel.* Jerusalem: Shikmona Publishing, 1983.

Madden, Thomas. *The New Concise History of the Crusades.* Lanham, MD: Rowman & Littlefield, 2005.

Madison.com. *Sterling Hall Bombing.*
http://www.madison.com/library/LEE/sterlinghall.html .

_____ *UW Students Arm Selves.* Wisconsin State Journal, August 26, 1970.
http://www.madison.com/library/LEE/08261970.pdf,

_____ *Wisconsin Socialists Condemn Bombing.*
http://www.madison.com/library/LEE/09051970.pdf

Malkin, Michelle. *Religion of Perpetual Outrage alert: Another Mohammed cartoon Riot.* February 11, 2008, 10:02 AM. http://michellemalkin.com/2008/02/11/religion-of-perpetual-outrage-alert-another-mohammed-cartoon-riot/.

Mallia, Joseph. *25 years later, photographer to meet his anguished subject.* Boston Sunday Herald, April 23, 1995.

Malone, Dumas. *Jefferson The Virginian.* Boston: Little, Brown and Company, 1948.

Maloney, Evan Coyne. *Cronkite Admits: Media Liberal,* Brain terminal, August 27, 2003.http://brain-terminal.com/posts/2003/08/27/cronkite-admits-media-liberal.

Mann, Peggy. *Golda, The Life of Israel's Prime Minister.* New York: Coward, McCann and Geoghegan, 1971.

Marcinko, Richard. *Rogue Warrior.* New York: Pocket Books, 1992.

Marshall, Peter, and David Manuel. *The Light and The Glory.* Grand Rapids: Flemming H. Revell, 1977.

Mason, Janet. *Caught In Time.* Life Magazine, May 1995.

McDowell, Stephen. *America, a Christian Nation? Examining the Evidence of a Christian Foundation of America.* Charlottesville: Providence Foundation, 2005.

McManus, Michael J. *Anti-Christian Bias In Media,* VirtueOnline, The Voice for Global Orthodox Anglicanism, http://www.virtueonline.org/portal/modules/news/article.php?storyid=3623

Media Research Center, *Media Bias Basics, How the Media Vote.* http://www.mediaresearch.org/biasbasics/biasbasics3.asp.

Meeks, Wayne. *The First Urban Christians.* New Haven, Yale University Press, 1983.

Meir, Golda. *A Land of Our Own, An Oral Biography of Golda Meir.* Marie Syrkin ed. New York: G.P.Putnam's Sons, 1973.

Meir-Levi, David. *The Nazi Roots of Palestinian Nationalism and Islamic Jihad.* Los Angeles: David Horowitz Freedom Center, 2007.

Mercer, Ilana. *Did Muhammad Invent Profiling?* WorldNetDaily, January 9, 2002. http://www.worldnetdaily.com/news/article.asp?ARTICLE_ID=25982.

Medieval Sourcebook. *The Battle of Pointiers, 732.* Anonymous Arab Chronicler. http://www.fordham.edu/halsall/source/arab-poitiers732.html.

MidEast Web Historical Documents. *UN Security Resolution 242*, November 22, 1967, http://www.mideastweb.org/242.htm.

_____ *Khartoum Resolutions*, September 1967. http://www.mideastweb.org/khartoum.htm.

Militant Islam Monitor. *From the Fuhrer to Florida: International terror organization founded by Hitler ally Al Husseini has office in Coral Gables.* August 8, 2005. http://www.militantislammonitor.org/article/id/926.

Millard, Alan. *Treasures From Bible Times.* Belleville, Michigan: Lion Publishers, 1985.

Moaveni, Azadeh. *Mahmoud Ahmadinejad.* Time Magazine. April 30, 2006. http://www.time.com/time/magazine/article/0,9171,1186909,00.html.

Mohsen, Zuheir . *Interview in the Dutch newspaper "Trouw".* March 1977. Article Republished March 6, 2006. http://forum.svt.se/jive//svt/report.jspa?messageID=82410.

Moore, Art. *Should Muslim Quran Be USA's Top Authority?* WorldNetDaily.com, May 1, 2003. http://www.worldnetdaily.com/news/article.asp?ARTICLE_ID=32341.

Moore, George F. *Judaism in the First Centuries of the Christian Era*, Vol. 1 Cambridge: Harvard University Press, 1927.

Morris, Charles. *Las Navas de Talosa.* http://www.mainlesson.com/display.php?author=morris&book=spanish&story=tolosa.

Moreorless. *Heroes & killers of the 20th century, Che Guevara.* http://www.moreorless.au.com/heroes/guevara.html.

MSN Encarta. *Six-Day War.* http://encarta.msn.com/encnet/refpages/RefArticle.aspx?refid=761570433.

Muhammad Ali, Maulana. *The Muslim Prayer Book.* Dublin, OH: Ahmadiyyah Anjuman Isha'at Islam, 5th ed.1992.

_____ *Muhammad and Christ.* Dublin, OH: Ahmadiyyah Anjuman Isha'at Islam, 1993.

Murray, David, Joel Schwartz and S. Robert Lichter. *It Ain't Necessarily So. How the Media Remake Our Picture of Reality.* New York:Penguin Books, 2001.

Muslim American Society. *What Is MAS.* http://web.archive.org/web/20021206132514/www.masmn.org/Other/About_Us.htm.

Mutaharri, Morteza. *Jihad and Shahadat: Struggle and Martyrdom in Islam*, edited and translated by Mehdi Abedi and Gary Legenhausen. Houston: Institute for Research and Islamic Studies, 1986.

Nahmias, Roee. *Lahad: Syria Behind Gemayel's Murder,* Nov. 26, 2006, Ynetnews. com, http://www.ynetnews.com/articles/0,7340,L-3332868,00.html#n .

Naval Technology. *Nimitz Class Nuclear-Powered Aircraft Carriers, USA.* Navaltechnology.com, http://www.naval-technology.com/projects/nimitz/.

Netanyahu, Benjamin. *A Durable Peace.* New York: Warner Books, 2000.

_____ *A Place Among the Nations, Israel and the World.* New York:Bantam Books, 1993.

_____ *Terrorism, How the West Can Win.* New York: Farrar Straus Giroux, 1986.

Netanyahu, Lt. Col. Jonathan. *Biography.* Official Website. http://www.yoni.org.il/.

Nasiri, Omar. *Inside The Jihad, My Life With Al Qaeda, A Spy's Story.* New York: Basic Books, 2006.

National and World Religious Statistics. *Largest Religious Groups in The United States of America.* Adherants.com, http://www.adherents.com/rel_USA.html#gallup

Nawar, Ibrahim. *Unexpected Gifts.* Al Ahram Weekly, Issue 788, 30 March-5 April, 2006.

New Advent. *Hammurabi.* http://www.newadvent.org/cathen/07125a.htm.

_____ *Cistercians.* http://www.newadvent.org/cathen/03780c.htm.

_____ *Saint Benedict of Nursia.* http://www.newadvent.org/cathen/02467b.htm.

Nosotro, Rit. *John Wycliffe, Morning Star of the Reformation.* http://www.hyperhistory.net/apwh/bios/b2wycliffejohn.htm.

Notable Names Database. *Ben Bradlee.* http://www.nndb.com/people/875/000022809/.

Nuclear Weapon Archives. *U.S. Nuclear Weapon Enduring Stockpile.* NuclearWeaponsArchives.org. August 31, 2007. http://nuclearweaponarchive.org/Usa/Weapons/Wpngall.html.

_____ *The B83 (Mk-83) Bomb.* http://nuclearweaponarchive.org/Usa/Weapons/B83.html

Obama, Barak. *Obama, Hagel, Cantwell, Smith Hail Committee Passage of the Global Poverty Act.* http://obama.senate.gov/press/080213-obama_hagel_can_1/.

Oren, Michael. *Power, Faith, and Fantasy: America in the Middle East: 1776 to the Present.* New York: WW Norton, 2007.

_____ *Six Days of War.* New York: Oxford University Press. 2002.

Ostrovsky, Victor and Claire Hoy. *By Way of Deception.* New York: St. Martin's Press, 1990.

Oulu University Library. *Ernest (Che) Guevara de la Serna (1928-1967).* http://www.kirjasto.sci.fi/guevar.htm

Ozick, Cynthia. *Where Hatred Trumps Bread, What does the Palestinian nation offer the world?* The Wall Street Journal, Monday June 30, 2003. http://www.opinionjournal.com/editorial/feature.html?id=110003690.

Palestinian Facts. *Why did Jordan expel the PLO in 1970?* http://www.palestinefacts.org/pf_1967to1991_jordan_expel_plo.php.
_____ *1948-1967 Six Day War Result.* http://www.palestinefacts.org/pf_1948to1967_sixday_result.php.
_____ *What Happened at the LOD Airport in 1972?* *http://www.palestinefacts.org/pf_1967to1991_lod_1972.php.*
_____ *Why did the United States immediately recognize the State of Israel?* http://www.palestinefacts.org/pf_independence_recognition_us.php.

Parsch, Andreas. *Lockheed Martin UGM-133 Trident II.* Directory of U.S. Military Rockets and Missiles. http://www.designation-systems.net/dusrm/m-133.html.

Pavilion. *Captured PLO Documents.* Philadelphia: Pavilion Press, 2004.

PBS Frontline. *Hunting Ben Ladin.* Broadcast, May 1998.

Peake, A. S. and R.G. Parsons editors. *An Outline Of Christianity; The Story Of Our Civilization.* 5 Vols., London: Waverly Book Company, 1926.

Pentecost, J. Dwight. *Things to Come.* Grand Rapids: Zondervan, 1979.

Perry, Richard. ed. *Sources of our Liberties.* Chicago: American Bar Foundation, 1978.

Pew Research Center for The People and the Press, October 15, 2000 Report. *The People and the Press, 2000.*

Pickthall, Marmaduke William. *The Meaning of the Glorious Qur'an: Explanatory Translation.* Arafat Kamil Ashi ed., Beltsville, MD: Amana Publications, 1996.

Pintak, Larry *Beirut Outtakes, A TV Correspondent's Portrait of America's Encounter with Terror.* Lexington: Lexington Books, 1988.

Pippert, Wesley. *Land of Promise Land of Strife.* Waco, Texas: Word Books, 1988.
_____ *An Ethics of News.* Georgetown: Georgetown University Press, 1989.

Podhoretz, Norman. *The Case For Bombing Iran.* Commentary Magazine. June 2007. Commentarymagazine.com,http://www.commentarymagazine.com/viewarticle.cfm/The-Case-for-Bombing-Iran-10882.

Poole, John H. *Tactics Of The Crescent Moon.* Emerald Isle, NC: Posterity Press, 2004.

Prarrieghosts. *Wisconsin's Psycho, The Deviant Life and Times of Ed Gein.* http://www.prairieghosts.com/ed_gein.html.

Pritchard, J.B. *Ancient Near Eastern Texts relating to the Old Testament.* Princeton: Princeton University Press, 1969.

Project for Excellence in Journalism: Understanding news in the Information Age. *Network TV Audience Trends, 2006 Annual Report Nightly Newscasts.* March 13, 2006, http://www.journalism.org/node/1190.

_____ Chart: *Evening News Viewership, All Networks, November 1980 to November 2005.* http://www.journalism.org/node/1190.

Prophet of Doom, *With Whom am I Speaking.* http://prophetofdoom.net/Prophet_of_Doom_07_With_Whom_Am_I_Speaking.Islam.

Qutb, Sayyid. *Milestones.* Salimiah, Kuwait: IIFSO, 1978.

_____ *The Right To Judge,* http://www.islamworld.net/justice.html.

Rabinovich, Itmar. *The War for Lebanon 1970-1983.* London: Cornell University Press,1984.

Reagan, Ronald. *We Will Be As A City Upon A Hill.* Speech at the Conservative Political Action Conference, Washington, DC, January 25, 1974. http://www.conservative.org/pressroom/reagan/reagan1974.asp.

_____ *Farewell Address to the Nation.* Broadcast from the Oval Office of The White House, Washington, DC, January 11, 1989. http://www.reaganlibrary.com/reagan/speeches/farewell.asp.

Richardson, Joel. *Antichrist, Islam's Awaited Messiah.* Enumclaw, WA: Pleasant Word Publishers, 2006.

_____ *Will Islam be in Our Future, A Study of Biblical and Islamic Eschatology.* AnsweringIslam.org.de: On line at AnsweringIslam, 2006. *http://www.answering-islam.de/Main/Authors/JR/Future/index.htm,*

RichardsonWorldHistory. *The Battle of Mulvian Bridge.* https://richardsonworldhistory.wikispaces.com/News+Story+-+The+Battle+of+Mulvian+Bridge .

Rodat, Robert. *The Patriot,* Mutual Film Company and Centropolis Entertainment, 2000. Directed by Roland Emmerich. DVD Columbia Pictures.

Rubin, Barry and Judith Colp Rubin. *Yassir Arafat, A Political Biography.* New York: Oxford University Press, 2003.

Rubin, Uzi. *Hizbollah's Rocket Campaign Against Northern Israel: A Preliminary Report.* Jerusalem Issues Brief, Vol. 6, No. 10. Jerusalem: Jerusalem Center For Public Affairs, August 31, 2006. http://www.jcpa.org/brief/brief006-10.htm.

Sadiq, Imam Jafar. *Kitab al-Kafi,* http://answering-islam.org/Index/index.html.

Samman, Ghada. *Beirut '75.* Translated by Nancy Roberts. Fayetteville: The University of Arkansas Press, 1995.

Schechtman, J.B. *The Mufti and the Fuhrer, The Rise and Fall of Haj Amin al Husseini.* New York: Thomas Yoseloff, 1965.

Schiff, Ze'ev and Ehud Ya'ari. *Israel's Lebanon War.* New York: Simon and Schuster, 1984.

Schihl, Robert J. *Some components of television station image projected and perceived through local news programs.* Thesis (Ph. D.)--State University of New York at Buffalo, 1982.

Seale, Patrick. *Abu Nidal A Gun For Hire.* New York: Random House, 1992.

Segev, Samuel. *The Iranian Triangle.* New York: The Free Press, 1988.

Selvage, Donald. *Che Guevara In Bolivia.* Abstracts of Marine Corps Command and Staff College, April 1, 1985. http://www.globalsecurity.org/military/library/report/1985/SDR.htm.

Shamir, Yitzhak. *171. Interview with Prime Minister Shamir on Israel radio, June 22, 1984.* Israel Ministry of Foreign Affairs, Historical documents 1982-1984, Volume 8: 1982-1984, http://www.mfa.gov.il/MFA/Foreign%20Relations/Israels%20Foreign%20 Relations%20since%201947/1982-1984/171%20Interview%20with%20 Prime%20Minister%20Shamir%20on%20Israel

Sharansky, Natan. *The Case for Democracy, The Power of Freedom to Overcome Tyranny and Terror.* New York: Public Affairs Press, 2004.

Shavit, Uriya. *Out of Jordan.* Haaretz Newspaper, May 28, 2002. http://www.eretzyisroel.org/~samuel/september.html.

Shoebat, Walid. *Israel and the World's Mock Trial, The Shame.* Monthly Pearl, March 2004, Edition 55. http://www.pushhamburger.com/mar04.htm.

———. *The Nazi Islam Connection.* Monthly Pearl, March 2004, Edition 55. http://www.pushhamburger.com/mar04.htm.

Schulimson, Jack. *Marines In Lebanon, 1958.* Washington, DC: Historical Branch, G-3 Division, Headquarters, U. S. Marine Corps, 1966. http://www.au.af.mil/au/awc/awcgate/usmchist/lebanon.txt

Shamoun, Sam. *Islam and Birth Control, Should Muslims Observe It or Not?* http://answeringislam.org/Muhammad/Inconsistent/azl.html.

Smith, Frank. *The Soviet Union Disintegrates.* Macrohistory and World Report. http://www.fsmitha.com/h2/ch33.htm .

Smith, Patricia and Gila Kahila. *Bones of a Hundred Infants Found in Ashkelon Sewer.* Biblical Archeology Review 17 (July-August, 1991) p.47.

Smith, William. *Smith's Bible Dictionary,* "Jerusalem" 1901. http://www.bible-history.com/jerusalem/firstcenturyjerusalem_smith_s_ bible_dictionary.html.

Spencer, Robert, *Religion of Peace, Why Christianity Is and Islam Isn't.* Washington, DC: Regnery Press, 2007.

———. *The Politically Incorrect Guide to Islam and the Crusades.* Washington, DC: Regnery Press, 2005.

———. *The Truth About Mohammed.* Washington, DC: Regnery Press, 2006.

———. *What American Needs To Know About Jihad.* Los Angeles: David Horowitz Freedom Center, 2007.

———. *Saddam, Just Before Execution, Shouts, "God is great. The nation will be victorious and Palestine is Arab!"* Jihad Watch: December 30, 2006. http://www.jihadwatch.org/archives/014615.php.

———. *Speaking of Playing Fast and Lose with History.* Dhimmi Watch: May 8, 2005. http://www.jihadwatch.org/dhimmiwatch/archives/006071.php.

Sperry, Paul. *Infiltration, How Muslim Spies and Subversives Have Penetrated Washington.* Nashville, TN: Nelson Current, 2005.

Stager, Lawrence. *"Eroticism and Infanticide at Ashkelon.* Biblical Archeology Review 17 (July-August, 1991) pp. 34-53.

Stalin, Joseph. *An Interview: Joseph Stalin and H. G. Wells, Marxism VS. Liberalism.* (New York, New Century Publishers, September 1937; reprinted October 1950.) http://www.rationalrevolution.net/special/library/cc835_44.htm

Stalinsky, Steven. *Dealing in Death.* National Review Online, May 24, 2004.

http://article.nationalreview.com/?q=MjdjMTcyMDQ1YmI3M2E2ZDdiYzY
5ZTgxNDYzMWRjM2Q=.

Stark, Rodney. *Cities of God*. New York: HarperCollins, 2006.
_____ *The Rise of Christianity*. New York: HarperCollins, 1997.
_____ *The Victory of Reason*. New York: Random House, 2006.

Strategy Page. *F-16 and F-18 Everywhere and Forever.*
http://www.strategypage.com/htmw/htairfo/articles/20051109.aspx.

Sublett, Kenneth L. *Sounding the Shofar.* Bible And History.
http://www.piney.com/Shofar.html.

Suren-Pahlav, Shapour. ed. *History of Iran, Cyrus Charter of Human Rights.* Iran
Chamber Society. http://www.iranchamber.com/history/cyrus/cyrus_charter.
php.

Tahiri, Amir. *Holy Terror: The Inside Story of Islamic Terrorism.* Bethesda, MD:
Sphere Books, 1987.

Tanner, Norman P. ed. *Decrees of the Ecumenical Councils, 2 Vols.* Georgetown:
Georgetown University Press, 1990. First Council of Nicea: 325 AD. http://
www.piar.hu/councils/ecum01.htm.

Taylor, Troy. *Dead Men Do Tell Tales.* Alton, IL: Whitechapel Productions, 2008.

The 9/11 Commission Report. *The Final Report of the Commission on Terrorist
Attacks Upon the United States, Official Government Edition.*
Washington, DC: USGPO, Dec. 5, 2005.
http://www.gpoaccess.gov/911/pdf/fullreport.pdf.

The British Museum. *The Cyrus Cylinder, A Declaration of Good Kingship.*
http://www.britishmuseum.org/explore/highlights/highlight_objects/me/c/
cyrus_cylinder.aspx .

The Byzantine Studies Page, *Byzantium.* Fordum University.
http://www.fordham.edu/halsall/byzantium/.

The Center for Media and Public Affairs and Harris Pole study in 1997.
What the People want from the Press.

The David Horowitz Freedom Center. *The Islamic Mein Kampf.* Los Angeles: David
Horowitz Freedom Center, 2007.

The Declaration of Independence, *The Unanimous Declaration of the Thirteen United
States of America, In Congress July 4, 1776.* ushistory.org, http://www.
ushistory.org/declaration/document/index.htm .

The Gallop Organization, Polls 2001-2005: *More See Media As "Too Liberal"* The
Missouri School of Journalism's Center for Advanced Social Research, *Results
2005, Key Findings;*

The Good News. *King Solomon's Reign: Israel's Golden Years, Enter the Queen of
Sheba.* http://www.gnmagazine.org/issues/gn15/archaeologysolomon.htm.

The Latin Chronicle of the Kings of Castile. *The Battle of Las Navas de Tolosa,
Chapter 24-26.* Translation by Joseph F. O'Callaghan. Medieval &
Renaissance Texts & Studies vol. 236: Tempe, AZ, Mrts, 2002.

The Los Angeles Times. *The Los Angeles Times Survey of Journalists and the Public,
1985.* Results published at MediaResearch.org: http://www.mediaresearch.
org/biasbasics/biasbasics2admissions.asp

The History Place. *An Unlikely Victory 1777 to 1783.*

http://www.historyplace.com/unitedstates/revolution/revwar-77.htm.

_____ *John Wycliffe, Morning Star of the Reformation.*
http://www.hyperhistory.net/apwh/bios/b2wycliffejohn.htm,

The Holy Bible, *The Amplified Bible.* Grand Rapids: Zondervan, 1965.

_____ *The New International Version.* Grand Rapids: Zondervan, 1984.

_____ *The New Living Translation.* Wheaton: Tyndale House Publishers, 2004.

_____ *The New King James Version.* New York: Thomas Nelson, Inc., 1982.

_____ *The Revised Standard Version.* New York: Thomas Nelson, Inc., 1954.

The Holy Qur'an. Translated by M.H. Shakir. Elmhurst, NY:
Tahrike Tarsile Qur'an, Inc., 1983.

_____ Translated by Abdullah Yusuf Ali. Elmhurst, NY:
Tahrike Tarsile Qur'an, Inc., 1999.

The Muslim American Society. *About MAS, When And Where It All Started.*
masnet.org. http://www.masnet.org/aboutmas.asp.

The Muslim Brotherhood. *The Principles of the Muslim Brotherhood.*
The Official English Website, June 8, 2006. http://www.muslimbrotherhood.
co.uk/Home.asp?zPage=Systems&System=PressR&Press=Show&Lang=E&
ID=4584 ;

The National Priorities Project. July 8, 2008. *The War in Iraq costs, 535 billion.*
http://www.nationalpriorities.org/costofwar_home.

The Pentagon. *U.S. Submarine Classes.* Millnet.com,
http://www.milnet.com/pentagon/subclass.htm.

The United States Constitution. *The Preamble.* The United States Constitution Online,
http://www.usconstitution.net/const.html#Preamble.

The United States Navy Fact File. *Fleet Ballistic Missile Submarines – SSBN.*
http://www.navy.mil/navydata/fact_display.asp?cid=4100&tid=200&ct=4

Think Quest. *Judaism, The Bare Essentials of Judaism.*
http://www.tqnyc.org/NYC052116/Judaism.htm.

Timeline of Bible History, *English Bible History: Timeline on how we got the English Bible,* http://www.greatsite.com/timeline-english-bible-history/ .

Thomas, Clarence. *Kelo v. New London.* 545 U.S. 2005, Kelo v. New London, Justice Thomas dissenting. http://straylight.law.cornell.edu/supct/pdf/04-108P.ZD1.

Thorton, Ted. *Islamic Conquests 623-661.* History of the Middle East DataBase.
http://www.nmhschool.org/tthornton/mehistorydatabase/islamic_
conquests_632.php.

Tierney, Brian. *The Idea of Natural Rights-Origins and Persistence.*
Northwestern University Journal of International Human Rights, Volume 2 (April 2004) paragraphs 15-16; http://www.law.northwestern.edu/journals/
jihr/v2/2/.

Time Magazine. *Fedayeen Leader Arafat.* December 13, 1968.

Trevor-Roper, Hugh. *Hitler's Table Talk 1941-1944.* New York: Enigma Books, 2008.

Truman, Harry S. *Harry S. Truman: Public Papers of the Presidents of the United States Containing the Public Messages, Speeches and Statements of the President---January 1 to December 31, 1950.* Washington, D.C.: USGPO, 1965.

Tuma, Laura. *Walter Cronkite, The Most Trusted Man in America,* Texas Tribute

(Spring, 1997). http://txtell.lib.utexas.edu/stories/c0003-full.html.

Twain, Mark. *The Innocents Abroad.* New York: Literary Classics of the United States, 1984.

United State Department of Defense Official Website, *The Battle for Iwo Jima* http://www.defenselink.mil/home/features/iwo_jima/iwo.html.

University of Colorado. *Report of the Investigative Committee of the Standing Committee on Research Misconduct at the University of Colorado at Boulder concerning Allegations of Academic Misconduct against Professor Ward Churchill.* May 16, 2006.

University of Wisconsin. *Enrollment, Faculty, staff and alumni at the University of Wisconsin, Madison.* http://www.wisc.edu/about/facts/community. php#community.

U.S. Court of Appeals, *Ehrenfeld v Ben Mafous* (USCOA, 2 No. 174) http://www.nycourts.gov/ctapps/decisions/dec07/174opn07.pdf

U.S. District Court, MN. *Shqeirat v U.S. Airways,* (U.S. District Court, MN. Civil No. 0:07 cv-01513-ADM-AJB) http://www.becketfund.org/files/f6db0. pdf

U.S.District Court, Northern District of Texas. *US v Holy Land Foundation.* 04-CR-240. Indictment. NDTX, July 27, 2004.

U. S. Supreme Court. *Church of the Holy Trinity v. U.S.*; 143 U.S. 457, 458, 1892.

Vatikiotis, P.J. *The History of Modern Egypt,* Fourth Edition. Baltimore: Johns Hopkins University, 1992.

Vecchio, Mary Ann. *Gillum Press Conference.* Emerson College, Boston, MA. April 23, 1995 transcript. http://www.may4archive.org/nyt_95.shtml.

Von Gelden, James and Siegelbaum, Lewis. *Seventeen Minutes in Soviet History, 1991: End of the Soviet Union,* http://www.soviethistory.org/index.php.

Von Harnack, Adolf. *The Mission and Expansion of Christianity in the First Three Centuries* Vol. 1. New York: Putnam, 1904.

Walker, Williston, Richard A. Norris, David W. Lotz, and Robert T. Handy. *A History of the Christian Church,* 4th edition. New York:Charles Scribner's Sons, 1985.

Wallach, Janet and John Wallach. *Arafat In the Eyes of the Beholder.* New York: Lyle Stewart, 1990.

Wars of the World. *The Six Day War 1967.* http://www.onwar.com/aced/data/9999/6day1967.htm.

Warraq, Ibn. *Why I Am Not A Muslim.* Amherst: Prometheus Books, 1995.

_____ *Leaving Islam, Apostates Speak Out.* Amherst: Prometheus Books, 2003.

Washington State University. *The Code of Hammurabi, English translation by L.W. King, 1910.* http://www.wsu.edu/~dee/MESO/CODE.HTM .

Walker, Benjamin. *The Foundations of Islam.* London: Peter Owen Publishers, 1998.

Walker, Williston, Norris, Richard A., Lotz, David W., and Handy, Robert T. *A History of the Christian Church,* 4th edition. New York: Scribner's, 1985.

Web Bible Encyclopedia, *Ur, The Moon City,* http://www.christiananswers.net/dictionary/ur.html.

Westman, Paul. *Walter Cronkite: The most trusted man in America.* New York:

CPSIA information can be obtained at www.ICGtesting.com
Printed in the USA
BVOW07s1630200913

331535BV00001B/45/P